The State
of the World's
Refugees
1993

UNHCR

The State
of the World's
Refugees
1993

The Challenge of Protection

UNHCR
United Nations
High Commissioner
for Refugees

PENGUIN BOOKS

PENGUIN BOOKS
Published by the Penguin Group
Penguin Books USA Inc., 375 Hudson Street,
New York, New York 10014, U.S.A.
Penguin Books Ltd, 27 Wrights Lane,
London W8 5TZ, England
Penguin Books Australia Ltd, Ringwood, Victoria, Australia
Penguin Books Canada Ltd, 10 Alcorn Avenue,
Toronto, Ontario, Canada M4V 3B2
Penguin Books (N.Z.) Ltd, 182-190 Wairau Road,
Auckland 10, New Zealand

Penguin Books Ltd, Registered Offices:
Harmondsworth, Middlesex, England

First published in Penguin Books 1993

10 9 8 7 6 5 4 3 2 1

The maps in this publication are not intended to be exact
representations. The designations on, and the presentation of,
the maps do not imply the expression of any opinion
whatsoever on the part of the United Nations concerning the
legal status of any country, territory or area, or of its
authorities, frontiers, or boundaries.
All figures referred to with a dollar sign ($) are in U.S.
dollars, unless otherwise stated. This report does not take
into account events occuring on or after 1 July 1993, unless a
later date is specified.

LIBRARY OF CONGRESS CATALOGING IN PUBLICATION DATA
The state of the world's refugees/United Nations High
Commissioner for Refugees
p. cm
Includes bibliographical references and index.
ISBN 0 14 02.3487 X
1. Refugees. I. Office of the United Nations High
Commissioner for Refugees. '
HV640.S675 1993
362.87   dc20   93–28920

Printed in the United States of America
Set in Times and Univers
Designed by Pentagram
Illustrations by Andrew Kingham, The Inkshed

This book is printed on acid-free paper.

Foreword

In 1970 there were 2.5 million refugees in the world. Ten years ago there were 11 million. In 1993, the number is 18.2 million.

The scale and complexity of today's humanitarian crises are a reflection of the instability of the period in which we live. The collapse of the old order has given rise to a more volatile world in which new refugee movements are likely to continue to occur. At the same time, the nature of the refugee problem has undergone fundamental changes which call urgently for new approaches.

Firstly, flight is more than ever before the product of vicious internal conflicts. Nationalistic, ethnic or communal tensions have become the predominant factor in refugee movements around the world, be it in the Horn of Africa and the Sudan, the former Soviet Union and the Balkans or in the Middle East and parts of the Asian sub-continent.

Secondly, the loosening grip of authoritarian regimes and the destructive effects of civil war are straining fragile state structures. This has led, in cases such as Somalia and Bosnia and Herzegovina, to the disintegration of states into territories controlled by competing factions, thereby greatly complicating efforts to protect and assist refugees and other victims.

Thirdly, internal conflicts are not only causing massive refugee flows but are also displacing inside their own countries large numbers of people who, in many cases, have the same need for protection and assistance as refugees. There are estimated to be about 24 million internally displaced people in the world today. Some of them are trapped by conflict and have no possibility of seeking asylum across an international border but many of them are potential refugees.

Fourthly, the widespread deprivation that continues to afflict the great majority of humankind is not only leading larger numbers of migrants to leave their homes in search of a better life; it is also exacerbating the social and political instability that produces refugees.

And fifthly, confronted by rising numbers of refugees and migrants, the traditional system for protecting refugees has come dangerously close to breaking down. The massive number of people on the move has weakened international solidarity and endangered, at times seriously, the time-honoured tradition of granting asylum to those in genuine need of protection.

In a world where persecution, massive human rights violations and armed conflict remain a daily reality, the need to protect refugees is greater than ever before. Asylum for those forced to flee must be preserved. But the current scale and nature of the refugee problem and limits to the absorption capacity of asylum countries mean that traditional methods of protection are no longer sufficient. They must be complemented by flexible approaches that respond to the present period of transition and upheaval in world affairs.

The pages that follow seek to define the current agenda of refugee protection. They attempt to analyze the issues that the international community urgently needs to address in coming to grips with the challenges of the refugee problem in the post-Cold-War world. This report examines evolving strategies which aim both to preserve asylum for those who need it and to address all stages in the development of refugee problems though preventive initiatives, emergency response, protection and the promotion and consolidation of solutions. In doing so, the report argues that humanitarian action must be firmly inscribed in a broader context of political initiatives to promote peace, human rights and development. Above all, it is an urgent appeal for international solidarity for humanitarian action.

The subject of refugees and displaced people is high on the list of international concerns today not only because of its humanitarian significance, but also because of its impact on peace, security and stability. The world cannot reach a new order without effectively addressing the problem of human displacement.

Sadako Ogata
Sadako Ogata
United Nations High Commissioner for Refugees

Contents

Team for the preparation of The State of the World's Refugees 1993

UNHCR Editorial Team
Raymond Hall (director),
Kathleen Newland (principal author),
Rupert Colville (editor), Jeff Crisp,
Jean-François Durieux, Erika Feller,
Sylvana Foa, Jan Henneman,
Fabrizio Hochschild, Irene Khan,
R. James Lattimer, Ekber Menemencioglu,
Waldo Villalpando.

External Advisory Committee
Marie-Angélique Savané (chairperson),
Claude Ake, Reginald Appleyard,
Jochen Blaschke, Gil Loescher.

Acknowledgments
The editorial team wishes to express its
appreciation to the many colleagues and
collaborators who provided assistance and
advice in the preparation of the report,
especially: Kwame Afriyie, Manoel de
Almeida e Silva, Robert Ashe, Helga Barabass,
Jeremy Black, Alessandro Casella,
Shunmugam Chetty, Gervase Coles,
Ertan Corlulu, Bryan Deschamp,
Jean-Marie Fakhouri, Anne Fati,
Carlos Antonio Garcia-Carranza,
Alejandro Henning, Anneliese Hollmann,
Bela Hovy, Kaj-Henrik Impola, Ivor Jackson,
Zakaria Kawi, Lennart Kotsalainen,
Marie Lobo, Martin Loftus, Donatella Luca,
Raya Meron, James Morwood,
Courtney O'Connor, George Okoth-Obbo,
Jennifer Otsea, Jovica Patrnogic,
Michael Petersen, Mary Petevi, Ron Redmond,
Annick Roulet, Sharon Rusu, Anne Skatvedt,
Linda Starke, Robin Stevenson,
Johannes Thoolen, Alwina Werner,
Jean-Nöel Wetterwald, Robert White
and Jonas Widgren.

The production of this book has been made
possible by a grant from the Japan Committee
for Refugee Relief Fund.

The World of Refugees

States with Refugee Populations of Over 5,000 on 31 December 1992

1 ARMENIA 300,000
2 AUSTRIA 60,900
3 AZERBAIJAN 246,000
4 BELGIUM 24,300
5 CROATIA 648,000
6 CZECHOSLOVAKIA 9,400
7 DENMARK 58,300
8 HUNGARY 32,400
9 FYR MACEDONIA 32,000
10 NETHERLANDS 26,900
11 FED. REP. OF YUGOSLAVIA 516,500
12 SLOVENIA 47,000
13 SWITZERLAND 26,700

14 KUWAIT 124,900
15 LEBANON 6,000
16 SYRIAN ARAB REPUBLIC 5,700
17 YEMEN 59,700

18 BURUNDI 271,700
19 DJIBOUTI 28,000
20 GHANA 12,100
21 GUINEA 478,500
22 GUINEA BISSAU 12,200
23 LIBERIA 100,000
24 MALAWI 1,058,500
25 RWANDA 25,200
26 SENEGAL 71,600
27 SIERRA LEONE 5,900
28 SWAZILAND 55,600
29 UGANDA 196,300

30 BANGLADESH 245,000
31 NEPAL 75,500
32 VIET NAM 16,300

33 EL SALVADOR 19,900
34 GUATEMALA 222,900

NORWAY 85,700
FINLAND 12,000
SWEDEN 324,500
RUSSIAN FEDERATION 17,100
UNITED KINGDOM 100,000
GERMANY 827,100
FRANCE 182,600
ITALY 12,400
SPAIN 9,700
GREECE 8,500
TURKEY 28,500
ISLAMIC REPUBLIC OF IRAN 4,150,700
AFGHANISTAN 60,000
CHINA 288,100
IRAQ 95,000
PAKISTAN 1,629,200
ALGERIA 219,300
EGYPT 5,600
SAUDI ARABIA 28,700
INDIA 258,400
MAURITANIA 37,500
MALI 13,100
SUDAN 725,600
BAHRAIN/OMAN/QATAR UNITED ARAB EMIRATES 15,200
THAILAND 63,600
BURKINA FASO 5,700
CÔTE D'IVOIRE 174,100
CENTRAL AFRICAN REP. 19,000
ETHIOPIA 431,800
CAMEROON 42,200
CONGO 9,500
KENYA 401,900
ZAIRE 391,100
UNITED REP. OF TANZANIA 292,100
ANGOLA 11,000
ZAMBIA 142,100
ZIMBABWE 137,200

See Annex I for a complete and more detailed list of countries hosting refugee populations.

Not all the numbers included on this map were collected on the same basis: see "The Problems with Refugee Statistics" in Annex I.

This map does not include the estimated 810,000 people who were internally displaced in Bosnia and Herzegovina on 31 December 1992.

* Dotted line represents approximately the Line of Control in Jammu and Kashmir, as agreed by India and Pakistan. The final status of Jammu and Kashmir has not yet been agreed.

The designations on, and the presentation of, this map do not imply the expression of any opinion whatsoever on the part of the United Nations concerning the legal status of any country, territory or area, or of its authorities, frontiers or boundaries.

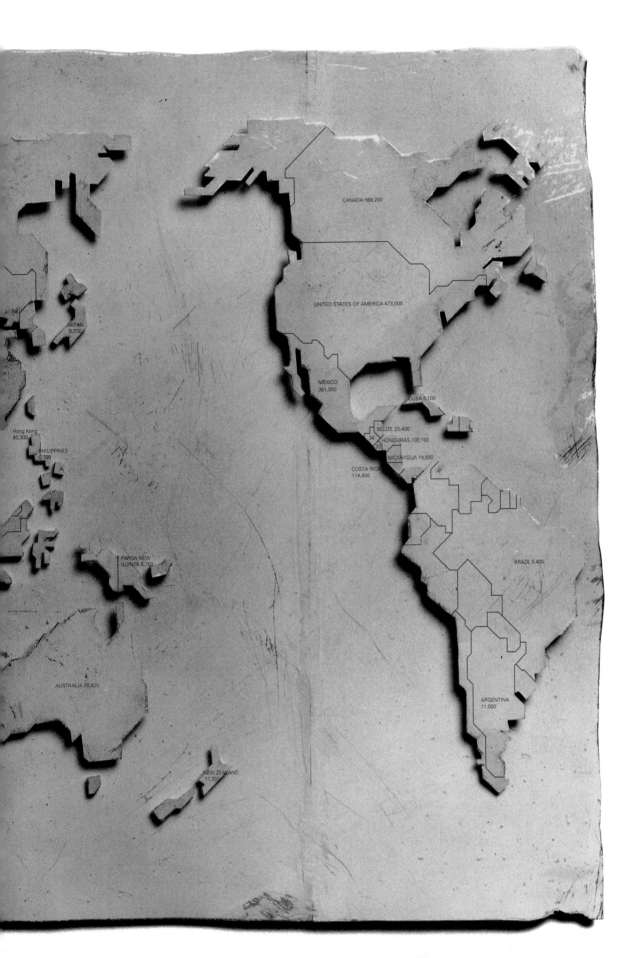

CANADA 568,200

UNITED STATES OF AMERICA 473,000

MEXICO
361,000

CUBA 8,100

BELIZE 20,400
34
HONDURAS 100,100
33
NICARAGUA 14,500
COSTA RICA
114,400

BRAZIL 5,400

ARGENTINA
11,500

JAPAN
8,200

Hong Kong
45,300

PHILIPPINES
0,700

PAPUA NEW
GUINEA 6,700

AUSTRALIA 35,600

NEW ZEALAND
17,300

Refugees from Myanmar. Teknaf, Bangladesh, June 1992.

Introduction

The Challenge of Protection

Refugees are the symptom of the ills of an age. The state of the world's refugees in 1993 shows the monumental challenges that need to be met before this decade can hope to earn a clean bill of health. As the year began, the number of people forced to leave their countries for fear of persecution and violence had risen to a total of 18.2 million.[1] To reach that painful sum, an average of nearly 10,000 people a day became refugees – every single day throughout the previous year.

Nearly four million people from the former Yugoslavia have come to depend on international emergency assistance since late 1991, as the term "ethnic cleansing" has joined the 20th century's lexicon of horrors. Fully one-tenth of Somalia's entire population is outside its borders, and is being helped to survive by international aid. Well over half a million Liberians have been in a similar situation since early 1990. New upheavals continue to drive out new victims: by June 1993, more than 280,000 people had fled from political repression in Togo, some 500,000 from the war between Armenia and Azerbaijan, 60,000 from clan-based struggles for power in Tajikistan and up to 100,000 from ethnic strife in Bhutan.

Refugees, by definition, are people who have left their countries. Many people who flee from violence and persecution do not become refugees for the sole reason that they do not – and in many cases cannot – cross an international border. Yet the needs, and the numbers, of the internally displaced are very similar to those of refugees. At a conservative estimate, some 24 million people are displaced within the borders of their own countries.[2] Adding their numbers to those of refugees means that, in a world population of 5.5 billion, roughly one in every 130 people on earth has been forced into flight.

The state of the world's refugees in 1993 is not one of unbroken gloom. Some of the conflicts that generated displacement within and across borders have subsided to the point where uprooted people feel able to go home. About 2.4 million refugees did so in 1992 alone. Returnees now far outnumber the remaining refugees in Central America. The last remaining refugee camp on the Thai border with Cambodia closed in April as its former residents went home in time to take part in the national elections in May. By mid-1993, over 1.6 million Afghan refugees had returned home from Pakistan and the Islamic Republic of Iran, despite very uncertain conditions in their native land; the total was expected to pass the two million mark well before the end of the year. And the repatriation of 1.3 million Mozambicans, the largest organized repatriation ever attempted in Africa, got under way in July. Meanwhile other solutions continue to be found for refugees unable to repatriate. Significant – if much smaller – numbers have been able either to integrate permanently in the countries where they first sought asylum or to resettle in third countries where they have begun new lives.

"The number of refugees continues, relentlessly, to grow"

The total number of refugees continues, relentlessly, to grow. The international framework for meeting the needs of these people, which includes the Office of the United Nations High Commissioner for Refugees (UNHCR), is being stretched to cover the new demands of larger and more complex refugee problems. It has at its core a simple but powerful commitment: refugees must be protected, and helped towards a lasting solution to their plight.

Today, the problems of refugees raise not only humanitarian and human rights concerns but also fundamental issues of international peace and security. This report will examine the challenge of protection amid the dynamics of changing political realities.

New realities

Wars, persecution and intolerance are ancient themes in the human drama, and refugees are perennial characters. If there is a dreadful sameness in the fact that people are still being forced to flee, there have been changes in almost every aspect of the framework in which their stories unfold. The problems of refugees have not changed, but the refugee problem has. Policy is being set against the background of radical geopolitical shifts, the enormous growth in refugee numbers, the prevalence of refugee emergencies in situations of armed conflict, and the shrinking opportunities for permanent large-scale integration in countries of asylum.

At the start of the 1990s, optimists foresaw a reduction in the number of refugees around the globe. Several long-standing armed conflicts had declined in intensity, apparently opening the way for the repatriation of millions of displaced people. But as the decade draws on, the euphoria that greeted the end of the Cold War has given way to a sober reassessment of how refugees are affected by the new geopolitical realities.

The reduction of East-West tensions has created new possibilities for international co-operation in the settlement of disputes. But the proxy wars of the previous decades have proved to have lives of their own after their patrons withdrew, leaving devastating armouries behind in the hands of rival factions. Many of the recently independent states that arose from the dissolution of the Soviet Union are experiencing violent clashes based on ethnicity, ideology or simple struggles for power. A number of states in other parts of the world have fragmented or imploded. In every region that is subject to these new or persisting forms of instability, people have fled their homes to escape persecution and violence. The same reduction of tensions that allowed recent conflicts to escape becoming Cold-War battlegrounds also meant that they – and their victims – could be neglected in the highest councils of international politics, especially when the perceived interests of influential powers were not at stake.

In 1978 there were only 4.6 million refugees looking to the international community for assistance and protection. The quadrupling of that number is placing serious strains on a system of protection that was conceived as temporary and finite. When UNHCR was set up in 1951, it had a projected life span of three years. It was assumed that the existing post-World War II refugees would be integrated into the societies in which they had found refuge, and that the organization could then be disbanded.

Local integration and third-country resettlement on the scale that would be needed to meet today's mass displacements are not realistic options. Permanent integration in countries of asylum has, in practice, only been available to a fraction of the displaced from the 1960s onwards. The vast majority of refugees sought and found sanctuary in neighbouring countries in the Third World, and returned home when conditions permitted.

As the total number of refugees continues to grow, temporary protection followed by voluntary repatriation is now seen as the most practical and, in the majority of cases, the most satisfactory means of protecting many of today's refugees, the great majority of whom are fleeing from armed conflict.

A policy of offering temporary protection, however, implies an active responsibility to pursue improved conditions in the country of origin, thereby allowing refugees to return voluntarily and in reasonable safety. Action on behalf of refugees is, therefore, becoming more closely tied to peace-making and peace-keeping efforts in their home countries. At the same time, states and international institutions are being compelled to address themselves to the causes of flight *before* it occurs. A new emphasis on prevention supplements the international community's earlier commitment to protect people and try to solve their problems *after* they have become refugees.

Fig. A
Global Numbers of Refugees: 1960 – 1992

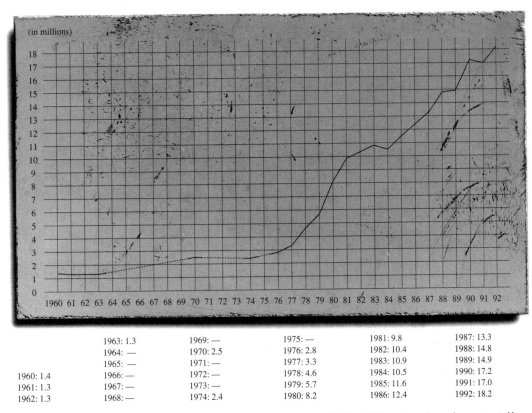

			1975: —	1981: 9.8	1987: 13.3
	1963: 1.3	1969: —	1976: 2.8	1982: 10.4	1988: 14.8
	1964: —	1970: 2.5	1977: 3.3	1983: 10.9	1989: 14.9
	1965: —	1971: —	1978: 4.6	1984: 10.5	1990: 17.2
1960: 1.4	1966: —	1972: —	1979: 5.7	1985: 11.6	1991: 17.0
1961: 1.3	1967: —	1973: —	1980: 8.2	1986: 12.4	1992: 18.2
1962: 1.3	1968: —	1974: 2.4			

Note: Totals are as of 31 December of each given year. Figures for the years 1964-69, 1971-73 and 1975 are incomplete, and are represented by a broken line. The total for 31 December 1992 does not include some 810,000 internally displaced people in Bosnia and Herzegovina. For a detailed breakdown of the totals for 1991 and 1992, see Annex I.1.

3

Box 1

Fridtjof Nansen: Pioneer of Protection

Fridtjof Nansen, who is widely regarded as the founding father of the international system of protection and assistance for refugees, was born in Christiania, now the city of Oslo, on 10 October 1861. After achieving considerable success as a zoologist in his early twenties, he went on to make similarly valuable contributions to marine biology, oceanography, geology, anthropology and sociology.

Not content with purely academic pursuits, he became one of the leading Arctic explorers of the period. In 1888, at only 26 years of age, Nansen led the first expedition to cross Greenland. Five years later, he set about proving his theory that the Arctic icepack flowed from Siberia to Greenland via the North Pole region. In June 1893, he set sail in the specially designed *Fram* which was duly caught up in the ice and began the long drift north. By March 1895, however, the ship had made much slower progress than anticipated, so Nansen and a companion, Hjalmar Johansen, started off on their own across the ice. Although they failed to conquer the Pole, they went further north than anyone else had been, before being forced to turn back. After surviving a long and perilous trek south, and an entire Arctic winter spent in a makeshift hut living off walrus and polar bear meat, they were finally rescued in June 1896 and arrived back in Norway to tremendous acclaim on 13 August – five days before the *Fram*.

As a scientist and explorer, Nansen acquired such enormous stature that his transformation to statesman was almost inevitable. In 1905, when the union between Norway and Sweden broke up, he used his diplomatic skills and prestige to help win international recognition of Norway as an independent state.

When the League of Nations was created in 1920, the world was still suffering from the ravages of World War I and the ensuing political and social upheaval. Nansen believed that the new world body provided an unprecedented opportunity for establishing peace and reconstruction in a devastated Europe. He set out to prove that it was not just an idealistic concept but a practical tool for improving the lot of humankind.

Over the next three years he took responsibility for no fewer than four huge humanitarian operations. First, on behalf of the newly-formed League, he organized the repatriation of half a million prisoners of war from 26 countries, mainly in south-eastern Europe and the USSR. Next, after a devastating famine struck the USSR during the winter of 1921, Nansen was asked by the International Committee of the Red Cross (ICRC) and a number of governments to supervise a massive relief effort for some 30 million men, women and children who were threatened with starvation.

In addition to the prisoners of war, World War I and its turbulent aftermath had left a legacy of 1.5 million refugees and displaced people scattered in a variety of countries. In the autumn of 1921, in order to provide a focal point for the co-ordination of relief efforts, the League of Nations appointed Nansen as the first High Commissioner for refugees – a role he was to perform tirelessly until his death.

One of the fundamental problems facing refugees and displaced people was their lack of internationally recognized identity papers. So in 1922 the new High Commissioner introduced the "Nansen passport", the forerunner of today's Convention Travel Document for refugees. It enabled thousands to return home or settle in other countries, and represented the first in a long and still evolving series of international legal measures designed to protect stateless persons and refugees.

In the same year, a war between Greece and Turkey caused several hundred thousand Greeks to flee from their homes in eastern Thrace and Asia Minor to Greece. Charged with finding a solution to this colossal dislocation, Nansen proposed a population exchange, as a result of which half a million Turks moved in the other direction, from Greece to Turkey, with the League of Nations providing compensation to help both groups reintegrate. This ambitious and unprecedented scheme took eight years to complete, but was ultimately successful.

In 1922, Nansen received the Nobel Peace Prize for his work on behalf of refugees and displaced people. He died on 13 May 1930 at his home near Oslo. His name lives on as one of the great humanitarian innovators of the 20th century and a powerful reminder to humankind of its moral duty to protect and assist refugees and others in similar distress.

The meaning of protection

What sets refugees apart from other people in need of humanitarian aid is their need for international protection. Most people can look to their own governments and state institutions to protect their rights and physical security, even if imperfectly. Refugees cannot. In many cases they are fleeing in terror from abuses perpetrated by the state. In other instances they are escaping from oppression that the state is powerless to prevent because it has lost control of territory or otherwise ceased to function in an effective way.

The protection that the international community extends to refugees recognizes the specific needs of people who have good reason to fear that their own governments will not or cannot provide safeguards against abuse. It provides a temporary substitute for the normal safeguards until the refugee can again benefit from national protection – either by returning voluntarily to his or her original country of nationality, or by assuming a new nationality. Until a solution of this sort is found, international protection also means that countries of asylum will not discriminate against refugees, allowing them at least the same civil and economic rights that are enjoyed by other legal immigrants.

The core of international protection is the principle that people should not be forced to return against their will to a country in which their lives or freedom would be endangered because of "race, religion, nationality, membership of a particular social group or political opinion". The legal term for this guarantee is *non-refoulement*. It can only be implemented through co-operation with governments at the political level, although extending protection according to the terms of international agreements remains a non-political, humanitarian act. A state can offer refuge without being seen to pass judgment on the country of origin. During the Cold War the criteria for recognizing refugee status were often highly politicized, and they remain so in some instances today. In principle, however, international protection is conceived as a response to the needs of the refugee rather than to the national interests of the country of asylum.

"Refugees must not be forced to return to a country where their lives or freedom could be in danger"

Protection must include physical security of refugees. There are two dimensions of physical protection. One is personal security from physical attack whether from armed forces, death squads, or lone assassins. Physical protection also means keeping people alive through humanitarian assistance. Food, water, sanitation and medical care are fundamental to survival. As more and more refugee crises erupt in the midst of armed conflict, the physical aspects of protection have assumed a compelling urgency.

The essential elements of international protection, then, are admission to safety, exemption from forcible return, non-discrimination, and assistance for survival. With growing numbers of people in need of protection, these principles are more important than ever. The increasingly volatile international context requires innovative strategies for implementing the traditional principles and extending them to cover new kinds of challenges.

Emerging issues in protection

The refugee problem is reaching critical proportions in almost all parts of the world, placing the structures and institutions of international protection under stress. The needs of refugees are too often seen as being at odds both with the interests of states and with political pragmatism. Many of the people in need of protection are fleeing from armed conflict, generalized violence, severe disruptions of public order or widespread abuses of human rights. Their claims to international protection are widely acknowledged, even though they may not always conform to the notion of persecution found in the 1951 Convention relating to the Status of Refugees (see Box 2). The situations from which they flee do not necessarily entail individually targeted persecution but do provide fertile breeding grounds for it.

New claims for international protection assert themselves in great numbers even as many old ones persist. The intermingling of refugees with economically motivated migrants complicates the effort to protect those who have a well-founded fear of persecution. Asylum countries must struggle with the pressing economic and political demands of their own populations, while fulfilling international obligations that at present seem much more likely to grow than to diminish.

These pressures on the established system of protection make it imperative to take advantage of the new possibilities for international co-operation. The difficult task under way is to preserve the principles of protection while devising new approaches that balance humanitarian needs and political realities.

"Traditionally, international protection was only seen to be necessary after a refugee had crossed a border"

The process of becoming a refugee is not instantaneous. It proceeds through the often slow growth of root causes to the sometimes quite sudden flash of an immediate catalyst that generates actual flight. Asylum follows when another state grants those in flight access to its territory and extends protection to them. Finally, for the more fortunate, a permanent resolution of their status is sought and found, and they cease to be refugees.

Traditionally, the need for international protection was seen to arise only after a refugee

had crossed a border and ceased to apply when a solution was found. Today, that truncated approach is seen to be inadequate. An effective strategy needs to address the entire continuum of refugee flows from causes through to emergency response, protection and eventual solution. A comprehensive policy must, therefore, be one that seeks to prevent the deterioration of conditions to the point where people are forced to flee. It must meet their needs for protection and assistance in flight and in asylum. It must also promote the resolution of problems and contribute to the safety and welfare of the refugees in the early stages of repatriation or settlement.

New issues have emerged from the changed circumstances and perceptions of the 1990s. They call for fresh strategies to meet the need for international protection. The chapters that follow in this report examine these emerging issues in depth. Seven of the most salient are highlighted here.

1. The climate of receptivity for refugees has cooled in many asylum countries. Economic difficulties, domestic political instability, the resurgence of ethnic tensions and the rolling up of the West's ideological welcome mat for refugees from communist countries are among the explanations for the less hospitable climate facing refugees. There is also a more general sense of weariness at the apparent intractability of refugee problems. In virtually all regions, the persistent growth in numbers of actual and potential refugees has prompted a more conservative approach. The authorities in many industrialized countries are increasingly inclined to interpret their obligations to refugees according to a narrow "persecution standard" and to apply a restrictive definition of what constitutes persecution. Part of the reason is that the asylum practices of the Cold-War period tended, in the West, to equate the grant of asylum with permanent settlement. Fewer asylum countries remain willing to accept what they see as an unlimited obligation to people fleeing violence.

2. Refugees are part of a complex stream of migration. The movement of refugees in search of safety takes place against a background of much larger migratory movements which engender unease among many people and xenophobic or racist reactions in a few. In many settings, refugees mingle with people who move not out of fear for their lives and freedom but in search of better opportunities or to escape from poverty. There is widespread anxiety in some countries that the special provisions made for the protection of refugees are being abused by people who have no valid claim to refugee status, and this is undermining support for generous provision of asylum in a number of recipient countries.

3. Refugees are often interspersed with other people who need humanitarian assistance. In the humanitarian emergencies that more and more often accompany political upheaval and armed conflict, refugees mingle with internally displaced people, victims of mass expulsion, returnees, demobilized soldiers and their families, as well as local people caught up in the same turmoil. Dealing with mixed populations of refugees and non-refugees poses serious practical difficulties as well as questions of principle. Does it make sense to ignore the humanitarian needs of non-refugees living in proximity to recognized refugees – for example, a local population severely affected by drought in a region where resources are further strained by an influx of refugees? Humanitarian agencies have been called upon to reach beyond their mandates in a number of situations where both categories face the same dire need for material help. Yet it remains essential not to lose sight of the distinction between those who require international protection and those who need only relief.

4. Humanitarian assistance is an increasingly important aspect of protection. The majority of today's refugees come from and find refuge in some of the poorest countries in the world. The combination of large numbers, remote and fragile environments, violence and extreme poverty can make the provision of humanitarian assistance both difficult and extremely urgent. With one refugee emergency following hard on the heels of another throughout the early 1990s, the capacity of the international community to mount adequate responses has been strained to breaking point. At the same time, valuable experience has been accumulated, and there is a new awareness of the need to address long-neglected problems. For example, women far outnumber men in most refugee populations, yet only recently has serious consideration been given to the ways in which their needs for both protection and assistance differ from those of men. The way in which assistance is provided can have an impact not only on the immediate safety and welfare of the refugees but also on the prospects for a durable solution.

5. Voluntary repatriation is occurring with growing frequency in conditions of continuing conflict and insecurity. Voluntary repatriation was traditionally thought of as the last stage in the process of return to normality, and usually took place after peace and stability had been restored to a country. Today's large-scale returns tend to occur in the midst of this process, and refugees themselves play an important role in peace-making and peace-building. Negotiations on the terms of repatriation are often an important early step in establishing contact between opposing parties to a conflict. The transition to stable government may depend on returning refugees being able to take part in elections or referenda on the form of government or its leadership. Repatriation in an unstable setting poses considerable risks for refugees, but they often make the decision to return despite the dangers that confront them.

6. The refugee problem is essentially a human rights problem. The right to seek and attain asylum is fundamental, but so is the right to live in peace and safety in one's own homeland. An actual or anticipated violation of rights is the direct reason for the departure of countless refugees. A pattern of violations is implicated in many of the conflicts that impel others to leave

Fig. B.1
AFRICA: Number of Refugees, 1980-1992

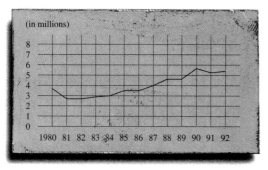

	1981: 2.7	1984: 3.0	1987: 4.0	1990: 5.6
	1982: 2.7	1985: 3.5	1988: 4.6	1991: 5.3
1980: 3.7	1983: 2.9	1986: 3.5	1989: 4.6	1992: 5.4

Fig. B.2
ASIA: Number of Refugees, 1980-1992

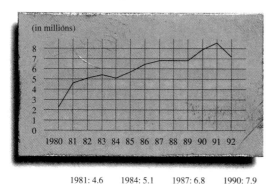

	1981: 4.6	1984: 5.1	1987: 6.8	1990: 7.9
	1982: 5.1	1985: 5.7	1988: 6.8	1991: 8.6
1980: 2.3	1983: 5.4	1986: 6.4	1989: 6.8	1992: 7.2

Fig. B.3
*EUROPE: Number of Refugees, 1980-1992

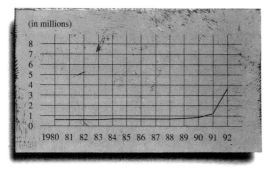

	1981: 0.6	1984: 0.7	1987: 0.7	1990: 0.9
	1982: 0.6	1985: 0.7	1988: 0.7	1991: 1.2
1980: 0.6	1983: 0.6	1986: 0.7	1989: 0.8	1992: 3.6

*The total for 31 December 1992 does not include some 810,000 internally displaced people in Bosnia and Herzegovina.

Note: See Annex I.1 for breakdown of regions by country

their homes. Safeguarding human rights is necessary to prevent conditions that force people to become refugees, and is a key element in protecting them. Improved observance of human rights standards is often of critical importance for the solution of refugee problems.

7. Prevention is preferable to cure. In the context of international protection, this does not mean erecting obstacles to refugee movements, which would constitute a denial of protection. Rather, it means addressing both the root and the immediate causes of flight. At the most fundamental level, prevention is not specific to refugees; it lies in the larger realms of peaceful resolution of conflict, respect for human rights, economic development, stable participatory government, a fair and independent judiciary and tolerance for diversity. Societies in which no one has cause to fear persecution or generalized violence do not produce refugees. The root causes of refugee flows are often very complex and difficult to identify precisely. The immediate causes may, however, be susceptible to more direct preventive strategies, including diplomacy, information campaigns and provision of training and advice on matters such as nationality law and communal relations.

Prevention should aim at arresting and rolling back the deterioration of conditions in a country that is, or seems to be, on the verge of producing refugees, so that people feel secure enough to remain in or near their homes. Preventive efforts should also seek both to persuade and assist the authorities in such countries to meet their obligations to protect the rights and security of their people to the best of their capacities – and should support them in strengthening those capacities in every way possible.

State responsibility

The new emphasis on prevention necessarily throws the spotlight on the conditions and events that force people to flee. Such attention was conspicuous by its absence in the first three decades after World War II, an omission that in part reflected the political paralysis of a bi-polar world. In the receiving countries of the West, anyone arriving from the Soviet Union or one of its allies was automatically granted some form of asylum; no detailed scrutiny of their reasons for leaving was felt necessary. In the Third World, too, it was almost impossible to address the causes of flight if the source country could call on the protection of one of the superpowers – and almost all could to some degree. In the system of refugee protection, the country of origin was shielded from scrutiny by the privileges of national sovereignty.

Refugee policy was thus limited to dealing with the manifestations of the problem, since the causes were beyond the reach of international co-operation. The approaches developed in this period concentrated exclusively on the roles and obligations of countries of asylum. In the 1951 Convention, no specific reference was made to the responsibilities of countries of origin.

The preventive approaches being developed today are based on notions of state responsibility. Countries of origin are being called upon to eradicate the causes of flight and to facilitate return. This is in keeping with a growing tendency for the international community to concern itself with conditions that until recently would have been treated as internal matters: violations of human rights, repression of minorities, indiscriminate violence and persecution. Such conditions can no longer be seen as falling exclusively within the realm of domestic concern especially when they affect other countries by causing an outpouring of refugees. Efforts are being made to draw refugee-producing countries into a framework of international co-operation aimed at preventing, halting and reversing the conditions that cause people to flee.

The focus of international protection of refugees has broadened gradually. The shift makes itself felt in an emerging emphasis, alongside the right to seek and to enjoy asylum, on the right not to be unjustly compelled to leave home. There is, in the idea of a "right to remain", a strong presumption against expulsion, denationalization, exile and denial of

Fig. B.4
LATIN AMERICA: Number of Refugees, 1980-1992

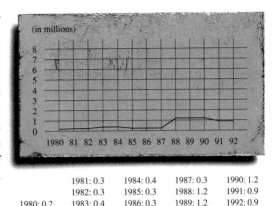

	1981: 0.3	1984: 0.4	1987: 0.3	1990: 1.2
	1982: 0.3	1985: 0.3	1988: 1.2	1991: 0.9
1980: 0.2	1983: 0.4	1986: 0.3	1989: 1.2	1992: 0.9

Fig. B.5
NORTH AMERICA: Number of Refugees, 1980-1992

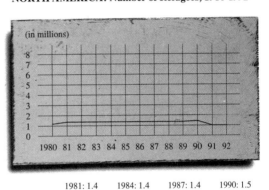

	1981: 1.4	1984: 1.4	1987: 1.4	1990: 1.5
	1982: 1.4	1985: 1.4	1988: 1.4	1991: 1.0
1980: 1.2	1983: 1.4	1986: 1.4	1989: 1.4	1992: 1.0

Fig. B.6
OCEANIA: Number of Refugees, 1980-1992

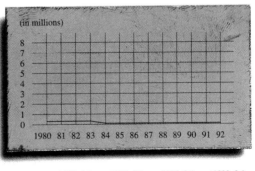

	1981: 0.3	1984: 0.1	1987: 0.1	1990: 0.1
	1982: 0.3	1985: 0.1	1988: 0.1	1991: 0.1
1980: 0.3	1983: 0.3	1986: 0.1	1989: 0.1	1992: 0.1

Note: See Annex I.1 for breakdown of regions by country

return – and even against ways of pursuing political or economic objectives that cause masses of people to fear so deeply for their lives or security that they become refugees.

"The responsibilities of countries of origin are only now emerging from the distorted political perspectives of the Cold War"

The emphasis on state responsibility is not limited to countries of origin. External forces, states and institutions often play major roles in triggering and sustaining refugee flows. They are even more strongly implicated in the deeper root causes of displacement such as economic inequality and deprivation, militarization and internal factionalism. An acknowledgment of shared responsibility can form the basis of broadly based political efforts to resolve refugee problems.

The principle of no forcible return of refugees to places where their lives or freedom would be threatened is essential to protect people whose right to remain at home has been violated. *Non-refoulement* has always been, and remains, indispensable to international protection. It is expressed as an obligation of states in the 1951 Convention, and has gained universal recognition through regional refugee instruments and as a part of customary international law. Despite broad acknowledgment of the principle, however, refugees continue to be refused entry or forcibly expelled, sometimes in very large numbers and to situations of grave danger.

The new emphases on prevention, repatriation and the responsibilities of states of origin do not in any way detract from this core principle of *non-refoulement*. Prevention is not prevention of movement but prevention of compulsion to move; repatriation of refugees must be voluntary and should not be encouraged until it is safe for them to go back. No country should act in a way that compels its people to flee but, in an imperfect world, the right not to be sent back is a crucial safeguard of life and liberty. Without it, there can be no meaningful international protection.

The responsibilities of asylum countries are well-established, even if they need to be constantly reaffirmed. The responsibilities of potential countries of origin, however, are only now emerging from the distorted political perspectives of the Cold-War period. The causes of refugee movements must now be urgently addressed in order to preserve the foundations of international protection – which could otherwise be overwhelmed, if only by the sheer numbers of claimants.

The conclusions now being reached seem self-evident in the cold light of current crises: the protection that the international community can offer to refugees is not an adequate substitute for the protection that they should receive from their own governments in their own countries. The generosity of asylum countries cannot fully replace the loss of a homeland or relieve the pain of exile. In this time of heightened tensions between peoples within states, displacement is in too many cases not a by-product of aggression but one of its fundamental aims. Making sure that human rights are respected where people live so that they do not have to flee to find protection is a matter of the greatest urgency.

Box 2

The Evolution of Refugee Protection

The international protection of refugees is a framework for promoting and defending the rights of people who have been forced to sever links with their home country. They know that they cannot rely, at home, on the protection of the police, access to a fair trial, redress of grievances through the courts, prosecution of those who violate their rights or help from their country's consular services when abroad. These are among the forms of legal and social protection that a properly functioning government is normally expected to extend to its nationals at home and abroad. They make up the content of "national protection".

Since refugees cannot count on national protection, and are unable to take advantage of the normal standards laid down by international law for the treatment of people outside their home country, special international standards have had to be defined to take account of their particular plight.

The foundations of international protection: 1921-47

The conviction that the international community of states – rather than individual governments or private charitable organizations – has a duty to provide refugees with protection and find solutions to their problems dates from the time of the League of Nations. The aftermath of World War I, the Russian Revolution and the collapse of the Ottoman Empire produced mass movements of people in Europe and Asia Minor. The League of Nations defined refugees in terms of specific groups of people who were judged to be in danger if they returned to their home countries. The League's first action on behalf of refugees took place in 1921, when it created the position of High Commissioner for Russian Refugees – and elected Fridtjof Nansen to fill it.

Over the following years, the League set up a succession of organizations and agreements to deal with new refugee situations as they emerged. The list of national categories was progressively extended to take in Assyrians, Turks, Greeks, Armenians, Spaniards and Austrian and German Jews among others. Starting with the problem of identity papers and travel documents, measures to protect refugees became more comprehensive as time went on, covering a wide range of matters of vital importance to their daily lives, such as the regularization of their personal status, access to employment and protection against expulsion.

When the United Nations replaced the League of Nations in 1947, it established a new body, the International Refugee Organization (IRO). The IRO's mandate was to protect existing refugee groups and one new category – the 21 million or so refugees scattered throughout Europe in the aftermath of World War II.

Initially, the IRO's main objective was repatriation, but the political build-up to the Cold War tilted the balance instead toward resettlement of those who had "valid objections" to returning home. Such "valid objections" included "persecution, or fear of persecution because of race, religion, nationality or political opinions".

UNHCR and the 1951 Convention

The IRO was replaced by the Office of the United Nations High Commissioner for Refugees (UNHCR) in 1951. By that time, international protection was firmly enshrined as the new organization's principal *raison d'être*. The Statute of UNHCR, adopted by a General Assembly resolution in December 1950, outlines the responsibilities of the Office, the most important of which are "providing international protection ... and ... seeking permanent solutions for the problem of refugees".

The 1951 CONVENTION RELATING TO THE STATUS OF REFUGEES was drawn up in parallel with the creation of UNHCR. It is a legally binding treaty and a milestone in international refugee law. It contains a general definition of the term "refugee" that no longer ties it to specific national groups: a refugee is a person who is outside his or her former home country owing to a well-founded fear of persecution for reasons of race, religion, nationality, membership of a particular social group or political opinion, and who is unable or unwilling to avail himself or herself of the protection of that country, or to return there for reasons of fear of persecution.

The Convention also clearly establishes the principle of *non-refoulement*, according to which no person may be returned against his or her will to a territory where he or she may be exposed to persecution. It sets standards for the treatment of refugees, including their legal status, employment and welfare.

The scope of the Convention, however, was confined to people who had become refugees as a result of events that took place before 1 January 1951, and signatory states were given the option of limiting its geographical application to Europe. In contrast, UNHCR was given a general competence to deal with refugee problems wherever they might arise, irrespective of date or location, as long as those concerned had a well-founded fear of persecution.

Subsequent decades demonstrated that movements of refugees were by no means a phenomenon confined to World War II and its immediate aftermath. As new refugee groups emerged, it became increasingly necessary to adapt the Convention in order to make it applicable to new refugee situations. In 1967, a **PROTOCOL** was introduced which abolished the dateline, making the Convention truly universal. By June 1993, 111 states had signed both the 1951 Convention and the 1967 Protocol, and a further seven had signed one or the other.

Regional initiatives

The Organization of African Unity (OAU) decided as early as 1963 that a regional refugee treaty was needed, in order to take account of special characteristics of the situation in Africa. The resulting 1969 **OAU CONVENTION GOVERNING THE SPECIFIC ASPECTS OF REFUGEE PROBLEMS IN AFRICA** expanded the definition of a refugee to people who were compelled to leave their country not only as a result of persecution but also "owing to external aggression, occupation, foreign domination or events seriously disturbing public order in either part or the whole of his county of origin or nationality".

In 1984, the Central American nations, joined by Mexico and Panama, adopted a declaration that built upon the OAU definition, adding to it the additional criterion of "massive violation of human rights". Although not formally binding, the **CARTAGENA DECLARATION ON REFUGEES** has become the basis of refugee policy in the region, and has been incorporated into the national legislation of a number of states.

The extended refugee definitions of the OAU Convention and the Cartagena Declaration have brought international protection to large numbers of people who may not be covered by the 1951 Convention but who are forced to move for a complex range of reasons including persecution, widespread human rights abuses, armed conflict and generalized violence. The extended definitions have been of particular importance in situations of massive influx where it is generally impractical to examine individual claims for refugee status.

The broadening of the refugee definition in response to regional considerations has provided much needed flexibility to international action on behalf of people forced to flee their countries. However, it has also introduced a new complexity in that a person recognized as a refugee in one country or region may not necessarily be considered one elsewhere.

Refugees and displaced people

The UN General Assembly and the Secretary-General have, on an *ad hoc* basis, frequently asked UNHCR to take care of groups of people – usually referred to as "persons of concern" – who are covered neither by the 1951 Convention, nor even by the extended regional definitions of a refugee. It has been recognized, for example, that some groups of internally displaced people need international protection, such as the Kurds in northern Iraq and civilians in parts of Bosnia and Herzegovina.

The international community continues to devise innovative ways to respond to the needs of people who cannot rely on the protection of their own governments. It is less likely, today, to insist that they must first cross an international border in order to find help. While such flexibility marks a welcome advance, it is vital that the core elements of the international refugee protection system are not diluted in the process.

Chapter one

The Dynamics of Displacement

There are as many reasons for moving as there are migrants. A particular set of reasons, involving persecution and the lack of national protection, distinguishes the refugee from other migrants. In practice, it is often difficult to pick out a specific cause for departure. People leave their homes as the result of a complicated mixture of fears, hopes, ambitions and other pressures which can be hard, if not impossible, to unravel.

Even for refugees, the reasons for flight are normally complex. The immediate cause of an exodus may be individual persecution, armed conflict, campaigns of repression, the violent collapse of civil society or a dozen variations on these themes. Behind these phenomena lie deeper and often interrelated patterns of political, economic, ethnic, environmental or human rights pressures, which are further complicated by the interplay between domestic and international factors.

The refugee problems of the 1990s are characterized by their complexity. They cannot be treated in isolation from the conditions that give rise to them – nor can those conditions be isolated from refugee concerns. If left unresolved, the problems of the displaced rebound upon the societies that send and receive them. Refugees often become an integral part of the dynamic that created them in the first place.

The situations that produce refugees also produce other forms of displacement, including people who have not crossed an international border but face the same fears and dangers as refugees. And they continue to affect people who have returned home to difficult and dangerous circumstances. In some settings, it is both unfair and counter-productive to assist refugees while ignoring the humanitarian needs of others in very similar predicaments, including people who have not even left their homes but who are subject to the same insecurity and deprivation. There remains, however, a crucial distinction to be made between people who need international protection, and those who can call on their own governments as a first line of defence.

In analysing a refugee flow, the problem is not simply to identify the multiple causes of flight but to understand the complex ways in which they interact. The stakes are high. A faulty or incomplete analysis may result in inadequate policies and inappropriate solutions. At worst, it can fuel the cycle of displacement it is meant to resolve.

Root causes

The international system of refugee protection was consolidated in the aftermath of World War II and during the tense early stages of the Cold War. To negotiators looking back to the Nazi persecutions and over their shoulders at Stalinist repression, the causes of the contemporary refugee problems did not seem excessively complicated. The governments of the countries that produced refugees were assumed not to be susceptible to international pressure concerning the treatment of their citizens. There was little to debate. A political consensus among Western democracies that the people of Eastern Europe were persecuted by their governments meant that the limited numbers who managed to flee were automatically granted asylum.

"Most conflicts in the world today are within rather than between states"

Conflicts over decolonization in the late 1950s and 1960s – such as those in Algeria, Angola, Rwanda and Zaire – generated large numbers of refugees but did not shake the disinclination to examine root causes. Again, the causes seemed self-evident. It was not until the numbers of refugees escalated sharply in the 1970s that the debate was joined. Some of the energy behind it was dissipated in argument over whether internal or external factors were chiefly to blame for refugee problems. It is now evident that both play major parts; further generalization is pointless. But the debate provided the stimulus for an analytical effort that is still going on. It has already, for example, borne fruit in the

specific approaches to the resolution of the very different refugee problems affecting Central America and Viet Nam.

1. Political roots

The 1951 Convention identified what is still a major root cause of refugee flows: persecution based on who the refugee is (race, nationality, membership of a particular social group) or what he or she believes (religion or political opinion). Persecution usually takes place in the context of fundamental political disputes over who controls the state, how society organizes itself, and who commands the power, privileges, patronage and perks that go with political control. These disputes are at their most heated during periods of intense change – in the aftermath of a revolutionary struggle (successful or failed), at the moment of a far-reaching change of regime or upon the emergence of a new state.

Entire social classes or ethnic groups may be presumed to hold political opinions in opposition to the state, such as the professional classes in Cambodia under Pol Pot, or the Kurds in Iraq under Saddam Hussein. Although the state usually has privileged access to the instruments of violence and persecution, it is not only states who indulge in acts that generate refugees. Armed opposition groups, such as the Shining Path in Peru, Renamo in Mozambique, the Khmer Rouge in Cambodia, and nationalist groups in Bosnia and Herzegovina, have also made life unbearable – or impossible – for their adversaries and for many innocent bystanders.

As the map in Box 1.1 shows, virtually all of the refugee-producing conflicts taking place in the world during the early part of 1993 were within states rather than between them. Weak states are especially prone to internal violence, as credible mechanisms for resolving conflicts peacefully or seeking redress for violations of rights are eroded or cease to function altogether. The lack of representative political institutions, an independent judiciary, impartial law enforcement or free elections may lead people to conclude that armed resistance is the only way to bring about change. However, the weakness of a state is very often mirrored by the weakness of opposition. Political conflict degenerates into anarchy, with the state just one of many contenders for the dwindling spoils, while the population is deprived of any form of national security. Somalia, with its tens of thousands of dead, hundreds of thousands of refugees and an estimated one million internally displaced, is today's template of this kind of nightmare – but elements of the pattern are familiar from Afghanistan, Haiti and Liberia.

As the superpower rivalry of the Cold War all too clearly demonstrated, external political involvement of the partisan variety complicates internal conflict and raises the level of violence. The largest refugee flows of the last three decades – Afghanistan, Viet Nam, Cambodia, the Horn of Africa, Angola, Mozambique – were exacerbated by superpower involvement. External intervention in local disputes often disrupts traditional processes of mediation by giving one party, clan or faction a definitive upper hand. Contenders are provided with additional firepower to enforce their will. An outside patron may prop up leaders who have little if any domestic legitimacy. An infusion of military aid increases the destructiveness of confrontation, while economic aid raises the stakes in the contest for control of domestic institutions.

The vast majority of refugees today, as in the past, are fleeing not from targeted acts of individual persecution but from generalized violence that endangers civilians and radically disrupts everyday life. These conditions are the products of instability, internally or externally generated, and are fed by political opportunism that seeks to exploit social divisions for political gain.

2. Economic roots

Economic tensions are among the major underlying causes of refugee flows, but the relationship is not as straightforward as might be assumed. It is too simple to say that poverty begets refugees. In relatively static situations, extreme deprivation is as likely to breed resignation as resistance. More combustible material springs from a deterioration of economic standing. Bitter disputes among national groups arise from efforts to preserve or advance the standing of one group at the relative expense of others. Disputes concerning the distribution of resources during general economic decline are the most politically explosive. Leaders, trying to avoid the blame for deteriorating economic conditions, frequently turn to scapegoating. Minority groups often provide the most convenient targets.

"Minority groups are often turned into scapegoats"

Poverty undoubtedly exacerbates ethnic and communal tensions. To know that the number of rural poor has doubled since 1950, that per capita incomes have fallen steadily in a number of regions and that malnutrition has risen, is to know that the stage is set for continuing refugee flows – but this is only one part of the dynamic of displacement. More than one billion people worldwide live in absolute poverty.[3] Only a small proportion of them will become refugees. In fact, the total number of refugees worldwide amounts to less than 2 per cent of the destitute. Nevertheless, economic deprivation interacts with other circumstances to heighten instability and aggravate conflicts.

In near-subsistence economies, violent conflict disrupts food production and distribution even as it displaces people. When the conditions of daily life, precarious to begin with, are disrupted by war, the ensuing famine and disease often become greater threats to the population than the fighting itself. In Sudan's civil war, for example, 600,000 people are thought to have died so far, many of whom have starved or succumbed to diseases that they would probably have been able to resist had the situation been more stable.

There is an obvious logic in the argument that stagnation and decline aggravate conflict. That rapid growth can have the same effect may be less apparent. Every process of change has

Box 1.1
Map of Conflict and Refugees

Country and region labels visible on the map: RUSSIAN FEDERATION, MOLDOVA, CROATIA, BOSNIA AND HERZEGOVINA, GEORGIA, ARMENIA, AZERBAIJAN, TAJIKISTAN, TURKEY, LEBANON, ISRAEL, IRAQ, AFGHANISTAN, KUWAIT, MYANMAR, SENEGAL, MALI, CHAD, SUDAN, DJIBOUTI, ETHIOPIA, SOMALIA, SRI LANKA, CAMBO[DIA], SIERRA LEONE, LIBERIA, TOGO, ZAIRE, RWANDA, ANGOLA, MOZAMBIQUE

⚜ Active conflict – Areas where fighting took place between 1 January
and 1 July 1993

⚜ Recent conflict – Areas where fighting has taken place since 1 January 1990,
but where no serious outbreaks occurred between 1 January and 1 July 1993

→ Active flows – An exodus of more than 1,000 refugees was recorded in period
1 January to 1 July 1993

⇢ Dormant Flows – An exodus of refugees occurred between 1 January 1990
and 1 January 1993, 5,000 of whom still remain outside their country of origin.

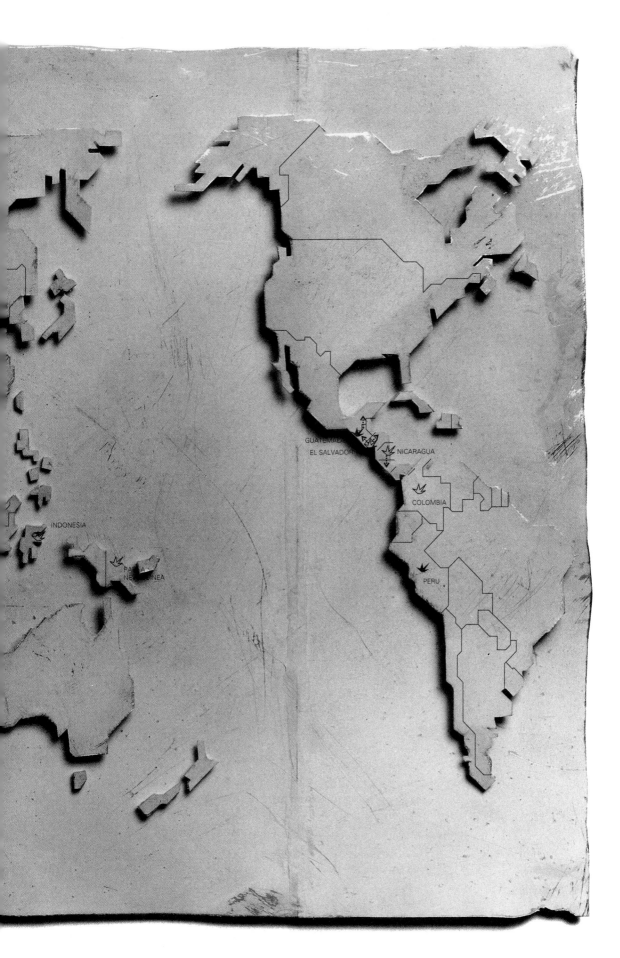

winners and losers. The dislocations of development result in imbalances, with some classes, regions or ethnic groups benefiting disproportionately. They may become the targets of resentment, or themselves assert a claim for self-determination in order to be free of what they see as the drag of less progressive elements of society. Either reaction may provoke violent confrontation.

3. Environmental roots

Millions of people have been forced to leave their homes because the land on which they live has become uninhabitable or is no longer able to support them. In some cases the cause is a natural disaster; in others, the catastrophe is caused by humans. The disruption to the habitat may be sudden, as at Chernobyl or Mount Pinatubo, or as gradual as the spread of a desert or the retreat of a forest.

"In extreme cases, destruction of habitat may be used as a deliberate weapon of war"

The terminology for describing environmentally induced migration is controversial. For many observers, "migration" does not convey the fact that the people affected are *forcibly* uprooted. To call them refugees seems to convey more accurately that they left their homes involuntarily, for reasons not of their own making. Accurate use of the term "refugee", however, implies a need for international protection. For most people whose usual places of residence have become uninhabitable, the first recourse remains their own governments and societies. People displaced by environmental degradation or natural disaster undoubtedly need assistance. They do not necessarily require the kind of international protection implied in the word "refugee".

There are, nevertheless, clear links between environmental degradation and refugee flows. The deterioration of the natural resource base,

coupled with demographic pressure and chronic poverty, can lead to or exacerbate political, ethnic, social and economic tensions which in turn result in conflicts that force people to flee. Africa, for example, accounts for 10 per cent of the world's population and hosts over 29 per cent of its refugees. It is no coincidence that those parts of the continent that are most affected by soil erosion, drought and other environmental problems are also the main theatres of armed conflicts, recurrent famine and consequent refugee movements.

In the Sahel and the Horn of Africa, the combination of rapidly expanding populations, drought and competition between nomads and settled agriculturalists has erupted into violence along a number of fronts. Disputes over irrigable land in the Senegal River basin have contributed to the flow of thousands of Senegalese and Mauritanians across their common border in both directions. In southern Ethiopia, incursions by certain clans into the traditional grazing lands of other clans have led to fierce and bloody clashes, and to a large, though temporary, flow of refugees into northern Kenya. Further south, in Mozambique, civilians already under severe pressure from the effects of civil war were pushed to the very edge of survival – and in many cases beyond it – by the effects of drought in 1992. More than 100,000 of them took refuge in neighbouring Malawi in that year alone.

Occasionally, the destruction of a habitat takes on the character of persecution – for example if it occurs as a result of deliberate governmental action or gross negligence and no effort is made to compensate or assist the people affected. Indigenous people are particularly vulnerable to this kind of assault, as their way of life is often closely connected to a particular terrain. In extreme cases, for example in Iraqi Kurdistan, destruction of habitat may be used as a deliberate weapon of war. People who are uprooted because of wilfully negligent or intentional destruction of the environment may indeed need international protection.

Long-term strategies of prevention should address environmental damage as a potential

A Bosnian Muslim in the Music School in Mostar, with portrait of Tito.
Bosnia and Herzegovina, September 1992.

contributor to refugee flows. There is no comfort in the fact that today only a minority of environmentally displaced people need international protection. The international community has every interest in responding to the need to preserve and rehabilitate the environment before degradation leads to violence and persecution – and a mass of displaced people who easily meet the conventional definition of refugees.

"Ethnic tensions are highly susceptible to political exploitation"

4. Ethnic tensions

Conflicts between ethnic groups have proliferated in recent years. Armenia and Azerbaijan, Bhutan, Burma, Ethiopia, Georgia, Iraq, Sri Lanka, Sudan and of course the former Yugoslavia are among a long list of examples. Very few modern states are ethnically homogeneous. The 190 or so independent states currently in existence contain at least 5,000 ethnic groups.[4] Ethnic diversity is part of human geography almost everywhere. As a consequence, the notion of an ethnically pure nation-state is almost everywhere a fantasy, which can only be realized at an unacceptably high human cost.

Ethnic tensions can be seen as a root cause of refugee flows for two reasons. First, they are highly susceptible to political exploitation. Factions seeking to mobilize support commonly seek to fan ethnic antagonisms for their own ends. Ethnic conflict is a likely outcome when control of the state is captured by a single ethnic group that uses its power to further its own interests at the expense of others.

Second, despite the fact that most states contain a variety of ethnic groups, the ethnic identity of a single group is all too often made into a defining characteristic of nationality. Some minority groups may be seen as an obstacle to nation-building, incapable of fitting into a homogeneous national identity. Ethnic Albanians and Bosnian Muslims, for example,

have no place in extreme nationalist visions of an Orthodox Christian "Greater Serbia". The ideology of apartheid in South Africa defined the non-white population out of citizenship. Members of groups other than the dominant one may be exposed first of all to discrimination, then to forced assimilation, persecution, expulsion or even genocide. In many refugee crises, ethnicity is the criterion according to which people are denied the protection of their national governments (see Box 1.2).

Recurrent conflict among ethnic or communal groups within a state calls for mediation by the central government. If the state is party to the conflict, or if it is otherwise unwilling or too weak to perform its mediating role effectively, "ethnic cleansing" or other forms of forcible unmixing of populations may be the result, leading to very large flows of refugees – as in Palestine and the Punjab in 1948, and in Bosnia and Herzegovina, Armenia and Azerbaijan today.

Ethnic tensions are also vulnerable to manipulation by external forces. Irredentism – the attempt to unite all territories occupied by a single ethnic group into one political entity – is the most obvious form, and has played a large part in refugee-producing conflicts, in the Horn of Africa and the former Yugoslavia, to cite two examples. Somalia's ambition to incorporate Somali-inhabited areas of the Ethiopian Ogaden led to a war in 1977, and the population of much of the region remains unsettled to this day, owing to a combination of political instability, ethnic tension, economic collapse and recurring drought.

Throughout the Cold-War period, superpower rivalry was a source of patronage for ethnic factions in numerous conflicts. Like European colonialism before it, the Cold War fostered or even created ethnic tensions. The recruitment of local factions into strategic alliances with East or West disrupted historical balances between groups, and artificially strengthened the position of client groups by arming them, arranging sanctuaries and providing diplomatic support for them. Members of certain disaffected ethnic groups were systematically co-opted to act as preferred proxies, intermediaries or fighters –

Box 1.2

The Ethnic Factor: The Nepalese of Bhutan

The ethnic origins of the refugees who have arrived in Nepal since 1990 are not in dispute. All agree that they are made up of a number of ethnic groups who fit comfortably under the generic label "Nepalese". For the most part Hindu by religion, they are commonly known in Bhutan as "Lhotshampas". This ethnic designation sets them apart from the Bhutan's northern population of Buddhist Drukpas. Almost everything else about the refugees is a subject of some controversy – be it the date of their migration to Bhutan, the validity of their claim to Bhutanese citizenship, the reasons for their flight and even, in some cases, whether they are coming from Bhutan at all.

The first refugees began fleeing to Nepal in early 1991, crossing malaria-infested jungles in India and arriving with little more than the clothes on their backs. During the first half of 1992, the influx increased sharply, with between 300 and 500 people arriving each day. By June 1993, estimates put their number at more than 100,000. Around 86,000 are in six camps in eastern Nepal and some 25,000 are scattered in India.

According to the refugees, they were forced to leave their homes as a result of abuses ranging from revocation of citizenship and property rights, to discrimination, persecution, torture and rape. The government of Bhutan denies the charges and says that many are recent illegal immigrants. However, in a public statement made in April 1993, the Bhutanese authorities estimated that 30 per cent of the population in the camps could be Bhutanese citizens.

The precise date of large-scale Nepalese immigration into Bhutan is also disputed. Some cite continuous migration eastwards since the 1700s, while others, including the Bhutanese authorities, say it is a much more recent phenomenon. Nevertheless, many of the Lhotshampas appear to have lived in the southern plains of Bhutan for several generations. Immigrants already in the country in 1958 were granted citizenship.

Bhutan says large-scale illegal immigration has continued since that date, and that measures to curb it are necessary if the Drukpas are not to become a minority in their own small country. Bhutan's official national population figures range dramatically from 600,000 to 1.4 million. The ethnic breakdown is similarly confusing. In a 1992 interview with Reuters, the King of Bhutan said that 28 per cent of the population were of Nepalese origin; other recent estimates have ranged between 45 and 53 per cent. A new citizenship act introduced in 1985 introduced more restrictive criteria and applied them retrospectively, thus endangering the acquired rights of many Lhotshampas, or those of their spouses and children.

The exodus to Nepal came after an edict was issued in 1989 requiring residents either to show proof of citizenship in accordance with the 1985 nationality law and the census which followed in 1988, or to leave the country by January 1992. Other measures – seen as discriminatory by the Lhotshampas – were introduced, including the compulsory wearing of national dress and the removal of the Nepalese language from the primary school curriculum. Growing unrest among the Nepalese population led to pro-democracy demonstrations in 1990 which, in turn, set off a government backlash conditioned by concern over Nepalese nationalist movements in Sikkim and India.

For Nepal, the refugees have posed a dilemma. Although many Lhotshampas have never visited Nepal and few have any family links there, they do regard it as their original home. There is concern that a prolongation of the situation may result in additional ethnic Nepalese returning to an impoverished homeland, where a demographic explosion is already threatening to become a national catastrophe. The majority of the refugees are located in the most politically volatile area of the country, and local resentment is on the rise. As a result, the government wishes to see rapid repatriation to Bhutan. In the meantime, Nepalese arriving after 1 June 1993 are being individually screened to ensure that only genuine refugees enter the camps.

Following a long period of stalemate, the Bhutanese and Nepalese governments agreed to resume talks on the problem in July 1993, giving rise to hopes of progress towards a solution. The longer the situation festers, the greater the danger that frustration will lead to increasing politicization and militancy which, if unchecked, could result in an ethnic upheaval involving not only Bhutan and Nepal, but also parts of neighbouring India.

for example, the Hmong in Laos or the Miskitos in Nicaragua – thereby exposing the whole group to retribution. Local impulses toward accommodation or reconciliation were sometimes submerged by a powerful patron's interest in continuing the conflict. Refugee populations themselves became pawns in disputes remote from their own immediate concerns.

"By the time massive abuses of human rights occur, the chances of averting refugee flows are slim"

If the Cold-War era was dominated by ideological conflict, the fear is widespread that the 1990s may be the start of a new era of ethnic violence that will uproot additional millions of people from their homes. Already, refugees from dozens of ethnic conflicts look to the international community for material assistance and protection. Supposedly ancient hatreds, to which many people attribute the savagery of ethnic conflicts, can be invented, revived or kept from dying a natural death by opportunists who see in them a vehicle for personal or political profit.

The challenge for modern states is to alleviate ethnic tensions through mediation and to prevent them from turning into violent conflict. This preventive role is set within a more positive responsibility: to manage ethnic diversity in a way that promotes tolerance within and beyond national borders.

Human rights and refugee flows

Coerced departure is a violation of the human right to remain peacefully in one's home. The direct denial of other basic rights, including the rights of civilians not to be targeted in military actions, often provides the immediate impetus for flight. Indirectly, protest about or resistance to human rights violations may provoke violent retaliation, or take a violent form itself. An accumulation of abuses accompanied by violence, which leads to further abuses and a generalized climate of fear, is a sequence that frequently produces mass exodus. In Iraq, Bosnia and Herzegovina, Myanmar, Guatemala and elsewhere, human rights violations have been at the core of major humanitarian emergencies.

The rights that states are obliged to protect are codified in the Universal Declaration of Human Rights, and are translated into binding form in the International Covenant on Civil and Political Rights and the International Covenant on Economic, Social and Cultural Rights. These instruments and others identify the sovereign state as the primary defender of rights such as the right not to be subjected to torture or to arbitrary detention and the rights to freedom of expression, thought and belief. The refugee's need for international protection arises from the violation of his or her rights combined with the state's palpable failure in its duty to defend citizens against such violations – which of course includes the duty to refrain from violations itself.

The responsibility of states towards their citizens is coming under closer scrutiny as refugee flows increase and come to be seen by many receiving states as a threat to international peace and security. Both humanitarian and security concerns have focused attention more sharply on the causes of mass exodus, bringing human rights out from behind the shield of national sovereignty. Indeed, the concept of the state's responsibility towards its citizens is being extended to encompass a responsibility towards the international community for the way those citizens are treated. Protection against the most threatening forms of abuse, such as arbitrary killings, detention, torture and disappearance, can have a profound impact on the cycle of violence and fear that impels so many people to flee (see Box 1.3).

Human rights violations do not occur in a vacuum. Like other causes of refugee flows, they exist in a complex environment of economic strains, political instability, a tradition of violence, ecological deterioration and ethnic tensions. One factor or another may dominate a particular situation while interacting with others. By the time serious and massive abuses of fundamental rights occur, the chances of averting refugee flows are slim indeed.

Catalysts

If it is possible to detect broad patterns in the root causes of refugee movements, the immediate triggers tend to be much more specific to the particular setting. In northern Iraq, the catalyst was a savage attack by government forces in response to a failed rebellion. In the former Yugoslavia, it was a series of localized (though co-ordinated) campaigns of terror against ethnic opponents, involving gross violations of human rights, forced displacement and indiscriminate destruction of lives and livelihoods. In Somalia, it was the disintegration of law and order, leading to the violent disruption of production and distribution, which left millions of people vulnerable to famine. In

Box 1.3
Victims of Torture

Among the most barbarous forms of persecution suffered by people who subsequently become refugees are physical and mental torture. Some victims never fully recover. The following is an extract from a recent account by one Middle Eastern refugee.

I'm sorry I couldn't come to see you earlier. I couldn't walk. In five days time I'll be 28 years old but my life is in ruins. Since my late teens I was indirectly involved in the activities of my parents, brothers and sister in opposition to the regime at home. Six years ago my sister was arrested, one year later my parents and brothers. I never heard of any of them again.

Following their disappearance, I took up the struggle for democracy. I quickly fell under suspicion and one night, as I was leaving the bakery where I worked, I was seized and thrust into a waiting car. I tried to escape at a traffic light but was shot in the leg.

Bleeding profusely and in great pain, I was blindfolded and taken to prison. There I was interrogated and beaten continuously for four or five hours. At first they beat me with their fists, then with a sort of steel-capped cudgel. When I started to lose consciousness, I was thrown into a cell with my hands tied behind my back. My torturers continued to beat me with electric cables on the soles of my feet. At last, I was given an injection and left alone. The following day I was again interrogated and taken to persuade women prisoners in the next cell to talk.

When the guards realized we were still not telling the truth, they took me to another room, tied me to a cross and poured petrol all over me. I was left there for hours on end under threat of being burned alive. When I still wouldn't co-operate, I was again beaten up and sexually abused by one of the guards. Two days later my kidneys stopped working and I was hospitalized. As my legs had been broken in several places, they had to put steel rivets in to hold the bones together.

When I was a little better, I was taken back to prison and tied up for hours in an unnatural position. Day after day, the torture continued. I was left hanging from the roof by one hand; I was beaten and burned with cigarettes; I almost lost my sight. Then I was forced to watch as women prisoners were tortured and raped. Many of them died. When I was again sent back to hospital, I realized that they did not want to kill me, just to destroy me mentally and physically.

While I was in hospital, one of the nurses drugged my guards and helped me to escape. He brought me to the border, travelling by night and hiding by day.

Three days after this interview, the narrator was resettled on emergency grounds in a European country where he underwent surgery and received specialized psychotherapy for torture survivors.

Each year, an average of 120 refugee victims of torture are recommended by UNHCR for priority resettlement in countries where their safety and rehabilitation can be assured. As resettlement places are available for only the most severely traumatized and vulnerable cases, these comprise a tiny percentage of the total number of refugees who have been subjected to torture or other forms of physically and psychologically damaging treatment.

Sudan, the imposition of laws and regulations which were unacceptable to a large segment of the population in the south of the country re-ignited a long-running secessionist struggle. In Haiti, a military coup against an elected government prompted a crackdown on civil and political expression as well as a regional economic boycott. In Afghanistan, the intervention of the Soviet Union in support of a client raised the level of violence in a civil war, which was further exacerbated by Western intervention to equip and fund opposition forces in exile.

"The immediate cause of flight is usually an imminent threat to life, liberty or security"

While the events that trigger refugee outflows are specific to each particular setting, certain common denominators are apparent. The immediate cause of flight is in most cases an imminent threat to life, liberty or security. Deliberate expulsion may present any or all of these threats. In situations of armed conflict, the perils to civilian life and security are not only accidental. Although non-combatants do inadvertently get caught in the cross-fire between opposing forces, the main dangers posed to civilians lie in the flagrant disregard of international humanitarian law (also known as the laws of war), which forbids attacks on the persons or livelihoods of non-combatants. The use of indiscriminate weapons, the adoption of scorched-earth policies in enemy territories and the denial of access to food supplies are among the violations of humanitarian law that have become major causes of contemporary refugee flows.

Refugees and non-refugees

The world's 18.2 million refugees are part of a complex migratory phenomenon. The United Nations has estimated that 80-100 million people worldwide live outside their countries of origin.[5] Legal labour migration accounts for 25-30 million of these. The number of undocumented economic migrants is understandably difficult to estimate, but is assumed to lie between 20 million and 40 million people. Each year, 150,000-300,000 people are accepted for resettlement on humanitarian grounds, and more than 2 million seek asylum in a foreign country.

Global migration thus proceeds across a spectrum of motivation, ranging from those who flee from persecution to those who flee from serious danger, those who are trying to escape from misery and those who wish to leave behind a lack of opportunity. The most privileged are able to move for reasons of personal preference or convenience. International obligations to allow people to remain in a country other than their own are clear at either end of this spectrum, but in the middle there is no consensus. At the one extreme, there is no legal responsibility, although there may be a strong interest, for a state to admit economic migrants. At the other, international law obliges a state to refrain from forcibly returning refugees, who have a well-founded fear of persecution. Some states, notably the signatories to the 1969 OAU Convention, have committed themselves to extending protection to people in danger from generalized violence, and many other states do so in practice. The appropriate response to misery is generally considered to be humanitarian assistance rather than international protection, unless of course misery is the result of persecution or violence and national protection is not available.

It can be difficult to make a clear distinction between refugees and non-refugees. It has always been common for large-scale economic migrations to be accompanied by politically motivated exile or flight, and vice versa. The level of economic discontent that gives rise to emigration also gives rise, in many cases, to protest or resistance against the system of government that perpetrates, tolerates or is powerless to correct conditions of deprivation.

The distinction between refugees and economic migrants is most difficult when people flee from countries where poverty is perpetuated by the political system. In Viet Nam, political repression was combined with economic stagnation (deepened by an economic boycott led by the United States) in a pattern that sustained an outflow of boat people for 15 years. Haiti is a case of debilitating poverty and repression feeding upon each other in a system of endemic corruption. Economic sanctions designed to underscore the government's lack of legitimacy may lead to results on the political level, but in the meantime they cause further deterioration of living standards in an already devastated economy.

Refugees and other migrants often use, or attempt to use, the same avenues for entry into another country. If labour migration channels are open, refugees may opt to avoid the bureaucratic rigours and uncertainties of asylum procedures and simply enter as workers. Labour needs in the industrialized countries have thus acted as an attraction for refugees as well as migrants. When, on the other hand, migration channels narrow, some economic migrants attempt to avail themselves of the asylum channels. In either case, previous settlement of members of the same ethnic or national group, whether as refugees or labour migrants, is one factor that helps direct the flow of people toward a particular destination.

The line between the voluntary migrant and the refugee is often a fine one. Yet it is important for states to be able to make the distinction in a fair and consistent manner so that people who genuinely asylum are granted it, and so that the protection system for refugees is not overwhelmed with economically motivated migrants.

Mixed populations

People in need of international protection include those who have left their countries for fear of persecution, victims of mass expulsions and people fleeing from a combination of violence, chaos and mass violation of human rights.

In addition to these international movements, the roughly 24 million people displaced within their own countries by armed conflict, the breakdown of public order, severe human rights violations and political persecution are displaced for the same reasons as refugees. The only difference is that they have not crossed an international border.

"No international institution has a general mandate to care for the internally displaced"

In Iraq, Ethiopia, Mozambique and other countries that have produced substantial numbers of refugees, the causes of external displacement have also created large numbers of internally displaced people. The geographical detail may seem trivial, but it can have life-or-death implications for the people affected. No international institution has the general mandate or the capacity to care for the internally displaced, even though they may have needs for protection and assistance that are indistinguishable from those of refugees.

In complex refugee situations where neighbouring countries import and export refugees, internally displaced people frequently coexist with refugees and suffering local inhabitants who have not been uprooted. The Hartisheik refugee camp in eastern Ethiopia illustrates the phenomenon of mixed populations vividly. By 1993 it had become one of the largest refugee concentrations in the world, with a population of some 250,000. The camp and surrounding areas contain Somalis who have fled the violence and disorder at home in Somalia; Ethiopians (some of Somali stock) who had been refugees in Somalia from the fighting in Ethiopia, and who were then driven back when the conflict in Somalia intensified; local people who were seriously affected by both the drought and the conflict nearby; and soldiers demobilized from the Ethiopian army after the defeat of the Mengistu regime. All of this diverse mix

Box 1.4
A Plan of Action for Viet Nam

A massive exodus from Viet Nam followed the collapse of the Saigon regime in 1975. The many who crossed the perilous seas of South East Asia became known as the "boat people". By July 1979, over 200,000 were languishing in camps in the region, and new arrivals were being prevented from landing, and were even being towed back out to sea. Confronted with this political and humanitarian crisis, the international community decided at the first conference on refugees from Indo-China, held in 1979, that Vietnamese boat people arriving in first asylum countries in South East Asia would be allowed to land in the region but would then be resettled in other countries. In the years that followed, nearly 700,000 people were resettled in the West under the 1979 burden-sharing arrangements.

The same year, in an effort to open up the possibility of legal emigration from Viet Nam and so reduce the number of clandestine departures (which had resulted in considerable loss of life at sea), UNHCR helped set up an Orderly Departure Programme, known as the ODP. This involved a complex procedure of matching the names of those accepted by Western countries with those proposed for departure by the Vietnamese government. The ODP provided a safer, officially sanctioned channel for emigration.

The numbers of boat people stabilized during the early 1980s. Resettlement countries were, however, growing reluctant to continue their open-ended commitment to resettle all boat people, and a backlog of those who did not meet increasingly restrictive resettlement criteria started to accumulate in camps. Nevertheless, the overall number of refugees in first asylum camps gradually declined.

In 1986, the situation changed dramatically as the result of a sudden and massive increase in clandestine departures from Viet Nam. The number of boat people in camps leapt from 31,694 at the beginning of 1986 to 65,349 by early 1989. Since there had been no significant deterioration in the human rights situation in Viet Nam, it was clear that the exodus, while retaining a refugee dimension, was increasingly driven by economic factors. A second International Conference on Indo-Chinese Refugees was convened in June

Fig. 1.A
Arrivals of Boat People in East and South East Asia: 1976-1992; and Orderly Departures from Viet Nam: 1979-1992

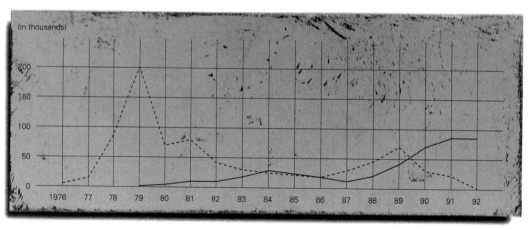

Arrivals of Boat People in East and South East Asia: 1976-1992 (- - - - -)

1976: 5,644	1979: 202,158	1982: 43,807	1985: 22,214	1988: 45,530	1991: 22,422
1977: 15,633	1980: 71,451	1983: 28,055	1986: 19,538	1989: 71,364	1992: 58
1978: 86,373	1981: 74,749	1984: 24,865	1987: 28,096	1990: 30,936	TOTAL: 792,893

Orderly Departures from Viet Nam: 1979-1992 (———)

1979: 1,979	1982: 10,057	1985: 24,940	1988: 21,275	1991: 86,444
1980: 4,706	1983: 18,978	1986: 18,418	1989: 43,177	1992: 86,121
1981: 9,815	1984: 29,154	1987: 12,961	1990: 70,411	TOTAL: 438,436

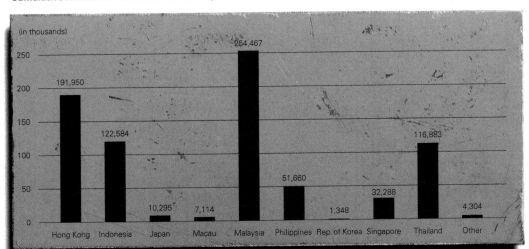

Fig. 1.B
Cumulative Arrivals of Vietnamese Boat People in East and South East Asia: 1976-1992

(in thousands)

Hong Kong	191,950
Indonesia	122,584
Japan	10,295
Macau	7,114
Malaysia	254,467
Philippines	51,660
Rep. of Korea	1,348
Singapore	32,288
Thailand	116,883
Other	4,304

1989. It adopted a Comprehensive Plan of Action (CPA), in an attempt to address the issue in a global and systematic way.

The CPA did away with blanket resettlement for all boat people – which was unique in the history of refugees – and introduced an approach that included the following elements:

• All Vietnamese boat people would be permitted to land in first asylum countries and would be screened for refugee status.

• All boat people who qualified as refugees would be resettled in a third country. Those who did not qualify would have to return to Viet Nam under a guarantee, monitored by UNHCR, that they would not be prosecuted for illegal departure.

• A programme would be set up by UNHCR to provide reintegration assistance to the returnees.

• The ODP programme would be expanded, its criteria liberalized and its procedures simplified to allow easier legal emigration for eligible groups such as family reunification

cases and former re-education camp internees.

• A "mass information campaign" would be launched in Viet Nam to inform the population of the provisions of the CPA, in order to discourage those who would not qualify as refugees from embarking on a life-threatening journey in the mistaken belief that they would automatically be resettled in the West.

Clandestine departures of boat people, most of whom would not be recognized as refugees under the CPA, continued at a high rate during the months prior to the adoption of the Plan. However, the implementation of the mass information campaign (see Chapter three, Box 3.5), and the beginning of voluntary repatriation back to Viet Nam soon brought about a substantial drop in the number of boat people. UNHCR is satisfied that the Vietnamese government's guarantees of non-prosecution and non-discrimination have been honoured.

In 1991, it became clear that many of the boat people still leaving Viet Nam were doing so

solely to acquire the repatriation allowance of $360. UNHCR suspended the grant for all those arriving in countries of first asylum on or after 27 September, 1991. Once this development had been publicized in Viet Nam through the mass information programme, numbers plummeted. By the end of the year, the exodus of boat people had virtually ceased. Only 58 boat people arrived in countries of first asylum in the whole of 1992, and 75 during the first five months of 1993. The introduction of repatriation under the CPA was controversial. The United States government argued that even those who failed to qualify for refugee status should be repatriated only on a voluntary basis until there was a change in political conditions in Viet Nam. However, faced with the choice between repatriation or an indefinite stay in camps with no chance of resettlement, many have opted to return. By 31 May 1993, 41,801 Vietnamese had gone home voluntarily, and 623 had been deported from Hong Kong.

of refugees, returnees, internally displaced, drought-affected locals and ex-soldiers face harsh conditions of extreme deprivation and similar needs for assistance.

One response to this kind of complex emergency is to abandon the attempt to categorize people according to their reasons for leaving home – or even according to whether they have left home or not. Instead, in such situations, need becomes the only criterion. A Programme of Action developed at the Horn of Africa Summit on Humanitarian Issues in April 1992 called for such an approach, based on non-discrimination among people in need in certain identified zones. Assistance programmes have been established on this basis in areas of eastern Ethiopia and southern Somalia.

"People should not have to struggle across an international border to get help"

This approach avoids making refugees a privileged class among people who are equally in need of assistance. Such people should not have to struggle across an international border to get help if the kind of assistance that they require can be provided closer to home. However, the overwhelming urgency of meeting the physical needs of people in these circumstances raises some troubling protection concerns. Not least among these is the danger that the availability of humanitarian assistance in the country of origin may be interpreted by the governments of neighbouring countries as a reason to refuse entry even though people my fear persecution as well as starvation. How can the asylum option be kept open, and the principle of *non-refoulement* remain uncompromised in such situations? The rapid growth of refugee populations amid circumstances that also expose local people to danger calls for innovative programmes – and for critical assessments of them.

Comprehensive responses

The complexity of refugee flows, both in terms of their causes and their manifestations, demands correspondingly complex responses. The totality of the problem – from causes through to solutions – requires careful examination. A comprehensive response must address all the reasons for flight, and the legitimate concerns of all the parties to a conflict. It will take into account, as appropriate, the rights and obligations of refugees and other affected populations, of the receiving countries and the countries of origin, opposition groups, third countries and international organizations.

Humanitarian agencies are being drawn more deeply into intricate political processes as a result of their involvement in comprehensive responses. Several plans have been developed and are being implemented, some under extremely precarious circumstances – as in the former Yugoslavia and Cambodia. Programmes for Viet Nam and Central America are more firmly established.

A comprehensive response includes several elements. The first priority is to deal with the immediate causes of displacement, for example by effecting cease-fires and negotiating internationally monitored agreements to stop persecution and violation of human rights. A second is to contribute to the development of structures for longer-term mediation, so that future disputes can be settled without resort to violence. A third element incorporates economic development plans to expand the resource base and to defuse issues arising from inequality of distribution. Refugees should be part of the process of rehabilitation and reconciliation at every stage.

The implementation of a comprehensive plan is not a task for humanitarian agencies alone, but for the entire international community. Solutions and protection for refugees are more durable if they are embedded in the wider processes of peace-keeping (or peace-making) and development. Issues such as access to the means of subsistence, protection of minority rights and representation of all parties in the councils of government are likely to be elements of a complex response. The Central American plan known as CIREFCA (see Chapter six, Box 6.5) provided an international framework for repatriation, reintegration and development. The Comprehensive Plan of Action (CPA) for Viet Nam was designed to tackle a mixed movement of refugees and economic migrants within a complex international political environment (see Box 1.4).

The largest UN operation of this kind to date, the UN Transitional Authority in Cambodia (UNTAC), combines peace-keeping, refugee repatriation, electoral registration and human rights monitoring with reconstruction assistance. The operation in the former Yugoslavia is if anything even more elaborate, with peace negotiations and humanitarian assistance taking place in the midst of a savage war.

The intricacy of a comprehensive response dictates that each plan must be individually devised to fit the needs of a particular situation. Certain basic elements, however, will be common to all. Respect for human rights, observance of *non-refoulement* and high standards of humane treatment for the displaced are the most important protection elements of such plans. Linkages with peace negotiations and development plans tie protection into the search for lasting solutions.

Effective responses to complex refugee problems present far-reaching challenges to the international community. Attempts to tackle root causes often run foul of claims that such internal questions are not matters of legitimate international concern, although arguments of this kind carry less weight as it becomes apparent that refugee flows frequently present significant threats to international peace and security. In the short term, negotiating and implementing solutions may be more difficult and expensive than merely containing apparently intractable problems. In the long run, however, there can be little doubt that neglect is the most costly of all possible approaches. Refugee problems left unresolved are not only an affront to humane values; they also feed back into the dangerous cycle of violent conflict and further displacement.

Somali boat people arriving in Mombasa.
Kenya, July 1992.

Chapter two

Asylum Under Threat

The number of people seeking asylum around the world has escalated sharply in the 1990s, imposing serious strains on the institution of asylum. In the aftermath of the war in the Persian Gulf, 1.8 million Iraqi Kurds fled to the border region of Turkey and to the Islamic Republic of Iran. More than 400,000 refugees flooded into Kenya to escape violence and anarchy in Somalia, civil war in the Sudan and endemic insecurity in southern Ethiopia. A quarter of a million Muslim refugees poured into poverty-stricken Bangladesh, reporting widespread harassment and repression in Myanmar's Arakan state – the second sizeable outflow from that part of Myanmar in the last 15 years. During the early part of 1993, a mass exodus of over 280,000 Togolese took refuge in Benin and Ghana, fleeing political upheaval in their home country.

Meanwhile, in the heart of Europe, over 1.2 million victims of the brutal conflict in the former Yugoslavia sought sanctuary in Croatia, Serbia, Montenegro, Slovenia and the former Yugoslav republic of Macedonia. At least 600,000 more took refuge outside the immediately affected region – a refugee flow unprecedented in Europe since World War II. The late 1980s and early 1990s saw a rapid increase in the number of asylum applicants in industrialized countries. In 1983, some 100,000 people requested asylum in Europe, North America, Australia and Japan. By 1992, the number had risen to over 800,000. In all, some 3.7 million asylum applicants were recorded during the period 1983-1992 (see Figure 2.A and Annex I.5).

The majority of those seeking asylum leave their own countries as part of a mass outflow and find refuge in a neighbouring country. Others make individual journeys to foreign lands, sometimes at a considerable distance from their homes. These two distinct patterns impose different – although in both cases grave – pressures on the institution of asylum. The first is the most common pattern in developing countries, where the pressures exerted by large refugee populations are taxing the hospitality of even the most generous countries. The second has engendered a crisis of confidence in the asylum system throughout the industrialized world.

The impulse to provide refuge to strangers in need is shared by virtually all cultures and religions (see Box 2.1). It is one of the most basic expressions of human solidarity. Like many forms of altruism, however, it is vulnerable in times of trouble, when individuals and states tend to become preoccupied with their own interests. Today, asylum remains the cornerstone of international refugee protection. It is the principal means through which states meet their obligations towards refugees on their territory. The grant of asylum removes the threat of forcible return and provides the refugee with sanctuary until a solution to his or her problem can be found.

"Everyone has the right to seek and to enjoy in other countries asylum from persecution"

Universal Declaration of Human Rights.
Article 14 (1)

For all its importance, the status of asylum in international law is ambiguous. According to the Universal Declaration of Human Rights, "Everyone has the right to seek and to enjoy in other countries asylum from persecution." Yet no binding treaty or convention obliges states to grant asylum. There is a gap between the individual's right to seek asylum and the state's discretion in providing it. In this legal no-man's land, each state makes its own decisions as to whom it will admit and why. In practice, of course, these decisions are constrained by circumstances beyond the control of the affected state. And when asylum-seekers cross a border in large numbers, the state receiving them may, at least initially, have little choice other than to give them asylum. As a result of legal and practical considerations, state practice in granting asylum varies widely. It shifts according to the

level of demand, the origins of the people who apply, the perception of their motives and other preoccupations and pressures of the time.

States that have signed the 1951 Convention and/or its 1967 Protocol – which by June 1993 included 120 of the 183 members of the United Nations – generally offer asylum to individuals who conform to the definition of a refugee in those texts. This extends to those who have a "well-founded fear of being persecuted for reasons of race, religion, nationality, membership of a particular social group or political opinion", who are outside their country of nationality and who are unable or unwilling to avail themselves of its protection.

But even here there is room for interpretation. What constitutes persecution? What evidence shows that a fear is well founded? What obligations are there to people who have a well-founded fear of being persecuted for reasons other than the five mentioned in the Convention? Canada, for example, recently included persecution on grounds of gender as a basis for asylum claims. Must the agent of persecution be a government, or can it be another party? This is an important question in situations where a state is no longer in control of all its territory. The German government, for example, maintains that a government must be implicated in the persecution if a claim for international protection is to be considered valid, while many other governments take a broader view of agents of persecution. And what about the huge movements of people trying to escape from wars, internal strife and general lawlessness, who make up the great majority of today's refugees?

Many states continue to grant asylum generously, despite the very real political, social and economic pressures created by large-scale refugee influxes. The costs of providing asylum weigh most heavily when they occur in countries already struggling with poverty, economic decline, political instability and environmental degradation – and yet these are the countries that have been most magnanimous in providing refuge to whole groups of people fleeing from

Box 2.1

The Origins of Asylum

The concept of asylum has been in existence for at least 3,500 years and is found, in one form or another, in the texts and traditions of many different ancient societies. In the middle of the second millennium BC, as entities resembling modern states with clearly defined borders began to develop across the Near East, several treaties were concluded between rulers which included provisions for the protection of international fugitives. For example, a Hittite king drew up a treaty with the ruler of a different country, in which he declared "Concerning a refugee, I affirm on oath the following: when a refugee comes from your land into mine he will not be returned to you. To return a refugee from the land of the Hittites is not right."[6] In the 14th century BC, another Hittite king, Urhi-Teshup, who had been deposed by his uncle, was given refuge by the Egyptian pharaoh, Rameses II.

In the 7th century BC, an Assyrian king, Assurbanipal, referred to a refugee from the land of Elam "who has seized my royal feet" – meaning that he had requested and been granted asylum.[7]

In Ancient Greece, numerous internal religious sanctuaries were established. However, the idea of external asylum also existed. Herodotus cites the case of a Phrygian, Adrastus, who fled to Sardis in Lydia (now Turkey) after accidentally killing his brother. He presented himself at the palace of Croesus, who welcomed him and told him he could stay as long as he wished. Asylum also features in

Ancient Greek drama: in Sophocles's tragedy *Oedipus at Colonus* the Athenian king, Theseus, gives a compassionate reception to the exiled Oedipus.

In AD 8, the Roman poet Ovid was banished by the Emperor Augustus to Tomis on the Black Sea (now Constanta in Romania), on the extreme edge of the Empire. As he records in *Tristia* (Sorrows), the Tomitans received him warmly. Although he continued to perceive them as "barbarians", Ovid was touched by their hospitality, learned their language – Getic – and remained among them until his death in AD 17.

The Old Testament Book of Numbers shows God instructing Moses to designate six cities as places of refuge, "both for the children of Israel, and for the stranger, and for the sojourner among them" (35: 9-15). In the New Testament, St. Matthew's Gospel portrays the infant Christ and his family as refugees fleeing into Egypt. Christian sanctuaries were first recognized under Roman law in the 4th century AD, and their physical scope was gradually extended. In the 6th century, the Emperor Justinian – anticipating modern asylum laws – limited the privilege to people not guilty of serious crimes.

During the early years of Islam, the Prophet Mohammed and his followers were forced to take refuge from those who felt threatened by the growing power of the new faith. The Hijra, his flight from Mecca to Medina in AD 622, marks the beginning of the Islamic era according to the religious calendar. The Koran spells out the importance of the notion of asylum in Islam: "Those

who have believed and have chosen exile and have fought for the Faith, and those who have granted them help and asylum, these are the true believers" (8: 74).

From early times, asylum had both political and humanitarian dimensions. The ancient practice of granting internal sanctuary – often on a temporary rather than permanent basis – in holy places reflected respect for the deity and the Church, while the grant of asylum by kings, republics and free cities was a manifestation of sovereignty.

As the power of the monarchy grew, the right to grant asylum increasingly became the prerogative of the state and the inviolability of internal asylum in holy places declined correspondingly. In the 16th century, for example, King Henry VIII of England abolished many religious sanctuaries and nominated seven "cities of refuge" in their stead.

The revocation of the Edict of Nantes in 1685, which forced 250,000 French Protestants (the Huguenots) to flee their country, marked the beginning of the modern tradition of asylum in Europe. It caused the Marquis of Brandenburg to issue the Edict of Potsdam allowing the settlement of Huguenots in his territory. After the French Revolution, the category of refugees fleeing political rather than religious persecution began to gain prominence. Although the first recorded use of the term "the Right of Asylum" occurred as early as 1725, asylum continued to be viewed more as a prerogative of the Sovereign than as an individual right to protection until the early years of the 20th century.

war and chaos. In industrialized countries, the steep rise in the number of asylum-seekers, the expense of judicial procedures to evaluate individual asylum applications and the welfare provisions for shelter and support of applicants while their cases are pending, have sent the costs of the asylum system soaring.

"Refusal to grant asylum can expose refugees to serious danger"

The fear of being inundated with asylum-seekers, or foreigners in general, elicits a number of reactions from states, some defensive, others more constructive. One is to prevent people from seeking asylum by making it difficult or impossible for them to reach or cross borders. A second is to attempt to deter further arrivals by lowering standards of treatment – a process that goes under the dubious label of "humane deterrence". Yet another is the tendency to restrict the grounds on which asylum is granted. A more positive response is to speed up and rationalize the determination process so that well-founded cases can be more easily distinguished from unfounded ones. In a number of countries, attempts are being made to set up faster and more consistent procedures which promise to unclog asylum channels, making it easier for states to meet their obligations to people in need of protection while exercising their sovereign right to control other forms of migration.

It is a sad fact that refugees, many of whom arrive deeply traumatized by what they have already gone through, may still face a succession of problems once they reach a place of refuge. Beyond the initial difficulty of gaining admission and access to asylum procedures, some refugees encounter insensitive and sometimes inhumane treatment by officials and members of the public. The process of deciding whether a person qualifies for asylum can, in certain countries, drag on for several years. In the meantime the refugee lives in a state of limbo, uncertain about the future and haunted by the past. Most serious of all, problems of expulsion and forced return still arise.

Denial of the right to seek asylum has taken a number of forms in recent years. Refugees have been prevented from crossing a frontier when they were in mortal danger from hostile forces, severe shortages of food and exposure to the elements. Others have been forcibly returned to a country where they fear persecution. People arriving at a hoped-for place of asylum by boat have been pushed off from the shore. Other "boat people" have been peremptorily returned to their country without screening to determine the soundness of their claims. Less draconian measures, which are aimed at deflecting illegal immigrants but also affect refugees, have been adopted by some governments, notably in the industrialized world. They include visa requirements for people arriving from countries afflicted by civil strife, and fines imposed on airlines that transport people without proper documentation (see Box 2.2).

Refusal to grant asylum leaves refugees without protection and can expose them to serious danger. On occasion, the international community responds decisively. For example, action taken to prevent Vietnamese boat people and refugees from landing on the shores of South East Asia following an upsurge in numbers during the late 1980s, triggered the development of a Comprehensive Plan of Action which has been largely successful in bringing the exodus of boat people to a satisfactory conclusion (see Chapter One, Box 1.4). The refusal of Turkey to allow Iraqi Kurds to cross its border in 1991 led to an unprecedented, multilateral military intervention on humanitarian grounds. By contrast, attempts to find countries that will accept Haitian asylum-seekers have made little headway (see Box 2.3).

Confronted with continuing influxes, a number of governments have sought to deter asylum-seekers by granting them less favourable treatment. Closed camps or other forms of detention or confinement – including the detention of children – have been introduced and access to employment removed. This has been the case, for example, in Hong Kong since 1982, in response to an influx of Vietnamese boat people which was judged to include an increasing proportion of economic migrants. Detention of certain groups of asylum-seekers has also been practised in Australia and the United States. A number of European countries have restricted employment opportunities and social benefits for asylum-seekers. Even in African countries of asylum, long the most hospitable in hosting refugees, an increasing unease and restrictiveness is evident. In Malawi, for example – a country that has extended an exemplary welcome to over a million Mozambican refugees – rising numbers coupled with the effects of drought and economic difficulties led, in 1992, to government plans to fence camps and restrict the movement of refugees. There are signs that the quality of asylum is deteriorating in many other parts of the world as well.

Some governments and judiciaries are also taking a more restrictive attitude towards the definition of a refugee contained in the 1951 Convention, requiring very high standards of proof from those who claim they fear persecution and placing unprecedented emphasis on the asylum-seeker's ability to demonstrate that he or she has been personally singled out for mistreatment. In addition, asylum-seekers may be required to demonstrate that they could not have sought safety in another area of their country of origin.

The asylum crisis in the West

Concern is widespread about the strains and pressures involved in granting asylum to large numbers of people. The most systematic debate on this subject is taking place within the European Community (EC) which, although it still hosts a relatively small proportion of the world's refugee population, has seen a sharp increase in the number of people seeking asylum in recent years. Wider consultations, including European states not members of the EC as well

as Australia, the United States and Canada, are taking place on issues of common concern.

During the 1970s, the average number of asylum-seekers arriving in Western Europe was around 30,000 a year. By the end of the 1980s, the annual figure had climbed to more than 300,000. In 1992 it surpassed 680,000. For a region that had seen the last of its post-World War II refugee camps closed in 1960, and had not experienced a mass influx of refugees since the Soviet invasion of Czechoslovakia in 1968, the numbers were sufficiently disturbing to set off a major public debate. Germany has been the most seriously affected by the sharp increase, with the number of asylum-seekers rising from 121,000 in 1989 to 438,000 in 1992. Moreover, the surge in asylum applications coincided with the strains, both social and economic, of German reunification.

"Asylum-seekers are increasingly being turned away without any attempt to determine the validity of their claim"

Since the mid-1980s, the pressures on the institution of asylum in Europe and North America have resulted in narrower interpretations of the definition of a refugee, more stringent determination procedures, and attempts to limit access to asylum channels. Austria, Germany and Canada have recently tightened their asylum laws; legislation for the same purpose has been introduced in the Netherlands, Spain, the United Kingdom and the United States. In some cases, people in need of protection have been forcibly returned to the country from which they fled. Particularly disturbing is a growing tendency to turn away asylum-seekers before any attempt is made to determine the validity of their claim to international protection.

What evoked these restrictive reactions? Previous crises had tended to broaden the basis for asylum – through the 1967 Protocol, the 1969 OAU Convention or the 1984 Cartagena Declaration – rather than narrow it.

Obviously, the increase in numbers is one part of the story. Another is the undeniable abuse of the asylum channel by growing numbers of people who are trying to enter the labour market rather than escape persecution or danger in their home country. A further important factor is that the majority of 1990s refugees are people in flight from war, generalized violence and chaos in their home countries.

There is no firm consensus among Western governments about how the needs of this group should be met. Although they have been willing to see such people recognized as refugees under regional arrangements in, for example, Africa and Central America, and to provide them with humanitarian assistance, Western governments are concerned by the prospect of large, spontaneous influxes into their own countries. Direct arrivals from South to North have heightened

racial and cultural tensions already in evidence as a result of labour migration in the 1960s. This concern has been exacerbated by the fact that the increase in the number of arrivals has coincided with the culmination of an extended period of low growth in Europe, punctuated by recessions, which has seen domestic unemployment continuing to rise even during the years of modest recovery.

The end of the Cold War has, moreover, removed the ideological basis of Western refugee policy, which was heavily geared towards offering asylum to people fleeing from communist regimes. In addition to the 3.5 million East Germans who moved to West Germany before the Berlin Wall was erected, Western countries accepted without question 200,000 refugees from the failed Hungarian uprising in 1956, 80,000 Czechs and Slovaks after the Prague Spring was crushed and 30,000 Jews from Gomulka's Poland.[8] The United States admitted half a million Cubans, tens of thousands of

Fig. 2.A
Asylum Applicants in 26 Industrialized Countries: 1983-1992

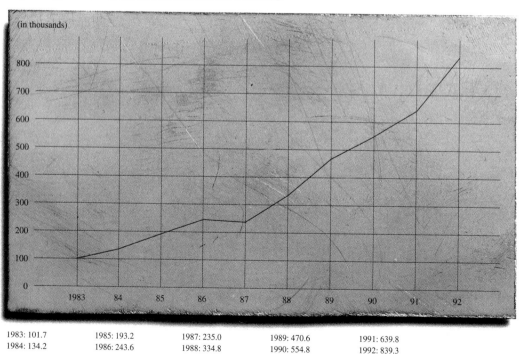

(in thousands)

| 1983: 101.7 | 1985: 193.2 | 1987: 235.0 | 1989: 470.6 | 1991: 639.8 |
| 1984: 134.2 | 1986: 243.6 | 1988: 334.8 | 1990: 554.8 | 1992: 839.3 |

Note: For a detailed breakdown of annual totals of asylum applicants in each of the 26 countries of asylum included in this graph, and a brief analysis of the trends, see Annex I.5.

Soviet Jews and thousands of other Eastern bloc citizens. More than 700,000 Vietnamese were resettled in the West after 1975. Exit restrictions normally limited the outflows from communist countries, but those who managed to leave were generally granted asylum without much inquiry into their motivation.

As Figure 2.B and Annex I.6 illustrate, the leading groups of asylum applicants in Western Europe, both immediately before and after the fall of the Berlin Wall, have for the most part come from other European countries. Ironically, the same regime changes in Eastern and Central Europe that lifted exit restrictions (and thereby brought a flood of asylum-seekers to Western Europe, especially Germany) also weakened the assumption that these people were in need of asylum.

In most Western countries, individual determination procedures to examine the claims of asylum-seekers are elaborate and costly, as are the social welfare obligations triggered by the arrival of an asylum-seeker. It is estimated that Western European countries alone spend the enormous sum of $7 billion a year on their asylum systems.[9] An individual petition may take years to work its way through the legal system, leading to long stays at the taxpayer's expense, even for people who do not in the end qualify for asylum. There is a growing public concern that the possibility of a lengthy stay in a wealthy country with generous welfare benefits is attracting people with very weak claims to asylum – or none at all.

Attempts to use asylum as a route for labour migration undermine both popular and official support for the institution of asylum. In 1992, of the 272,000 individual applications considered in Western Europe, only 25,000 (9 per cent) were granted refugee status under the 1951 Convention. An additional 29,000 people were allowed to stay on humanitarian grounds. Yet by no means all rejected claims are cynical abuses of the asylum system. Among unsuccessful applicants are people who at another time (before the political changes in Central and Eastern Europe) or in another place (one of the

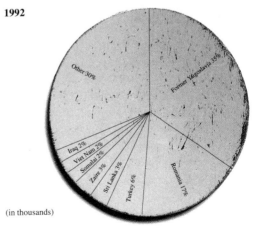

Fig. 2.B
Leading Nationalities of Asylum Applicants in Ten European Countries

1988

(in thousands)

Poland 39.2	Islamic Rep. of Iran 17.4	Zaire 6.7
Turkey 34.8	Sri Lanka 8.1	Lebanon 6.6
Yugoslavia 24.0	Romania 7.0	Other 72.1

1990

(in thousands)

Romania 60.4	Lebanon 29.5	Poland 13.3
Turkey 47.0	Sri Lanka 19.0	India 11.6
Yugoslavia 33.0	Islamic Rep. of Iran 17.6	Other 164.7

1992

(in thousands)

Former Yugoslavia 229.6	Sri Lanka 19.0	Viet Nam 13.6
Romania 114.2	Zaire 17.4	Iraq 13.4
Turkey 36.9	Somalia 14.0	Other 203.4

Note: See Annex I.6 for a complete listing of the top ten nationalities of asylum applicants in each of the ten European countries concerned.

37

states signatory to the OAU convention, for example) would have been admitted as refugees.

The lack of opportunities for legal labour migration increases the pressure on asylum procedures. Western Europe closed regular migration channels (except for family reunification and limited openings for certain skilled professionals) in the early 1970s in response to the severe economic downturn that followed the first oil crisis. The period of painful economic adjustment that followed has not yet come to an end. Western European unemployment rose from 9 million in 1979 to more than 17 million in 1993.

"Policies intended to deter economic migrants may also affect refugees"

North American and European states generally permit anyone who reaches their borders to request asylum. There are no formal limits on the numbers who may be granted refuge if they meet certain criteria. The widespread perception that the asylum channel is being abused by would-be economic migrants, and the spectre of virtually unlimited numbers of people in need of international protection because of violence and chaos at home, inspire fear in many industrialized countries. This fear is reflected in the Maastricht Treaty on European Union, which permits signatory states to impose visa restrictions in order to prevent mass inflows in case of an emergency outside the Treaty territory.

Domestic pressures create a political imperative for the governments of receiving countries to be seen to be in control of the asylum process. The fear of a deluge of poor and alien people overwhelming prosperous and relatively homogenous societies is an old one, which tends to gain momentum during times of economic insecurity. Unfortunately, in many countries, there are individuals and political parties eager to exploit such anxieties, and to direct confusion and insecurity into the path of xenophobia.

The free movement of people is an element of closer European integration. With the abolition of internal border controls between certain countries within the European Community, common standards for granting admission at the external borders are considered crucial. Elements of such standards are embodied in the Schengen Agreement and the Dublin Convention (see Annex II). The agreements guarantee that all asylum requests will be examined, and determine which of the participating states will be responsible for dealing with each application. Part of their purpose is to avoid disruptive movements of applicants from one country to another, in search of more generous asylum policies or looser procedures, and also to discourage individuals from choking the already overloaded screening process by making simultaneous asylum applications in different countries.

At the same time, EC governments are currently engaged in broader efforts to harmonize their immigration and asylum policies and practices. Their goals include the adoption of common standards for determining and processing manifestly unfounded claims for asylum, as well as a consistent application of concepts such as first asylum and safe countries of origin.

The legitimate efforts of states to streamline and harmonize asylum policies have given rise to a number of concerns. The chief danger is that policies intended to deter economic migrants from using the asylum channel could, without counterbalancing measures, be equally effective in deflecting refugees with a genuine need for international protection.

The dilemma of the screened-out

The majority of asylum-seekers who go through individual procedures to determine the validity of their claim are found not to have a "well-founded fear of persecution" under the terms of the 1951 Refugee Convention. However, in most states, only a small proportion of the rejected cases are actually deported.

Box 2.2
Obstacles to Asylum

Many industrialized states have introduced increasingly tough measures to prevent people from abusing asylum procedures for immigration purposes. While reflecting legitimate concern over irregular immigration, such measures can raise obstacles for people in genuine need of asylum.

Procedures devised to prevent entry or simplify expulsion are numerous. They include heavy policing, as on the eastern borders of Austria, and legal or administrative provisions for rejection of unwelcome visitors before they cross the frontier. France and Spain are among countries that have used the legally questionable concept of "international zones" at airports for intercepting and expelling unwanted aliens. In June 1992, a US presidential Executive Order allowed the summary return of all Haitian boat people intercepted on the high seas, without any examination of their asylum claims. In May 1993, Germany – which in 1992 received more asylum-seekers than all the other European countries combined – revised its constitution to permit asylum-seekers to be sent back to neighbouring countries considered by the German authorities to be safe countries of asylum. Similar changes of practice have occurred elsewhere – including the Scandinavian countries, traditionally among the most liberal in Europe. These measures were, by mid-1993, leading countries such as the Czech Republic, Hungary and Poland to tighten their own admission policies.

The return of an asylum-seeker to a safe country is not, in principle, objectionable. But when it occurs without the consent of the country concerned, asylum-seekers may end up "in orbit", shuttling between airports or railway stations only to be refused admission at each successive destination.

This was the fate of two Somali sisters who, accompanied by four young children, arrived in Switzerland in July 1992. Having spent a brief period in Kenya after fleeing Somalia, they travelled to the Maldives and Zurich, hoping to make their way to Canada to join a step-daughter. In Zurich, they were found to be travelling on forged documents and, after a week in detention, were deported back to the Maldives. From there, they were immediately sent on to Sri Lanka, on the basis of forged visas in their passports, then – in an increasingly desperate shuttle from one closed door to another – back to the Maldives and back again to Sri Lanka. Finally, they and their children were detained at Colombo airport. Their detention lasted until 17 September 1992, when one of the sisters was admitted urgently to hospital where she gave birth to a baby daughter. In early 1993 a solution was finally found when Canada – the country they were trying to reach in the first place – accepted them for resettlement. They arrived there safely on 15 March 1993, a year after their odyssey began.

Where possible, governments prefer exclusion to expulsion. Strict visa requirements, coupled with heavy penalties against airlines carrying passengers whose documents are not in order, have made movement more difficult for both migrant and refugee. Many Sri Lankan Tamils, for example, have been prevented from reaching Western Europe in this way. In some countries immigration officials have boarded incoming aircraft in order to screen out and return any passenger who might be intending to apply for asylum. There have been well-documented instances of people – notably Kurds and Tamils – being summarily deported in this way to countries where they have subsequently been detained, tortured or otherwise mistreated. In other cases, immigration officials have been dispatched to refugee-producing countries to show airline check-in staff how to spot passengers with suspect papers – or motives – and prevent them boarding. Slip-ups by ground staff can result in punitive fines against offending airlines. In 1990, in the United Kingdom alone, the government issued 9,521 fines of £1,000 to airlines.[10]

Radical changes in the international environment have led to increased population movements. The response of asylum countries should not be to devise ever more ingenious ways to close their doors. Instead, they need to develop procedures that distinguish rapidly, fairly and effectively between those who need protection and those who move for other reasons, while at the same time working to create conditions in countries of origin that permit as many asylum-seekers as possible to return home safely.

In the United Kingdom, for example, in 1991 only 15 per cent of applications were granted refugee status under the 1951 Convention. In all 48 per cent were permitted to remain. The overall EC acceptance rate for asylum-seekers was below 20 per cent in 1991 for all statuses combined.[11] Yet an estimated 80 per cent of asylum-seekers stayed on, some illegally and some under special dispensations. An inter-governmental study found that only 25,000 of 110,000 cases rejected in 1990 had left volun-tarily or been deported.[12]

"The failure to solve the non-refugee problem has adversely affected the position of genuine refugees"

Some people look at the high proportion of non-refugees who stay on and see a malfunc-tioning screening system that fails to discrimi-nate between those who need international protection and those who do not. To others it appears to be a laudably flexible practice that permits humanitarian responses to displacement without stretching the conventional definition of a refugee.

States have the unquestionable right to deport people who enter their territory illegally and are found not to be refugees. A number of countries do not hesitate to exercise that right, at least in the case of certain groups, even though depor-tation is often difficult to implement for practical and political reasons. Some groups of asylum-seekers have strong advocates in the receiving countries who, for political or humanitarian reasons, vociferously oppose deportation.

It is widely acknowledged that the failure to solve the non-refugee problem has undermined the credibility of the asylum channel generally and has adversely affected the position of refugees, who genuinely need international protection. The treatment of rejected asylum-seekers varies considerably from country to country. This lack of consistency, and the uncer-tainty that afflicts many of those whose asylum applications have failed, creates a number of serious difficulties. New measures to bring coher-ence and effectiveness to the treatment of reject-ed asylum cases are welcome, as long as they are consistent with human rights standards and do not jeopardize the safety of the people involved. The prospect of a more orderly system of return makes it even more imperative that screening is fair, thorough and based on sound knowledge of conditions in the country of origin.

Temporary protection

The majority of the world's refugees today are fleeing from violent conflict and chaotic break-down of civil order in their home countries. They need, at a minimum, international assistance and protection for the duration of the violence and disorder that displaced them, followed by assistance to reintegrate in their own societies when conditions permit them to return. Permanent exile is neither necessary nor desir-able for most people in these circumstances.

During the Cold War, asylum tended to be linked either to permanent settlement in the country where refuge was first sought or to resettlement in another country. At the time, safe return was not viewed, among Western governments, as a realistic possibility for refugees coming from most communist coun-tries. The provisions of the 1951 Convention that relate to the economic and social rights of refugees were therefore seen as tools to promote their integration in the country of asylum. Today, the opportunities for permanent integra-tion in receiving countries are limited. It seems very unlikely that people who have fled *en masse* to a neighbouring country will in the future be offered large-scale resettlement else-where, as happened in the case of the Vietnamese boat people in the 1980s and that of the Hungarians three decades earlier.

Most asylum countries in the developing world suffer from increasing pressure on land and water resources, employment and public services. Local integration is correspondingly less practical, both in economic and political terms. A number of asylum countries that have hosted large refugee populations for extended periods, such as Kenya, Malawi, and Pakistan, are chafing under their very real burdens. They do not view asylum on their territory as permanent but as a temporary and pragmatic response to humanitarian emergencies offered until such time as refugees feel safe to go home voluntarily.

Western governments, too, are increasingly resorting to temporary asylum. A number of them make provision for temporary protection in their national legislation, although its content and implementation vary considerably from country to country. It goes under a variety of names: in Europe, "B or C status", "Duldung" (tolerance), "exceptional leave to remain" or "humanitarian status"; and in the United Sates, "temporary protected status". Falling short of full refugee status, these alternative classifications allow asylum-seekers who might not qualify for refugee status to remain at the discretion of the authorities until it is deemed safe for them to return home. They are used for two distinct but related purposes. They provide a mechanism that allows people who would be denied refugee status under the 1951 Convention – but who would face danger if returned to their country of origin – to remain on a temporary, though often renewable, basis. More rarely, they are used to relieve the members of certain national groups from having to apply for refugee status by giving them leave to remain until conditions in their own country stabilize. In the latter case, judgment is suspended on the question of whether the people concerned would qualify as refugees under the 1951 Convention. This practice has developed in Western Europe in response to the need to provide asylum to large numbers of people fleeing from the war in the former Yugoslavia and, under this impetus, has become more systematic.

For all its benefits as a pragmatic response to situations of compelling humanitarian urgency, there are fears that temporary asylum, while broadening refugee protection, may also weaken it. It protects those who need a safe haven but might not qualify for Convention status. Some observers feel, however, that it also eases the pressure on governments to apply the Convention along with its wide range of economic and social rights. "Humanitarian status" and its equivalents are administrative measures adopted at the discretion of individual governments. They can be granted but also revoked more easily than refugee status.

"Some asylum countries hosting large refugee populations are chafing under their burdens"

The argument in favour of temporary protection can be cast in philosophical as well as practical terms. In a number of conflicts today, displacement of people is not the by-product of war but one of its primary purposes. In the face of this grim reality, encouraging permanent resettlement of refugees can mean abetting forcible expulsion. In a setting such as Bosnia and Herzegovina, it is important to keep alive the idea of return in order to avoid collaborating, however unwillingly, in the crime of "ethnic cleansing". The need to deter such practices has to be weighed carefully against the humanitarian duty to relieve suffering. Clearly, people should never be prevented from escaping extreme danger.

The time has come for temporary protection to be given broader, more coherent and consistent recognition as a legitimate tool of international protection. In order to be accepted, temporary asylum must conform to certain minimum standards of protection against discrimination, *refoulement* and expulsion. It should also come with clearly defined guarantees of humane treatment and fundamental human rights, such as the right to family unity.

Box 2.3
Haitian Boat People

On 30 September 1991, a military coup overthrew the first democratically elected president of Haiti, Jean-Bertrand Aristide. The coup was roundly condemned by the international community, which refused to recognize the new government. As repression spread throughout the country over the next few months, more than 38,000 Haitians risked their lives at sea in an attempt to reach the United States. This precipitated a major crisis and threw a spotlight on the long-standing US practice of interdicting Haitian "boat people" at sea.

Ten years earlier, in 1981, the United States and Haiti had concluded an agreement that allowed the US Coast Guard to board Haitian vessels on the high seas and send back those whom US authorities determined did not have a credible basis for an asylum application. Between 1981 and September 1991, the Coast Guard intercepted 24,600 Haitians. Only 28 of them were found by the Immigration and Naturalization Service (INS) to have

a reasonable asylum claim and allowed to enter the United States. The rest were returned to Haiti. The low admission rate aroused serious concern among many human rights groups in the United States and elsewhere.

In the eight months following the September 1991 coup, more Haitians were interdicted at sea than had attempted to leave during the whole of the previous decade . Under pressure from litigation challenging the validity of screening carried out on Coast Guard cutters on the high seas, the US government opened a camp at its military base in Guantanamo Bay, Cuba. According to official INS statistics, 34,841 interviews with Haitians were conducted at Guantanamo Bay from November 1991 to June 1992 and 11,062 people were found to have a "credible fear of persecution", the necessary grounds for seeking asylum. While this gives an average recognition rate of 31.6 per cent, the rate fluctuated widely during the period, even though political conditions in Haiti did not change significantly. Those not recognized as having

reasonable grounds for filing an asylum claim continued to be returned to Haiti.

In May 1992, President George Bush issued Executive Order 12807 which halted the screening and ordered the immediate repatriation of all Haitians interdicted at sea. Efforts were simultaneously launched to monitor the situation of returnees and to screen applicants for refugee status in Haiti itself. A federal court found that the executive order violated section 243(h) of the 1980 Refugee Act, and imposed an injunction against return. But the US Supreme Court allowed the order to stand while it decided on the case. On 21 June 1993, it ruled 8-to-1 in favour of the Executive Order.

The summary return of all Haitians to their country of origin appears to be in direct contravention of the widely recognized right to leave one's country to seek asylum from persecution. According to the State Department's 1992 annual report on human rights conditions, the level of political violence declined in Haiti in 1992 but widespread human rights abuses continued. They included extra-judicial killings by security forces, disappearances, beatings and other mistreatment of detainees, as well as political interference with the judicial process.

It has been recognized that an effective response to the Haitian crisis needs to revolve around intensive efforts to find a political solution to the situation in Haiti and to address the root causes of the refugee outflow. The United Nations and the Organization of American States, with the support of the US administration, have

Fig. 2.C
Haitians Interdicted at Sea: 1981-1992

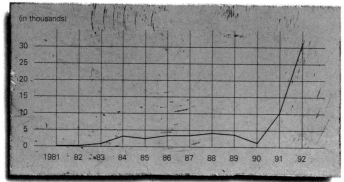

1981: 187	1984: 2,942	1987: 3,541	1990: 1,124	*Source:*
1982: 193	1985: 2,411	1988: 4,614	1991: 10,086	US Coast Guard
1983: 762	1986: 3,388	1989: 3,737	1992: 31,401	TOTAL: 64,386

been undertaking intensive diplomatic efforts to resolve the political crisis, restore democracy and promote human rights monitoring through an expanded international presence.

In the meantime, UNHCR has continued to express its concern that asylum should remain open for people who are obliged to flee. The set of standards and safeguards that are spelled out in the 1951 Convention and 1967 Protocol should apply to Haitians who qualify as refugees.

Fig. 2.D
Haitians Interdicted at Sea and Those Found to have Plausible Asylum Claims: 1991-1993

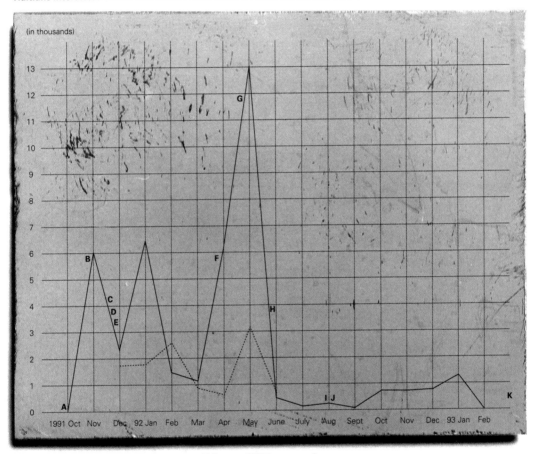

Haitians interdicted at sea: October 1991 to February 1993 (————)

1991	1992				
October: 19	January: 6,477	April: 6,144	August: 252	December: 772	TOTAL: 41,141
November: 6,012	February: 1,401	May: 13,053	September: 84	**1993**	
December: 2,346	March: 1,158	June: 473	October: 714	January: 1,354	
		July: 160	November: 713	February: 9	

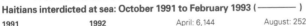

Haitians found to have plausible claim to refugee status: December 1991 to June 1992 (··············)

December: 1,703	February: 2,263	April: 598	June: 674
January: 1,742	March: 897	May: 3,185	TOTAL: 11,062

Sources: US Coast Guard; Immigration and Naturalization Service

Haitian Boat People: A Chronology of Events
A 30.09.91 Aristide deposed by military coup
B 28.10.91 First post-coup boat of 19 Haitians intercepted by US Coast Guard
C 14.11.91 US Naval Base at Guantanamo (Cuba) opened as screening centre
D 18.11.91 Coast Guard returns 538 Haitians
E 19.11.91 Miami court issues temporary restraining order barring repatriation. Ruling subsequently overturned by Circuit Court
F 27.03.92 New York Federal Judge issues temporary restraining order blocking repatriation from Guantanamo
G 22.04.92 Supreme Court lifts restraining order and returns case to Court of Appeals
H 24.05.92 Executive Order ends screening: orders direct return of all interdicted Haitians
I 29.07.92 Court of Appeals overturns Executive Order and reimposes injunction against return
J 01.08.92 Supreme Court stays injunction, pending ruling on the merits of the case
K 21.06.93 Supreme Court rules in favour of Executive Order

Cessation clauses

International protection is meant to be an interim measure to bridge the gap between the time when refugees leave their own country and the time when they can again benefit from national protection, either through repatriation or through acquiring the nationality (and therefore the protection) of a country of asylum. The 1951 Convention includes a series of "cessation clauses", which present guidelines on when a state may cease to provide protection without violating international obligations or exposing individuals to danger. These include repatriation and resettlement, as well as the situation when a refugee "can no longer, because the circumstances in connection with which he has been recognized as a refugee have ceased to exist, continue to refuse to avail himself of the protection of the country of his nationality". The latter is known as the "ceased circumstances" clause.

"The designation of 'safe countries' is controversial and often highly politicized"

Invocation of the ceased circumstances clause has been fairly rare for several reasons, one of which is obvious: the paucity of long-standing, dramatic changes of circumstance in refugee-producing countries. There are some encouraging examples of its application, however. Democratization in Argentina and Uruguay, following the overthrow of brutal regimes with a record of human rights violations, allowed the clause to be applied to refugees from those two countries. More recently, it has been applied to a number of Eastern European countries including the former Czechoslovakia, Hungary and Poland.

As a result of concern about the growing number of asylum-seekers and the new emphasis on temporary protection, interest in the cessation clauses in general, and the ceased circumstances clause in particular, is increasing. Any resort to the clause, however, requires a careful and exhaustive examination of conditions in the country of origin. It is vital that the changes that might justify an application of the clause are profound and durable. They should be reflected in human rights practices and institutionalized in legislative, political and constitutional structures. Above all, they must not be easily reversible. Consistent standards for determining when circumstances justify a change need to be developed, along with humane procedures for returning people as a result of the application of the ceased circumstances clause. In addition, the 1951 Convention provides that individuals should be allowed to appeal for exemption because of continuing fears or past traumas.

"Safe countries"

Along with the renewed interest in cessation of refugee status, the concept of a "safe country" is also gaining currency among officials in some asylum countries. In the context of the asylum debate, a "safe country" is one where there is no serious danger of persecution. A safe country of origin is one that does not produce refugees. The term can also be applied to countries of asylum, meaning that refugees who enter are neither threatened with danger in that country nor with *refoulement* from it.

The concept of a safe country of origin can be applied in two ways. One of these can be useful in evaluating individual asylum claims. The other is potentially a dangerous obstacle to the right to seek asylum, with a questionable basis in international law. The designation of specific countries as "safe" is both controversial and often highly politicized.

If the concept is used as part of an asylum determination procedure, it creates a presumption of ineligibility which the applicant must refute. As long as the opportunity for a rebuttal exists, this presents no great departure from normal practices. Most screening processes incorporate information on the general conditions in an asylum-seeker's home country as necessary background for assessing the individual's claim.

Box 2.4
Resettlement

Fig. 2.E
Departures for Resettlement, by Region of Origin: 1992

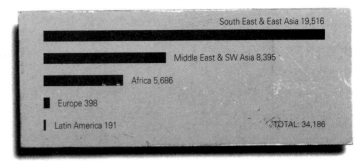

South East & East Asia 19,516

Middle East & SW Asia 8,395

Africa 5,686

Europe 398

Latin America 191

TOTAL: 34,186

Resettlement, which involves moving refugees from one country to another, is often considered the least satisfactory solution to a refugee problem because of the difficult cultural adaptations involved. It is normally turned to only as a last resort, when there is no other way to guarantee protection and safeguard fundamental human rights.

Resettlement may be necessary to ensure the security of refugees who are in danger of being deported to their country of origin, or those whose physical safety is seriously threatened in the country where they have sought sanctuary. It is also used to provide humanitarian protection to particularly vulnerable groups, or to reunite refugees with close relatives.

Although resettlement receives extensive publicity, it applies to only a minute fraction of the international refugee population. Just over 34,000 of the world's 18.2 million refugees were resettled in 1992.

Historically, large-scale resettlement has been rare, the most spectacular exception being that of Indo-Chinese refugees. In 1979, in order to preserve temporary asylum which was severely threatened in South East Asia at the time, Western countries agreed to accept large numbers of refugees. Over 700,000 Vietnamese boat people were resettled under these arrangements.

Other refugees who have recently needed resettlement have included torture victims among the Iraqi refugees in Turkey and Saudi Arabia, and Somali refugees in Kenya suffering from torture or war-related disabilities. Significant numbers of women at risk are found among Ethiopian refugees in Sudan and Somalis in Kenya. Many have suffered from sexual abuse and other forms of violence.

Resettlement has traditionally been viewed as a permanent solution. The great majority of today's refugees, however, are victims of conflict rather than political persecution, and as a result there may be a corresponding growing need for temporary resettlement outside the immediate region. Opportunities of this type have been urgently sought for particularly vulnerable groups from the former Yugoslavia, such as former detention camp inmates and their families.

While the major immigration countries such as Australia, Canada and the United States have continually provided the lion's share of resettlement places, some smaller countries – notably the Netherlands, the Nordic countries, New Zealand and Switzerland – have been particularly generous in providing resettlement opportunities for difficult cases.

Fig. 2.F
Numbers Accepted for Resettlement, by Receiving Country: 1992

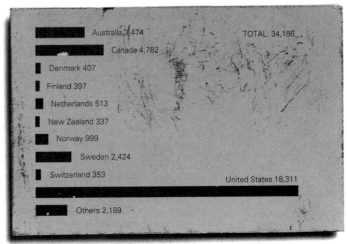

Australia 3,474

Canada 4,782

Denmark 407

Finland 397

Netherlands 513

New Zealand 337

Norway 999

Sweden 2,424

Switzerland 353

United States 18,311

Others 2,189

TOTAL: 34,186

45

The dangers of the safe country concept arise if it is used to exclude entire national groups from consideration for asylum. The political and human rights situations in many countries are difficult to assess with precision, can change very rapidly and may vary from one social or ethnic group to another. The combination of an imperfect classification of safe countries and a rigid refusal to consider asylum cases originating from them could expose individuals to *refoulement* and subsequently to great personal danger.

> ## "Although people have the right to seek asylum, they do not have the right to pick and choose where they do so"

The designation of safe countries of asylum is intended to prevent people from submitting asylum applications in several countries simultaneously or moving from one country where they have already been granted refuge to another which they happen to prefer. Although people have the right to seek asylum, they do not have the right to pick and choose where they do so. It is not the prerogative of asylum-seekers to decide how the burdens of providing refuge will be shared. Refugees are supposed to apply for asylum in the first safe country they reach. There are some difficulties in applying this concept, however. How long does an individual need to have stayed in a country before it is considered a place of first asylum? In an age of long-distance air transport, is a transit stop sufficient? Both forms of safe country – those of origin and of asylum – suffer from the same fundamental problem: determining what constitutes safety.

In a number of cases, measures have been adopted by states to shift the responsibility for examining applications for refugee status to other countries through which the applicants have passed. In the UK it has become increasingly common for asylum-seekers to be sent back when such countries are judged by the authorities to be safe. Although applicants can appeal against this decision, they can only do so from abroad. In France, as a result of pre-screening procedures carried out in designated "waiting zones" at ports and airports, asylum-seekers have on a number of occasions been denied access to French territory because they have transited for a few hours or days in a country where they could have sought asylum. Similarly, in Greece, applications for asylum are not accepted unless the applicants come directly from a country where their lives or freedom are endangered. Measures for returning asylum-seekers to neighbouring transit countries were part of the recent constitutional debate in Germany, which resulted in revision of the article governing the terms of asylum.

There is legitimate concern over disruptive movements of asylum-seekers between countries. Nevertheless, measures to shift the responsibility for examining applications back to countries through which the applicant may have briefly passed – without any attempt being made to verify whether he or she will indeed be re-admitted and given a hearing – sometimes place refugees in danger of *refoulement* to their country of origin or to other places where their life or freedom is threatened. It is therefore essential that arrangements of this nature are surrounded with the appropriate safeguards. If they are not made within in a framework of burden-sharing, they may amount simply to burden-shifting.

Protection in asylum

Even in asylum, refugees encounter threats to their security and well-being that are specific to their status as refugees. Some of these have to do with the peculiar vulnerability of refugee camps to external attack. Others arise from the isolation and dependency that often afflict camp populations, making them prey to manipulation and exploitation by petty officials or self-appointed "leaders". Finally, those who

Who Protects the Palestinians?

The Palestinians have suffered displacement longer than any other refugee group of comparable size. Since the 1948 Arab-Israeli War and the creation of the State of Israel, subsequent wars in the region have uprooted many Palestinian families two, three or even four times.

The United Nations Relief and Works Agency for Palestine Refugees in the Near East (UNRWA) was created in 1949 by UN General Assembly resolution 302(IV), with a mandate to provide humanitarian assistance to refugees from the 1948 war.

Originally, UNRWA looked after three-quarters of a million Palestinian refugees. By 1993, mainly as the result of an additional outflow following the 1967 Arab-Israeli War and natural demographic growth, this figure had increased to 2.7 million Palestinians living in Jordan, Syria, Lebanon, the West Bank and Gaza.

Although no single refugee group has attracted more international attention than Palestinians, their protection falls uncomfortably between the mandates of the two refugee agencies, UNRWA and UNHCR. UNRWA's mandate focuses on relief. It does not explicitly include either the protection of refugees or the promotion of solutions to refugee problems. UNHCR's mandate, on the other hand, has protection at its core but excludes Palestinians under the responsibility of UNRWA as a result of specific reservations raised by governments during the drafting of UNHCR's Statute in 1951.

Nevertheless, the UN Secretary General, in his report of 21 January 1988 to the General Assembly, proposed the expansion of UNRWA activities in the Occupied Territories to include a limited protection function. Subsequent General Assembly resolutions supported this approach. UNRWA has taken a series of steps to provide a degree of passive protection for the population in the Occupied Territories, including the initiation of a legal aid scheme, the recruitment of additional international and local staff and the publication of reports. However, regular abuses of the basic rights of Palestinian refugees continue, both in the Occupied Territories and in a number of other countries in the region.

The fourth generation of Palestinian refugees is now growing up living in camps constructed by their great-grandfathers with UNRWA's help. UN Security Council Resolution 194, adopted in 1948, states that the Palestinian refugees should be permitted to return to the homes they left during the 1948 Arab-Israeli war and that compensation should be paid to those who choose not to return. For many this is not a realistic option. The world cannot afford to let another generation grow up without the firm prospect of a satisfactory end to one of the worst chapters in refugee history.

settle within local communities in asylum countries, as is commonly the case in the West, often experience discrimination. Some have been subject to physical violence and even murder. Among the most exposed are refugees who have not yet been given official recognition.

Refugee camps are a highly visible target. They house large concentrations of people, often identified with one side of an armed conflict. The inhabitants are frequently suspected (rightly or wrongly) of plotting against the government of their country of origin. Armed forces representing both countries of origin and countries of asylum sometimes attack refugee camps. Among the best-known incidents are the South African raid on Kassinga camp in Angola in 1978, and the 1982 massacre in the Palestinian refugee camps at Sabra and Chatilla in Lebanon – but such attacks occur more often than is commonly supposed. For example, Cambodian camps in Thailand, Afghan camps in Pakistan, Salvadorian refugees in Honduras, Guatemalans in Mexico and, more recently, Somali camps in Kenya have also drawn fire. Refugee camps in which civilians and armed combatants mingle are particularly vulnerable. Often, raids on camps are proclaimed as justifiable military actions, on the grounds that the camps are providing shelter for armed combatants.

There are two principal ways of dealing with this problem – both of them vigorously but not always successfully promoted by UNHCR. The first is to ensure that camps are located at a sufficient distance from international borders – an approach sometimes resisted by both governments of asylum countries and by refugees themselves. The second is to ensure that camps are strictly civilian in character and humanitarian in purpose. This is easier said than done, as many refugee communities are highly politicized and deeply engaged in the conflicts that caused their displacement. Internal camp organization is often in the hands of factional leaders who see the refugee camp as a resource in their struggle, in terms of provisions and recruitment, and as a sanctuary for wounded or exhausted fighters as well as civilian bystanders. The demilitarization of camps is a prerequisite for the protection of their residents. It is also essential for the preservation of the non-political and humanitarian character of refugee status which is clearly incompatible with military activity.

Even if external attack is not an imminent danger, refugee camps can still be hazardous. The residents are susceptible to manipulation and coercion by ruthless elements from among their own numbers, or by local officials.

"The 1951 Convention states that refugees escaping danger should not be penalized for entering a country illegally"

Women are particularly at risk. Such protection as exists for women under normal circumstances is commonly subsumed under family law; the disruption of family circles inherent in forcible displacement leaves many women outside the usual structures of familial and community protection, with enlarged responsibilities and few resources. There are innumerable instances of refugee women being subject to sexual coercion in exchange for normal entitlements such as food and medical services for themselves and their families.

Sexual assault is common in some settings, along with violations of basic rights such as equal access to education and freedom of movement. Women who speak out in defence of women's rights have, in some camps, been targeted for abuse.

Ethnic and tribal tensions often follow refugees into a camp setting, and spark off fighting among different groups. Banditry is commonplace. The enforced idleness (for men particularly) and frustration of prolonged camp existence contribute to a heightened level of tension and violence. Law enforcement authorities in host countries are often reluctant to become involved in refugee-on-refugee crime unless it has political or security dimensions.

One of the most contentious protection issues for asylum-seekers is detention. It is the practice in a number of countries to keep applicants in prison-like facilities as they wait for their cases to be heard, or at least until a preliminary hearing has decided whether they have a plausible case to make. Some states cite security concerns as a reason for keeping refugees in closed camps. The 1951 Convention says that refugees should not be penalized for having entered a country illegally if they have come directly from a place where they were in danger and have made themselves known to the authorities. While limitations on the movements of asylum-seekers may indeed be necessary during an initial evaluation of their cases, the conditions of detention often make it look and feel like punishment, and as such violate the requirement of humane treatment for refugees.

Refugees who have the opportunity to settle in an affluent society are, in relative terms, fortunate. But they too have special needs for protection in asylum. Some of these derive from the difficulty of gaining access to public services, including law enforcement, because of language and cultural barriers. One London borough, for example, reported in 1992 that one in ten of its residents was a refugee, and that 90 per cent of this group could not communicate in English and therefore had little or no access to

Rwanda: A Generation of Exile

The estimated half-million Rwandese refugees, almost all members of the minority Tutsi tribe, are among the oldest refugee populations on the African continent. After three decades in exile, many people who in 1959 fled the Hutu-led "social revolution" that preceded independence in 1962 have been integrated to varying degrees in neighbouring countries of asylum. But refugee numbers have continued to swell as a result of natural demographic growth and additional outflows of Rwandese caused by periodic eruptions of inter-ethnic violence. With the Rwandese government long maintaining that it had neither the land nor the resources to permit large-scale repatriation, the situation continued to fester, souring relations with neighbouring countries.

Tensions flared into open conflict in October 1990, when the Rwanda Patriotic Front – an organization composed mainly of refugees and exiles – launched an attack from across the Ugandan border. The conflict and its disturbing implications for regional security prompted a number of summit meetings of regional heads of state, culminating in the Dar es Salaam Declaration of 19 February 1991.

The Declaration, signed by Burundi, Kenya, Tanzania, Uganda and Zaire (all countries with sizeable populations of Rwandese refugees), as well as by Rwanda itself, recognizes that a solution to the 30-year-old refugee problem is essential to any viable peace agreement. Therefore it calls on the OAU and UNHCR to draw up a Plan of Action to identify solutions for the refugees, including voluntary repatriation or integration in asylum countries, following the establishment of a cease-fire and the initiation of a national process of political dialogue. A number of detailed surveys have since been carried out to investigate the possibilities for repatriating those refugees who wish to return home, and arranging local integration for those who do not. Effective implementation of the plan, however, depends on the establishment of peace and suitable conditions for return.

The introduction of a new constitution and a multi-party system in Rwanda should have been important steps towards political reconciliation and a definitive solution to the problem of Rwandese refugees. So should the 9 January 1993 agreement on power-sharing within a broad-based transitional government, signed by the present government and the Rwanda Patriotic Front. The peace process, however, remains volatile, and has been shaken by a new outbreak of fighting in the north of the country. This has led to a further exodus of refugees and, by June 1993, to the internal displacement of nearly one million people throughout the country. Once again, the prospects for a permanent solution have been set back.

---

health care.[13] Again, this is a problem that affects refugee women disproportionately.

More serious even than lack of access to public services are the discrimination, hostility and physical assault that have become a distressing feature of refugees' experience in a number of asylum countries, including the most affluent. The number of assaults on refugee centres and individuals – including mob attacks – has escalated with the growth in numbers of asylum-seekers, as racist and xenophobic groups of the extreme right make a particular target of refugees and asylum-seekers. Governments have sometimes responded firmly, if belatedly, but serious protection problems remain.

Long-term refugees

The emergence of new and urgent refugee problems tends to monopolize the headlines, but long-standing problems like those of the Afghan refugees in Pakistan and Iran still merit the attention of the international community. Such situations become increasingly serious as time passes and people remain separated from normal community life, often "warehoused" in desolate and crowded refugee camps where the stresses on individuals are acute.

A refugee situation that persists for years or even decades is not only a prescription for dependency, debilitation and demoralization, but also a continuing formula for instability. No state with a sizeable dispossessed population encamped on its borders, or even at considerable distance from them, can feel secure. The longest-standing of today's refugee problems, those of the Palestinians and the exiled Rwandese, are sobering reminders of the potential for conflict inherent in unresolved displacement (see Boxes 2.5 and 2.6). Perhaps the most disturbing element is the maturing of new generations who have known nothing other than the limbo of refugee life. Conflict is the central ordering principle of their lives.

Countries of first asylum that are unwilling to make a permanent place for refugees on their territory often compound the frustrations of life in exile by resisting any developments that imply local integration. They thus deny refugees a chance to engage in productive activity and deny themselves the benefits of refugees' contributions to the local economy. Even social infrastructure projects, such as schools and improved medical facilities, may be discouraged for fear that they will tempt refugees to remain in camps rather than repatriate at the first available opportunity. The tendency to keep camps inhospitable in order to discourage long stays exacts a heavy human cost. Children are denied irreplaceable opportunities to learn and develop, while their parents grow dependent and embittered.

Asylum is not a solution. It sometimes leads to one, if a refugee is allowed to and wishes to apply for citizenship and thereby ceases to be a refugee. This sequence, which is foreseen in the 1951 Convention as the norm, has ceased to be an option for most of the world's refugees. For them, there is no alternative but a negotiated end to hostilities and the commencement of reconciliation.

Conclusion

Pressure on the institution of asylum comes from a number of different sources. It stems not only from abuses by would-be economic migrants – a well-founded concern in industrialized countries – but, more generally, from the fear of receiving countries that they cannot absorb the number of refugees to which a consistent application of conventional asylum practices would expose them. In the West, lack of consistency was justified in the past by the political motivations of the Cold War. Even then it was challenged by human rights and refugee advocacy groups.

The depoliticization of refugee issues has made possible the application of a broader and more consistent humanitarian standard. But the current refugee system cannot absorb the numbers of people facing persecution and political violence in the world today. As a result, that system has already begun to change. As the process continues, two factors in particular are crucial to a successful adaptation: preservation of the core principle of asylum for victims of persecution, and an effective regime of temporary protection for victims of generalized political violence. The viability of temporary protection depends on an active search for political solutions to refugee-producing conflicts, and greater exertion of co-ordinated pressure to bring the solutions to fruition. Otherwise, temporary protection may simply become another name for prolonged exile.

Asylum remains the cornerstone of international protection. For too long, however, it has been taken to be the entire edifice. Restrictions on access to asylum, and on the definitions of those entitled to it, have been justified by beleaguered governments as necessary for the preservation of the institution. A surer way to accomplish that goal is to embed the practice of asylum in a comprehensive response to refugee flows, which attempts to address the entire continuum from initial causes and preventive actions, through emergency response and international protection, aiming finally to arrive at satisfactory solutions.

Chapter three

Information as Protection

On 7 November 1992, a vessel slipped away from the Somali port of Marka carrying a desperate human cargo: 3,302 refugees from the brutal civil war that had plunged their country into anarchy and famine. Distress signals from the ship, which carried little food or water, were picked up five days later, as it headed for the Gulf of Aden. No port in the region was willing to accept another shipload of Somali boat people – until the press was alerted and began to write and broadcast news of the impending tragedy. World attention focused on the lost ship, and states with forces in the region launched a week-long air and sea search until it was located. Yemen, already host to 50,000 Somali refugees, opened the port of Aden. The ship, jammed with hungry, thirsty, frightened people, docked safely on 18 November.

A late 20th-century cliché holds that information is power. Information is also protection. Neither the general public nor officials can respond adequately to refugee problems they know nothing about. Gathering information and communicating it effectively are central to the assistance and protection of refugees.

Radical changes in the information environment, the result of the technological revolution, have made it less likely that humanitarian tragedies will unfold completely unnoticed by the outside world. There are other risks, however. The consumers of modern media are exposed to enormous quantities of information from multiple sources. Refugees and other humanitarian issues compete with an array of topics, ranging from local to global concerns and from the momentous to the trivial. "Compassion fatigue" has often been predicted, but attention fatigue is as great a danger. The impact of media coverage on public opinion and the impact, in turn, of public opinion on the political process make it vital that refugee issues get a hearing.

The camera – especially the television camera – has proved to be a powerful advocate for people in need, including refugees. But the arrival of photographers and television crews usually occurs at a late stage of refugee-generating crises, after the exhausted victims of violence, persecution and terror have fled their homes and gathered together where their plight can be more easily observed. The cameras seldom stay on beyond the onset of the next crisis, although the victims generally do. On television screens and in the headlines, Liberia is erased by the crisis in the Persian Gulf, the problems in Iraq by the tragedy in Bosnia and Herzegovina.

Information can play a role in protecting refugees right from the beginning of a crisis. If exposure starts early enough, and draws an effective response, it may even prevent people from having to become refugees. Failing that, once displacement has occurred, sustained attention may help foster solutions.

"Information draws attention to policies and practices that create refugees"

Information is both a resource and a tool for the protection of refugees. It is the resource that alerts governments, international agencies and private groups to the need to assist people who have had to flee. It is often the tool that persuades such entities to act and convinces members of the public to support their actions. Information is also a resource for people who are contemplating movement. It may help refugees choose the safest and most appropriate channels for departure, and the most opportune moment to return. For people who are not under the kind of compulsion that would give them a claim to international protection, accurate information about their chances of being admitted as immigrants may influence their decision to leave home.

One function of information is to draw attention to the policies and practices that create refugees and to identify those responsible. The media often provide the setting for the "court of public opinion", as well as the instrument for relaying the evidence. In countries of asylum and resettlement, information channels – which include informal networks as well as conventional news media – perform an important function in building public awareness of the meaning of refugee status and encouraging humanitarian attitudes in general.

False or incomplete information – whether unintentional or deliberate – can be as dangerous as good information is helpful. It can result in inadequate policies or, in the refugee's case, a potentially fatal course of action. The circumstances from which refugee crises emerge are typically the most difficult in which to gather reliable, objective information. Governments and opposition groups, relief agencies and advocacy groups have become increasingly sophisticated in the presentation of data to illustrate their own points of view. There is sometimes a fine line between selectivity and manipulation; outright fabrication of events by partisans is not unknown. And of course the media have their own biases, reflected not only in the content of news reporting but also in the definition of what is news.

The best information base is built by including as many different sources as possible, while remaining fully aware of the biases or limitations of each. For conveying the genesis and dynamics of forced displacements, few sources can compete with the refugees themselves.

Drawing attention to refugee-creating abuses

One of the purposes of public information is to galvanize international opinion through continuous monitoring and reporting of conditions that lead to refugee movements. The proliferation of information channels facilitates this task. Often, there is a *de facto* alliance between informal or unofficial observers in the field and the media. The former, with intimate knowledge of the situation on the ground, can provide first-hand descriptions of events, while the latter can deliver it to a global audience. For example, the desperate plight of villagers and townspeople under siege in eastern Bosnia during the winter of 1992-93 was in part brought to light by local amateur radio operators. Their reports, while not always accurate, were monitored by international news media and brought in external observers better equipped to assess humanitarian needs. Refugees provided the first accounts of pirate attacks on refugee boats in the South China Sea, of civilian massacres by government forces in El Salvador and of inhumane detention camps and widespread rape in Bosnia and Herzegovina. Their stories were relayed by humanitarian workers and picked up for further exploration by news media (see Box 3.1).

The use of refugee reports as a source of information makes special demands on humanitarian agencies and the media. It requires skilled and compassionate listeners, as well as sensitivity to the victims' right to privacy. Often the retelling of an ordeal can be an additional trauma, particularly for torture victims and women who have been raped. Piecing together a consistent and objective account of events from hundreds of highly personal, emotional tales is difficult, and relaying anecdotal evidence of abuses has its dangers. Yet it is just such personal accounts that humanize the abstractions of refugee issues, and that are the most powerful instruments for mobilizing public determination to assist the victims.

The manipulation of information by the

Box 3.1
Breaking the Story of the Bosnian Detainees

Pictures of emaciated prisoners, their hollow stares framed by the barbed wire of a Serbian detention camp, flashed across television screens around the globe in August 1992. Shocked by these images, and by graphic newspaper accounts of atrocities in the camps of northern Bosnia and Herzegovina, the world reacted with outrage. Within days, the commanders of the prison camps – men who would normally spurn public opinion – were forced to begin closing them. Such is the protective power of information.

The day the first firm information on some of the camps was received by the UNHCR Press Office in Geneva, it was shared – on a background basis – with a number of journalists, including Roy Gutman of *Newsday*, the American reporter who broke the story. UNHCR also helped corroborate some of the evidence gathered independently by Gutman, who subsequently earned a Pulitzer Prize for his reporting on the camps.

Not all the information provided was background. On 27 July – a week before Gutman's prison camp story made world headlines – UNHCR had published details of some shocking human rights abuses, including an unconfirmed but credible report it had received concerning Omarska prison camp. These were distributed to more than 4,300 journalists, diplomats and humanitarian organizations worldwide. Of Omarska camp, a source was quoted: "Guards ... boasted that they will not 'waste bullets' on their detainees, who have no food, water or shelter and who are beaten twice a day. 'They will starve like animals,' one guard said."

The UNHCR report and additional background information helped convince the editors at *Newsday* to publish Gutman's story on 2 August. Television cameras, the first from the UK's Channel 4 News, followed. On 4 August, the UN Security Council issued a statement demanding that the ICRC and other international bodies be allowed to inspect the camps and prisons in former Yugoslavia. Within a week, international observers began entering the camps; shortly afterwards, arrangements to close them and transfer the detainees out of the country got under way.

By early July 1993, over 5,500 detainees had been released under ICRC supervision, 4,647 of whom had been given asylum abroad along with 6,383 family members. The detention centres in Bosnia and Herzegovina, however, were by no means a thing of the past. Of the 8,238 detainees notified to the ICRC in 1992, 2,416 were still being held prisoner by the three warring parties, despite repeated agreements reached with the ICRC. Furthermore, additional civilians were reportedly still being taken prisoner. There is every reason to fear that civilians continue to be held under harsh conditions in Bosnia and Herzegovina, out of reach of the scrutiny, and therefore the protection, of outside observers.

parties to a conflict is a perennial problem. A former ambassador in Belgrade, before the break up of Yugoslavia, recalls receiving the same graphic, illustrated "reports" of atrocities from both sides of the Serb-Croatian conflict, each claiming them as evidence of the horrors perpetrated by the other. This practice has, if anything, occurred with even greater frequency during the war in Bosnia and Herzegovina. In one of the most blatant examples, Belgrade television claimed that the 56 people, including 15 children, killed by Serbian shelling in the besieged town of Srebrenica on 12 April 1993 were in fact captured Serbs who had been tortured to death. UN officials in Srebrenica immediately and unequivocally denounced the report as "a shameless lie".

"Subtle forms of media bias can have far-reaching effects on international perceptions and policies"

Such crude distortions of reality are relatively easy to discredit. More subtle forms of bias hold greater dangers, as they fuel the hatred and the will to fight of the warring parties, and can have far-reaching effects on international perceptions and policies. The old debate about who is a "terrorist" and who is a "freedom-fighter" is the one of the most obvious examples. For years, the word "Palestinian" was hardly ever to be found in the Western media without words such as "terrorist", "bomb" and "hijack" nearby. The word "Israeli" has suffered much the same fate in the Arab and Islamic press. Almost all the world's media are guilty of stereotyping directly or by implication. Even objectively provided information can be subject to political manipulation. Right-wing demagogues, for example, frequently use immigration figures to inflame xenophobic and racist reactions. Information employed in this manner can feed and perhaps even cause persecution and conflict.

Humanitarian organizations are not only users of information about refugees and their problems; they are also among the main sources of it. Providers of assistance and protection in the field have unrivalled access to refugees and their stories of how they came to be uprooted. Reporters and observers who visit refugee camps, many of which are in remote and inaccessible parts of the world, commonly find themselves dependent upon relief organizations for both logistical support and an interpretation of the situation. Yet being seen as major conduits for information, especially on sensitive issues such as human rights, can place relief workers at risk of being thrown out of the area where they work, or even of physical attack. On the other hand, in some situations, contact with the press may provide them with a degree of protection.

The ability to communicate is indispensable to humanitarian agencies, almost all of which depend on awareness of refugee problems to generate public or official support for their work. Some organizations exist solely for the purpose of disseminating information about refugees and exerting pressure on governments to adopt certain policies. Others combine advocacy work, public education, fund-raising and direct assistance. Each of these roles uses information in a different way. For example, the main purpose of some public information activities is to build constituencies for humanitarian organizations and mobilize funds for refugee assistance. Others aim to arouse public opinion to demand certain responses from political leaders. All organizations have to be selective when choosing material to disseminate, and the act of selection will inevitably sometimes raise doubts about the fairness and balance of the picture that is being presented. In a similar vein, public exposure by relief workers of abuses may lead to charges that they are stepping beyond the bounds of their non-political, humanitarian role.

In the age of the hand-held video camera, the fax machine, the cassette recorder and the computer disk, information is difficult to suppress. The mere fact that an attempt to do so

The world's most under-reported disaster. Sudan, December 1988.

has been made can provide a clear warning signal of potential humanitarian problems. Yet some of the worst and most sustained occurrences of deliberate deprivation, persecution and indiscriminate violence have occurred in areas shielded from international observation: for example in Cambodia under the Khmer Rouge government and in remote areas of Mozambique. Access for observers, reporters and, as the next chapter will discuss, relief workers, is an essential ingredient of protection.

"A true information vacuum is rare, but a certain volume and momentum are needed to stimulate and sustain a response"

A true information vacuum is rare, but a certain volume and momentum are needed to stimulate and sustain a response. The war of attrition that the government of Iraq has been waging against the Shi'ites and Marsh Arabs in southern Iraq and the no-holds-barred civil war taking place in southern Sudan have both received coverage by the media and have been raised in international fora such as the General Assembly and the UN Commission on Human Rights. However, the volume of information has been slow to reach critical mass. Reports appear sporadically, people are shocked and then, when no more information is immediately forthcoming, the spotlight moves on to other, more accessible catastrophes.

The dynamics of information in such situations are hard to unravel. Journalists have proved time and time again that they are prepared to go anywhere, however dangerous, to cover a story. By June 1993, for example, more than 30 journalists had been killed while reporting the war in Bosnia and Herzegovina, many of them as a result of deliberate targeting. Editors – who tell their reporting staff where to go – make their decisions on the basis of perceived levels of interest among their audiences. The likelihood of international political or military engagement also plays a role in such decisions. Iraq, Somalia and the former Yugoslavia have all captured and retained the headlines in the West at various times, partly because Western involvement was seen first as a genuine possibility and then as a fact. Meanwhile, equally grim human catastrophes unfolding in places such as Liberia and the Sudan, remained relatively unnoticed outside the immediate region. Just as information can be an important factor in generating political action, the potential interests of powerful states can play a central role in determining the focus of the mass media.

More consistent reporting, including eye-witness accounts, is needed if the continuing crisis in the Sudan, for example, is to receive the sustained attention it desperately requires. Conditions in the south of the country – the scene of one of the world's most under-reported humanitarian disasters – are dire, owing to the fighting between the Sudan People's Liberation Army (SPLA) and government troops and, more recently, the fierce infighting between southern factions. The economy has been ruined by nearly 30 years of civil war; 1.7 million people are believed to be displaced by the lethal combination of drought and conflict; 7.2 people million are reportedly in need of assistance; 600,000 lives are thought to have been lost already. Some estimates put the numbers far higher. The situation has many parallels with that in Somalia but has received relatively little attention, in part because both government and rebel authorities have tended to bar independent media from entering the area. In mid-1993, however, access became a little easier. Aid agencies stepped up their activities and news of the crisis in southern Sudan began to appear more frequently in Western media.

One inhibitor of the free flow of information that is entirely beyond the media's control is, of course, the denial of access. Regimes and factions engaged in the systematic murder of large numbers of people in remote and inhospitable locations have often shown great skill in playing the information game. Relief agencies and NGOs are refused entry, the media barred, often under the pretext that it is for their own safety – a claim that on occasion comes close to being a threat. The true story will likely emerge in the end but, as in the case of El Salvador's Truth Commission, it may be years before credible hearsay is shown to be fact by mass graves and documentary evidence uncovered during the course of a systematic investigation.

It is not enough for information on refugee-producing events to become widely available. A willingness to act upon it must exist if exposure is to have a practical protective function. The fear of disclosure of abuses can have a deterrent effect in certain situations, for example when antagonists are competing for international legitimacy. In all circumstances, however, information is at least the beginning of protection, showing where and why it is needed.

Stimulating response to the needs of refugees

When awareness of a refugee crisis is aroused, practical response to the needs of the displaced often begins with material assistance. The most pervasive images of refugees are associated with physical need: pictures of emaciated children, wounded civilians, frightened and destitute families seeking to escape threats to their lives. These powerful images are what news media, especially television, need to tell a story; they are also what people respond to most directly: digging into their own pockets, expressing their sense of urgency through local media or grass-roots organizations and lobbying their political representatives.

Media coverage of the plight of Kurds on the Iraq-Turkey border in 1991 and of widespread starvation in Somalia in 1992 provoked massive responses at both public and political levels. Probably the most renowned case of public response stimulated by the media dates back to the Ethiopian famine of 1984-85, and to the BBC film footage that brought the starvation of internally displaced people to the television

screens of the West. It generated an outpouring of sympathy and financial contributions from private citizens, and revitalized the attention of governments to the unfolding tragedy.

It also demonstrated the important role of non-conventional and non-news media in drawing attention to humanitarian issues, as the initial news coverage was amplified by, among other things, rock concerts that subsequently became a benchmark of solidarity with people in need. Popular music, drama and fiction have now all become means of raising awareness. Celebrities such as the late Audrey Hepburn (for UNICEF), and Barbara Hendricks and Sophia Loren (for UNHCR) have put their ability to command attention at the service of refugees and victims of famine and war.

"Public opinion can be aroused by exposure to a refugee problem but meet a blank wall in terms of policy response"

A generous public response to campaigns for refugee assistance makes it possible for NGOs to respond to emergencies, often more rapidly and flexibly than official agencies can. Nonetheless, the resources available through governments are much larger. Therefore the relationship between public information, public opinion and government response is an important one, although by no means as direct as some simple formulations would have it.

The notion that information, reflected in news media, acts on public opinion and through it drives policy-making does not do justice to the complexity of the relationship between information and policy. Public opinion can be aroused by exposure to a refugee problem but meet a blank wall in terms of policy response. A government may explain inaction in terms of national interest, conflicting goals or pragmatic constraints. Then again, an activist policy may

Box 3.2
Racism and Xenophobia

"There are only 90,000 of them here but they are a disgusting and painful abscess on the body of our nation. An ethnic group without any culture, moral or religious ideals, a nomad mob only robbing and stealing. Dirty, full of lice, they occupy the streets and railway stations. Let them pack their dirty tatters and leave forever!"

From a wall poster in Central Europe

In some countries, incidents of criminal violence committed against asylum-seekers have risen by as much as 400 per cent in the early 1990s. They cannot be treated as a marginal phenomenon. In too many countries it is no longer considered unacceptable for political leaders to publicly flaunt racist or xenophobic sentiments.

Racial persecution is a major cause of refugee flight. The number of refugees around the world can be seen as a barometer of human intolerance. Ironically, these very refugee flows are today being cited as a cause of the new xenophobic trend. Racism, and the violence that goes with it, all too often haunt refugees even after they have found asylum.

Equally disturbing, public hostility towards what is seen as an endless tide of immigrants has convinced policy makers in many industrialized nations that their constituencies have reached saturation point. This has led many countries to adopt more restrictive approaches to asylum, sparking fears that the centuries-old tradition may be crumbling at a time when it is needed most.

Germany has confronted its xenophobia problem more openly than most other nations. It recorded 4,587 attacks against foreigners in 1992, compared to 2,462 such incidents in 1991. The 1992 figure included 548 incidents of arson directed at accommodation centres for foreigners and asylum-seekers. Seventeen people died in racially-motivated attacks. Anger at the sheer number of asylum-seekers – Germany found nearly 440,000 on its doorstep in 1992 – led to increased support for far-right fringe parties. An economy in recession and massive unemployment fuelled resentment over the generous benefits the state accords to those seeking sanctuary, the majority of whom are found, after lengthy legal proceedings to have no claim to refugee status. The animosity displayed by the extreme right reached such a high pitch that Japanese companies in Berlin began giving employees tips on how to dress and behave to ensure they would not be mistaken for Asian refugees. On the positive side, in an encouraging and heart-felt public expression of revulsion at the wave of xenophobia, hundreds of thousands of Germans have taken part in a series of massive demonstrations across the country.

Germany is most often cited in treatises on xenophobia because of its high-profile public debate on the issue and its meticulous record-keeping. But the problem of xenophobia is widespread throughout Europe and elsewhere. The Nordic countries, once considered bastions of tolerance, have not been spared xenophobic acts of violence. Nor have Belgium or Switzerland. In France, a 1992 government survey found that 40 per cent of French people admitted they held racist sentiments, while 21.2 per cent characterized themselves as "very racist". And in Japan, thousands of posters appeared in Tokyo in early 1993 urging fellow Japanese to "Get rid of the delinquent foreigners who are destroying our nation's culture, tradition and safety."

The wall poster quoted above could have been found almost anywhere. The "ethnic group" it attacks could be one of a hundred. Disturbed by the rising tide of racism and xenophobia, some governments and human rights organizations have joined hands with the media to counter-attack. There have been strong manifestations of public disgust in response to the racial attacks in Germany and the Nordic countries. Several other nations have mounted public awareness campaigns aimed at confronting mounting xenophobia head on.

A total of 76 organizations, including UNHCR, have participated in a Spanish campaign organized around the theme "Democracy is Equality". With financing from the Ministry of Social Affairs, the campaign used TV spots, full-page advertisements in national newspapers and subway posters to combat the ignorance that breeds racism. The campaign – which generated extensive public debate – was both controversial and courageous in that it used racist epithets to fight deep prejudices against refugees, immigrants, gypsies and all people of a different race.

Media initiatives in other countries have included a message broadcast between commercials by a Netherlands TV station, which stated "If you too think that foreigners must leave the country, then we prefer to do without you as viewers of RTL 4." Also in the Netherlands, Radio 3, a rock-music radio station, launched a concerted campaign against racism and other forms of discrimination in early 1993.

Elsewhere in the world, politicians and local media are often failing to combat – and in some cases actively fuelling – rabble-rousing attempts to blame the ills of society on foreigners or minority groups. While it would be simplistic to claim that information campaigns like those cited above can, by themselves, cure such deeply ingrained problems as racism and xenophobia, they can certainly be useful in encouraging greater tolerance and positive humanitarian attitudes towards people in need.

For the sake of society at large, including refugees and asylum-seekers, it is important that certain obvious messages – which are sometimes forgotten by the general public and politicians alike, particularly in the context of the immigration debate – are broadcast loud and clear. Foreigners do not cause economic decline. They do not invite racism. On the contrary, they are the principal victims.

be formulated not in response to expressed public opinion but in anticipation of it. Information conveyed in the media may act directly on policy-makers, unmediated by a wider public debate. It is relatively rare that information generates a direct demand for action from an aroused public and thereby moves foreign policy – but it can make the public more receptive by explaining the need for action. Consequently information in the service of refugees must work on several levels at once: on general public opinion, on groups with a special interest in refugee affairs, on "opinion makers" and on those directly involved in setting policy.

Building public awareness

It is easier to explain the physical needs of refugees than the requirement for other kinds of protection. Food, water, shelter, medicine and immediate physical security from fighting and shelling are tangible in a way that the need to ensure the legal protection of refugees and to safeguard and promote their rights are not. As a result, legal protection measures are often less comprehensible to the public at large and more likely to cause resentment than relief assistance.

Public ambivalence is exacerbated by a blurring of the distinctions between refugees and other migrants, and by a failure to comprehend the specific needs of different groups. Effective communication can be used to clarify these distinctions, while promoting humane attitudes toward all those in need. It can also explain the obligations to protect refugees that states accept under international law. Explaining what it means to be a refugee is particularly important at a time when so many man-made and natural disasters claim public attention. Some elements of the mass media create an image of a never-ending stream of undifferentiated victims, or of an impending deluge of economically motivated immigrants. Information conveyed by local and national governments, international agencies, citizens' groups and NGOs has a central part to play in restoring perspective and accuracy to public perceptions of refugee inflows.

The most worrying aspect of the misapprehensions about refugees is the manifestation, in many countries, of xenophobic or racist reactions against foreigners (see Box 3.2). Many attacks have been directed specifically against housing and other facilities for asylum-seekers, although the perpetrators generally do not make distinctions among refugees, temporary labourers and long-term foreign residents. An encouraging counter-trend can be seen, however, in

Box 3.3

Refugees and the Nobel Peace Prize

UNHCR's first High Commissioner, Dr Gerritt van Heuven Goedhart, was perpetually strapped for cash. "What does international protection mean for a man who dies of hunger?" he asked in his first report to the General Assembly. "Passports are necessary but hunger can't be stilled by them."

Insisting that UNHCR was not in business merely to "administer misery", van Heuven Goedhart was impatient with the slow response of donors when it came to providing material assistance to destitute refugees. Taking matters into his own hands, he sold a bar of gold inherited from one of UNHCR's predecessors, the Nansen Office for Refugees. He got $14,000 for the gold, which the Nansen Office had purchased with funds from its 1938 Nobel Peace Prize.

The Nobel Peace Prize figures prominently in the history of refugees. The Norwegian Nobel Committee has decided to highlight efforts made on behalf of refugees at least four times. Prior to the 1938 award to the Nansen Office, Fridtjof Nansen himself had received the prize in 1922 for his work on behalf of Russian refugees. UNHCR has been honoured twice, in 1954 and in 1981.

The 1954 prize, awarded only three years after the founding of UNHCR, cited the agency's work on behalf of the 2.2 million refugees and displaced people in post-war Europe. High Commissioner van Heuven Goedhart told the committee that UNHCR's objective, like Nansen's, was to create "a state in which no people of any country, in fact no group of people of any kind live in fear or need". To his 99 staff members he said: "Everybody could say that he was one per cent of the Nobel Prize winner."

In 1981, when the number of refugees had risen to nearly ten million, the Nobel Committee praised UNHCR for dealing with "a veritable flood of human catastrophe and suffering, both physical and psychological" despite substantial political difficulties. The committee drew attention to the "tremendous and increasing number of refugees" in the world, mentioning those who had fled Afghanistan, Ethiopia and Viet Nam.

"The stream of refugees ... creates serious problems in relations between states, and for this reason the activities of the Office of the High Commissioner is serving the interests of humanity and peace," the committee said. The High Commissioner at the time, Poul Hartling, called the award "a statement to the world's refugees that you are not forgotten".

The Nobel Committee has also presented the award on five occasions to individual refugees who rose above their personal tragedies to make exceptional contributions towards peace – underlining the fact that a bundle of meagre belongings is not necessarily the only thing a refugee brings to his or her new country.

- Ludwig Quidde, a prominent German pacifist, was co-winner of the 1927 Nobel Peace Prize. Quidde, a strong opponent of the revival of German militarism, escaped to Switzerland in 1933 after the Nazis came to power.

- Willy Brandt, who had fled to Denmark and Norway from his native Germany in order to escape the Gestapo, later became Chancellor of West Germany. He received the Nobel Peace Prize in 1971 for his policies of peace and reconciliation with the East.

- Romanian-born American novelist Elie Wiesel, deported by the Nazis in 1944 to Auschwitz, received the 1986 Nobel Peace Prize for his spiritual leadership in an age when "violence, repression and racism continue to characterize the world".

- The Peace Prize recipient in 1989 was the Dalai Lama, Tibet's exiled spiritual leader. He was recognized for his opposition to violence in his struggle to preserve the historical and cultural heritage of his people.

- The 1992 Nobel Peace Prize went to Rigoberta Menchú, a Guatamalan Mayan Indian who had sought asylum in Mexico, in recognition of her crusade for social justice and ethno-cultural reconciliation based on respect for the rights of indigenous people.

popular campaigns to reject and condemn such attacks and the attitudes behind them.

Public information also has a role to play in presenting a more complete picture of refugees than that contained in the stereotype of a mass of ill-educated, helpless victims. Many refugees bring skills, energy and high motivation to the countries that offer them asylum (see Box 3.3). Isabel Allende, Bertolt Brecht, Marlene Dietrich, Albert Einstein, Sigmund and Anna Freud, Gabriel García Márquez, Rudolf Nureyev and Sir Georg Solti are just a few of the many refugees and exiles whose work has enriched humankind.

Providing a basis for decision-making

The importance of information as a tool for educating and mobilizing the public is equalled by its importance as a resource for making decisions. Any decision-maker is constrained by what he or she knows about the available options and the likely consequences of a chosen course of action – whether that person is a government minister, an asylum officer trying to determine if a particular individual should be granted refugee status, or someone deciding whether or where to seek asylum. A sound information base is a prerequisite for sound decision-making.

In situations where applicants for asylum are screened individually, the determination of refugee status under the 1951 Convention requires an assessment of whether the reasons for the asylum-seeker's flight are included among those covered by the definition of who is a refugee, and whether the applicant's fears are well-founded or not. Organizations and individuals who work with refugees – particularly those who must determine if a person or a group needs international protection – depend on clear, accurate and up-to-date information on circumstances in the country of origin, including human rights practices and the treatment of ethnic or religious minorities.

In most cases, the challenge is not lack of information. A huge amount of data exists. The challenge is to identify what is credible, reliable and relevant – and then to locate and retrieve it so that it can be used in situations where it is needed. The range of relevant material is broad. Information on political, economic, social and legal structures is important, as are reliable facts about human rights problems. Several layers of information are needed: not only about what the law of a certain country says, but also about the relationship between the law and usual practice.

The vast array of factual and analytical material available about countries of origin, and the importance of finding the most trustworthy information to support judgements, gives information technology a key role in protection. Modern communications technology accomplishes in a matter of seconds, tasks that consumed much time and manual labour in the past. Computerized data banks allow researchers to conduct "on-line" searches and to retrieve information over great distances. To take advantage of these new capabilities, international refugee information networks have been established and are being steadily augmented.

"Quantity of information is not a substitute for quality of analysis"

The International Refugee Documentation Network (IRDN) is one example. It was set up in 1986, with the purpose of developing tools for the rapid exchange of information between international and non-governmental organizations dealing with refugees. It has established an electronic mail system known as the International Refugee Electronic Network (IRENE) which allows instant electronic contact between centres around the globe, from Denmark to South Africa. The Human Rights Information and Documentation System (HURIDOCS) – now used by more than 350 refugee and human rights documentation centres – is another system designed to make data more accessible and compatible. Through such co-

Box 3.4

Trading in Human Misery

Human smuggling is big business. In many instances, organized crime is involved at both ends of the journey. Crime syndicates operating in China, for example, charter ships, recruit passengers with promises of easy riches and then ensnare them by providing loans to pay the extortionate sums charged for illicit passage – as much as $30,000 per person. To pay off the debt, many people end up as virtual bonded slaves to the smuggling syndicates. Working illegally in restaurants, laundries, prostitution rings and gambling halls, they are disciplined by fear both of their employers and of the authorities. Wages of 70 cents an hour – less than one fifth of the legal minimum in the United States – have been reported.

Smuggling rackets find a ready market for their services not only among would-be migrants seeking to bypass immigration controls, but also among the persecuted. Denied passports or exit permits, people in flight from persecution may have little choice but to turn to rings of organizers who arrange their departure for profit. Refugees fleeing from Viet Nam during the first wave of "boat people" in the late 1970s often paid large sums of money to secure their passage. More than a few were swindled in the process.

Smuggling operations vary from country to country – the common theme being the exploitation of human misery. Moscow reportedly has become a staging post for

movements from the Middle East (especially Iraq) and East Africa.[14] Russian racketeers demand high prices for passage to the Nordic countries via Russia or the Baltic states. Sweden, with its liberal asylum laws, is the favoured destination. In January 1993, several Latvian boats, containing mainly Iraqi Kurds, were intercepted by the Swedish authorities. Other countries have been affected as well. In the same month, the bodies of five Tamils were found dumped at a motorway parking lot in Austria. They had died of suffocation in the cargo container of a truck that was smuggling them from Moscow to Italy.[15]

Recently, criminal syndicates have moved to make their smuggling operations more efficient. Large ships have been used to transport cargoes of up to 400 people, often by long circuitous routes, to Western countries. Sweden, Australia and the United States have had to deal with several such cases. In one of the worst known incidents, in May 1993, a freighter carrying 397 Chinese ran aground in its approach to New York City. Ten people drowned while trying to swim ashore.

In early July 1993, three other boats carrying 659 Chinese were intercepted off California by the US Coast Guard. A diplomatic imbroglio ensued which kept the Chinese at sea for days while the United States sought to avoid admitting them and to persuade the Mexican government to allow disembarkation. They were eventually permitted to transit in Mexico pending rapid deportation to China. One person, identified as having a valid asylum claim was

admitted to the United States.

Tens of thousands of Chinese have been smuggled into the United States since the early 1980s. But controls are getting tougher and more people are being caught. Significant numbers of them, upon being apprehended, claim political asylum. The US government holds that the situation in China cannot justify a blanket determination that none of those brought in illegally have a well-founded fear of persecution if returned home. Indeed, Chinese asylum-seekers in the US have had much higher rates of approval for refugee status than most other national groups. The Chinese authorities, alarmed about the criminal syndicates operating the trade, have publicly stated their desire to eradicate it.

Ironically, most of the Chinese originate from the relatively prosperous provinces of Guangdong and Fujian. The unequal distribution of wealth brought about by rapid industrialization and privatization, compounded by distorted information about the outside world, help the racketeers win the confidence of would-be migrants. One way of fighting this kind of exploitation is through an information counter-attack aimed at alerting people to the dangers and misery that likely await them during and after an illicit voyage.

In the meantime, those who seek asylum remain entitled to a fair hearing. For it is not only migrants seeking a better life who fall victim to racketeers, but also people in genuine fear of persecution who have been driven by desperation into the hands of smugglers for lack of alternative escape routes.

operative efforts, many smaller organizations now find it much easier to share information and services with a worldwide audience.

Information on asylum applications and countries of origin is increasingly being exchanged among governments, international agencies and private organizations. Plans and mechanisms for information-sharing have proliferated in the industrialized countries in recent years. In Europe in particular, governments have set up a range of information systems designed to help prevent multiple applications and disruptive movements of asylum applicants between European countries, as well as to harmonize refugee determination procedures. The new systems are specifically geared to sharing data on trends in asylum applications, countries of origin, legal and migration issues and even individual case files.[16]

Various international organizations have also set up related computerized information projects, including the International Organization for Migration and UNHCR whose Centre for Documentation on Refugees continues to maintain and develop its databases on refugee-related case law, legislation, international instruments, country-of-origin information and more general literature. Lack of access to information is rapidly ceasing to be a constraint on the development of refugee policy.

As noted earlier, however, information is not a neutral commodity. Its usefulness does not depend on compilation alone. The user must be able to recognize what is important and judge the reliability of content and the biases in reporting. The importance of these factors point to the potential dangers of databases: quantity of information is not a substitute for quality of analysis.

The decision-makers on the front lines of refugees flows are, of course, the refugees themselves. Accurate information can be a life-giving resource for them, although refugees in flight have limited choices about how to respond to what they hear. Refugees are deeply affected by decisions such as the closing of the Turkish border to Kurdish refugees in 1991, the US decision in 1992 to return all Haitian asylum-seekers directly to Haiti without asylum hearings and the policies of European and other states that asylum claims should be processed in the first "safe country" entered. Individuals under pressure to flee are helped by having access to information about conditions that may affect their prospects for securing protection.

"Accurate information can be a life-saving resource for refugees"

Access to information continues to be important once refugees have reached an asylum country. They need to know their legal rights and obligations as well as what resources are available to assist them. Material of this sort, in the refugee's own language, can lay the basis for a successful adaptation to new circumstances, whether temporary or permanent. Voluntary repatriation depends very heavily on feedback about conditions in the home country; only on this basis can a refugee make an informed decision to return home.

Information of concern to refugees also has a role to play in the decision-making of other migrants. Particularly unfortunate are the many people who travel under a mistaken impression that they will be received as refugees and allowed to resettle abroad, but who do not satisfy the criteria for refugee status. People leave their homes ill-informed about the conditions and likelihood of being allowed to enter or remain in a country of asylum. Often, they invest heavily in the journey, which may itself subject them to danger. People who travel by boat are particularly at risk, as are those who entrust themselves to unprincipled and extortionate smuggling networks (see Box 3.4).

The policies and practices that affect such people should be broadcast widely in order to spare those who have virtually no chance of gaining refugee status the perils of a fruitless journey – and to avoid overburdening the

Box 3.5
Mass Information Campaigns for Prevention

Contemporary flows of refugees and migrants involve a nexus of push and pull factors which are not always easy to disentangle. It is increasingly clear, however, that illusions and misinformation play a major part in persuading large numbers of people who do not qualify for refugee status to seek asylum. Such people often put their lives and those of their families at risk. Moreover, the magnitude of their numbers imposes a large financial and social burden on the international community. More importantly, it represents a major threat to the principle of asylum, as governments tend to react by introducing restrictive measures which may hamper genuine refugees' efforts to gain admission to a safe country.

Just as misinformation, illusion and misunderstanding about economic opportunities and immigration possibilities in the industrialized world can be an important factor in fuelling irregular movements of people, accurate information can play an important role in containing them. When the ending of automatic resettlement in the West for Vietnamese boat people and the subsequent adoption of the Comprehensive Plan of Action for Viet Nam in 1989 (see Chapter One, Box 1.4), initially failed to stem the exodus – which by then was of a largely migratory nature – an urgent attempt was made to address the problem at its source.

A mass information campaign was launched in Viet Nam using local television, radio and press, backed up by outside media, notably the BBC and Voice of America. This aimed to give the Vietnamese accurate and credible information about the new conditions for reset-tlement, and to explain the Orderly Departure Programme (ODP), the direct migration channel. It was hoped that, after gaining a clearer understanding of the realities of their situation and prospects, people who were intending to leave clandes-tinely for non-refugee related reasons would think better of their plans.

The campaign began with repeat-ed television broadcasts of a film made by Vietnamese television, under UNHCR sponsorship. It illustrated conditions in the camps in Hong Kong and featured UNHCR and government officials explaining that only recognized refugees would be resettled. Within six weeks of the initial broadcast, the arrival rate in Hong Kong had dropped by 87 per cent compared with the previous year. By the end of 1992, the combined effect of the repatriation of non-refugees to Viet Nam, the expanded ODP and the mass information campaign, which publicized these and other developments in Viet Nam, had brought the clandestine exodus to an end.

The impact of mass information on departures from Viet Nam has led to an extension of the approach to other situations. In 1991, as a multi-party system began to emerge in Albania and exit restrictions were lifted, more than 40,000 Albanians poured into Italy. As, by this stage, the motivation was chiefly econom-ic misery rather than continuing political persecution, steps were taken to establish direct dialogue with the population at large in Albania through weekly radio pro-grammes on Radio Tirana, again backed up by the Voice of America and the BBC. As in Viet Nam, infor-mation is being provided to the pop-ulation about the criteria for granting asylum and refugee status, as well as the possibilities for legal departure. In 1992, the number of asylum-seekers arriving in Italy dropped to 2,493. The mandatory repatriation of some 17,000 Albanians by the Italian authorities the previous year undoubtedly played a key and controversial role in stemming the exodus, but the volume of enquiries received by the mass information programme sug-gests that it, too, played a significant part and that Albanians are continuing to take its message seriously.

Mass information has become a valuable tool that helps dissuade people from leaving their countries for reasons other than those that would qualify them for refugee status. Clearly, such programmes have to be carefully planned and closely monitored in order to avoid any risk of their being exploited as a means of discouraging people who are genuinely in fear of persecution from leaving the country in which a mass information campaign is operating. If a campaign is to be effective, the information it provides has to be – and be seen to be – impartial and therefore credible to its target audience. For this reason, campaigns are launched only in certain very specific situations, and are closely supervised by UNHCR throughout.

asylum channels with non-refugees. The arrival of large numbers of asylum-seekers without valid claims prejudices public opinion in receiving countries to the detriment of those who do need international protection. Mass information programmes have been implemented in Viet Nam and Albania to alert people to the conditions and prospects of asylum in receiving countries (see Box 3.5). To the extent that these strategies persuade non-refugees to forego the asylum channels, they enhance the protection of refugees.

The intelligent use of good information is the key to good decisions, whether in determining the refugee status of an individual, planning preventive strategies or devising solutions such as voluntary repatriation for large groups. It also helps identify people who are not at risk, and thus provides a basis for developing fair and effective methods for dealing with the misuse of asylum procedures. Credible information, broadly based and widely shared, supports and strengthens the system of international protection.

Reuniting Cambodian refugees with their families.
Kao-I-Dang Camp, Thailand, October 1989.

Chapter four

Protection in Times of Armed Conflict

The majority of today's refugees and displaced people are being uprooted by armed conflict. Some have fled from the fighting itself – which usually causes more civilian than military casualties – and others from the complete disruption of their livelihoods. Disturbance of food production and the confiscation of food supplies by armed forces are often instrumental in forcing people to move. The upheaval and dislocation frequently kill more people than the bombs and bullets.

Forced displacement is commonly used as a military strategy. By depopulating a rural area, one party to a conflict may hope to deny its opponents a major source of support and recruitment. Although expressly forbidden by the Geneva Conventions, uprooting all or part of a population in some cases is a goal in itself.

Insurgent groups usually aim to disrupt lines of communication and other infrastructure, both to demonstrate their own power and to undermine the government's control. Social institutions such as schools and clinics are also seen by some groups as symbols of central authority, and therefore as targets. Such attacks on the fabric of civil society contribute heavily to the impulse to flee.

People who have fled from the effects of war are not necessarily seen as conforming to the refugee definition of the 1951 Convention. Yet they are recognized in regional instruments, in national practices and in popular perception as people in need of international protection until circumstances permit them to return safely to their home countries. Most modern refugees fall into this somewhat ambiguous category. Some of the new thinking about refugee issues discussed elsewhere in this report – such as protective prevention, in-country assistance, country-of-origin responsibility, monitoring, early warning and comprehensive approaches – is drawing humanitarian institutions more and more deeply into situations of armed conflict.

The victims of conflict include refugees, internally displaced people and people trapped behind siege lines or geographical barriers. Those who manage to escape across an international border have a good chance of gaining at least temporary refuge and international assistance. Whether or not the internally displaced gain access to protection or assistance depends on the vagaries of national and international politics – even though distinguishing between refugees and internally displaced people with identical protection and assistance needs is illogical and counter-productive, to say nothing of inhumane. The plight of those who are prevented from becoming refugees is often the most tragic. The same forces that impede their movement may cut them off from external aid or even the observation of the outside world. International agencies that normally work with displaced people, including UNHCR, try to assist and protect these would-be refugees in a number of settings. However, because of the inadequacy of international mechanisms specifically geared to the internally displaced, the response to their plight remains uneven, to say the least.

"Assistance for victims of war must be neutral, impartial and humanitarian"

Those uprooted by armed conflict in one country are increasingly likely to include people who are already refugees from another. For example, after the Mengistu regime in Ethiopia collapsed in 1991, Sudanese refugees living in camps in western Ethiopia were attacked. Up to 380,000 people spilled back across the border straight into a combat zone within Sudan, where they were attacked by Sudanese government troops, or got caught in the cross-fire between government and rebel forces. Other refugee groups have similarly been compelled to return to unsafe areas. Some 500,000 Ethiopian refugees streamed back into drought-devastated eastern Ethiopia, along with fleeing Somalis, because of fighting and the collapse of public order in Somalia during 1991-1992.

Armed conflict imposes political and logistical constraints on the provision of assistance

and protection to the displaced. During civil wars or armed uprisings, recognized governments may object to assistance being given to civilians in territory controlled by opposition forces. Under these conditions, protection and assistance are inextricably linked – in particular over the question of access to those in need of assistance, and over the location and conditions governing the provision of relief. The presence and actions of international humanitarian workers in the field may provide a certain degree of indirect protection. Aid workers are also in a position to take more active protective measures by drawing attention to abuse or discrimination affecting displaced people. As a result they are frequently obstructed and harassed, and are sometimes physically attacked, taken hostage or killed.

The protection of civilians in armed conflicts is amply provided for in international law (see Box 4.1). The 1949 Geneva Convention Relating to the Protection of Civilian Persons in Time of War, which has been ratified by 181 states, provided the foundation, which was built upon by the two Additional Protocols of 1977. Protocol II, with 116 ratifications, deals with the protection of civilians in internal armed conflicts. Among other things, it prohibits the use of starvation and forcible population transfers as weapons of war. The mandate of the International Committee of the Red Cross (ICRC) extends beyond the treaties and provides a mechanism for putting them into operation. ICRC and UNHCR frequently work alongside each other in conflict situations.

International guidelines for the provision of assistance to victims of armed conflict emphasize that help must be neutral, impartial and humanitarian. Neutrality implies a refusal to take sides. Impartiality implies that aid is given solely on the basis of need. The humanitarian principle upholds the protection of life and the relief of human suffering as the sole purpose of outside interference.

Assistance and protection are more and more frequently being provided to displaced people in the midst of active hostilities. Armed conflict not only creates refugees but also erects sometimes insurmountable obstacles to assistance efforts. It is almost inevitable that one or all parties to a conflict will politicize humanitarian aid, viewing it as a factor that could affect the outcome of the dispute. When warring parties believe their objectives or military tactics will be advanced by harming the civilian population, they nearly always see humanitarian relief efforts as a form of external interference obstructing the successful realization of their plans. Humanitarian assistance becomes a means of protection in precisely this way: its purpose is to remove the misery of non-combatants from the tactical calculus of war, and to

Box 4.1

International Humanitarian Law

Since the middle of the last century, international law has progressively acquired more humane and compassionate dimensions in an effort to ensure the fundamental protection of human beings both in times of peace and of war. This development is reflected in three distinct but interrelated branches of international law – human rights law, refugee law and humanitarian law – all of which are important means of preventing potential refugees flows.

International human rights law provides a set of universal standards which states must observe in their treatment of people under their jurisdiction.[17] Human rights conventions do not grant rights directly to individuals. Instead, they impose obligations on signatory states to grant such rights.

International refugee law seeks to protect people who have been forced to flee their home country because of persecution or violence, and whose own governments are unwilling or unable to protect them or to safeguard their basic human rights.

In its specialized sense, international humanitarian law provides aid and protection for victims of war. Its origins go back to 1864, when the first Geneva Convention was adopted at the instigation of the International Committee of the Red Cross (ICRC).[18] It is now codified in the four 1949 Geneva Conventions and in two Additional Protocols adopted in 1977. By June 1993, 181 states had signed the Geneva Conventions, thereby giving them almost universal validity, while Additional Protocols I and II had been adopted by 125 and 116 states respectively.

At the heart of international humanitarian law lies the principle of respect for human life and dignity. The Geneva Conventions stipulate that all those who are not taking an active part in hostilities – be they civilians or former combatants – must be respected, protected against the effects of war and provided with impartial assistance.

Most contemporary refugee flows result from armed conflict. International humanitarian law should, therefore, be of increasing relevance both for the protection of refugees caught up in fighting and for preventing refugee outflows by safeguarding the rights of civilian populations, including internally displaced people.

An important limitation of international humanitarian law, however, lies in the fact that it does not cover all armed conflict situations and that its application is more likely to be disputed in situations of civil war. Protocol II, which deals with internal conflicts, specifically excludes internal disturbances and tensions, such as riots, or isolated and sporadic acts of violence. Consequently, a number of situations in which the safety and well-being of civilians are seriously at risk fall outside the scope of humanitarian law or are unilaterally declared to do so by the governments concerned.

As internal conflicts proliferate, humanitarian law is violated with increasing frequency. Torture, rape, hostage-taking and "ethnic cleansing" are daily occurrences in war-torn areas throughout the world, and the impartial humanitarian assistance which victims have the right to receive is often obstructed.

An urgent question facing the international community today is how to halt such violations and to ensure that those responsible for war crimes are brought to justice. Unless ways are found to ensure that the principles and rules of humanitarian law are respected and properly implemented, the world is likely to continue to see refugees spilling across national boundaries in flight from the ravages of war.

confine the conflict solely to the opposing military forces.

The difficulties of providing protection and assistance in armed conflict are multiplied in situations of armed anarchy, when a government has collapsed and there is no central authority. It becomes virtually impossible to negotiate terms for the provision of relief that have meaning beyond the immediate time and place – and sometimes not even that. Under such circumstances relief operations proceed, if at all, in conditions of extreme uncertainty and insecurity. In the extreme case of Somalia, humanitarian relief operations were virtually paralyzed for many months until the UN-sanctioned military intervention in November 1992.

Box 4.2

Rape as a Form of Persecution

"While there has been steady progress in women's rights in many countries, a reversion to barbarism has occurred in others. Some countries have seen the use of systematic sexual violence against women as a weapon of war to degrade and humiliate entire populations. Rape is the most despicable crime against women; mass rape is an abomination." (Boutros Boutros-Ghali, International Women's Day, 1993).

Refugee women are vulnerable to rape before, during and after flight. During the 1980s, the most widely publicized example of sexual violence against refugees was the brutal rape and, in many cases, subsequent murder of Vietnamese women by pirates preying on boat people in the Gulf of Thailand. In many other parts of the world, however, women have been and continue to be victims either of random acts of sexual violence or of politically motivated rape.

Sexual attacks on women are commonplace in times of conflict or of heightened political or inter-communal tension. A review of European asylum case law indicates that a deplorably high number of Tamil refugee women had been raped in Sri Lanka. In interviews carried out by UNHCR Protection Officers among the quarter of a million Muslim refugees who fled from Myanmar to Bangladesh in 1992, allegations of rape figure prominently among the reasons given for flight. The conflict, banditry and anarchy that have characterized much of the Horn of Africa in recent years have resulted in large numbers of refugee women being raped or sexually abused prior to flight and, in some instances, after arrival in a country of asylum.

Sexual violence may be targeted directly at women themselves or, through them, at their families. Often, the aim of rape is to inflict deep and lasting damage on entire communities. There have been reliable reports of rapes being carried out in front of whole villages in order to spread terror and force people to flee.

An exact numerical assessment of rape cases is always difficult. Because of the stigma attached to its victims in many cultures, rape is one of the most under-reported crimes even in peace-time. Always highly emotive, in times of war and social breakdown the subject of rape is prone to manipulation for propaganda purposes.

Since April 1992, the former Yugoslavia has undoubtedly provided the most publicized example of rape being used as a weapon to further war aims such as "ethnic cleansing". Exactly how many rapes have been committed since the beginning of the conflict will never be known, although extensive evidence gathered by independent sources leaves no doubt that rape has occurred on a massive scale. All the warring parties have been implicated, though to varying degrees. A European Community team of investigators that visited the former Yugoslavia in December 1992 concluded that large numbers of Muslim women and girls in Bosnia and Herzegovina had been raped as part of a systematic campaign of terror.

Over the years, governments of countries admitting refugees have increasingly, though by no means uniformly, recognized that sexual violence can be used as an instrument of persecution, thereby providing valid grounds for claiming refugee status. Women who have suffered, or who have a well-founded fear of suffering, sexual violence because of their membership of a particular social group deserve to be granted international protection and recognized as refugees under the 1951 Convention.

Refugees and international security

Refugee groups are not necessarily passive victims of armed conflicts. Often they support or even participate in the fighting. Refugee camps are supposed to be respected as neutral, humanitarian zones and UNHCR refuses, as a matter of principle, to provide its protection to people actively engaged in armed hostilities. Nonetheless, in reality combatants often mingle with civilian populations, greatly complicating the task of protecting those not involved in the fighting. It is well known that Cambodian guerrillas operated from refugee camps not under UN control in Thailand, and that the Afghan *mujaheddin* based themselves among refugees in Pakistan, as did the Nicaraguan *contras* in Honduras.

The presence of "refugee warriors" sometimes provokes military retaliation. Fighting between different opposition factions may subsequently be repeated on a smaller scale within refugee camps. Even if the camps are not actively used as bases, they may still offer valuable support in the form of food supplies, medical care and rest for wounded or exhausted fighters. The host country is on occasion a willing accessory to this pattern, using refugee communities to forward its own foreign policy or security agenda.

Refugees' freedom of movement is sometimes constrained by their own military or political leaders, who for strategic reasons either prevent them from returning home or urge them to do so before conditions are safe. External forces also attempt to manipulate displaced people for political purposes.

It is vital that planners and field workers understand the military strategies, tactics and weapons employed in the fighting, as well as the politics of the underlying disputes. They need to know who controls which areas of the country of origin, and the relationships that exist between various factions and different refugee groups. A grasp of the local and international security dimensions of a conflict will allow the current and future protection needs of the displaced to be more effectively addressed. It is also essential if sound judgements are to be made concerning the risks and dynamics of assisted or spontaneous repatriation.

"Humanitarian assistance is sometimes drawn into the centre of disputes"

In almost all cases of displacement due to armed conflict, the first step towards a solution to the refugee problem is negotiation to end the fighting. Even this truism raises a dilemma for organizations that assist and protect the displaced. To what extent should they become engaged in efforts to bring about peace? Some see their work as creating a "humanitarian space" enabling adversaries to identify fundamental shared needs before moving on to more difficult political issues. Others see involvement in peace efforts as a dangerously political act which may compromise the neutral character of relief efforts.

Given all this, it is scarcely surprising that humanitarian assistance is sometimes drawn into the centre of disputes. Siege and starvation are two of the oldest weapons. Humanitarian assistance can also be a weapon, whether those providing it like it or not. Relief supplies reinforce the credibility and authority of the people in charge of civilian populations. Humanitarian aid can even fuel hostilities: passively, if it permits a military force to continue fighting while the civilians are cared for by international relief; actively, if relief supplies are diverted to military forces. Humanitarian assistance is sometimes accused of providing short-term help that may in the long term do more harm than good – by prolonging conflict, stimulating further displacement or diverting attention from a crying need for concerted political action to achieve peace.

Negotiating access

The provision of relief and the monitoring of the safety and welfare of displaced people depends on access: both the access of humanitarian agencies to people in need and vice versa. Access tends to be the subject of the most difficult and protracted negotiations between humanitarian agencies and warring parties in virtually all conflicts, both great and small.

The obligations of states to permit humanitarian access are well established in international law. Article 59 of the Geneva Convention Relating to the Protection of Civilian Persons in Time of War obliges all parties to an international conflict to allow free passage for humanitarian assistance such as food. Protocol II requires that medical personnel and transport be protected. Although these provisions apply only to states that have ratified the instruments, they are widely acknowledged – though not necessarily implemented – by governments and insurgent groups that wish to be accepted as members of the international community.

"The international community is becoming more insistent that warring parties permit access"

While the law on humanitarian access is clear, the record of implementation, particularly in internal conflicts, is very poor, and methods of enforcement are far from straightforward. States accept obligations such as those set out in the Geneva Conventions as necessary proof of their legitimacy and sovereign authority, and yet frequently invoke sovereignty as a means of preventing actions intended to hold them to their obligations. Barring humanitarian agencies from war zones has a twin effect. It stops presumed supporters of opposition groups from receiving relief and assistance, and it excludes independent observers who might witness and report mistreatment of civilians at the hands of government forces. Rebel movements in control of territory often react in an identical fashion.

Nonetheless, even in the midst of brutal fight-

ing, most states continue to acknowledge their humanitarian obligations. For example, in April 1992, a summit meeting of heads of state and governments in the Horn of Africa produced a Declaration of Commitment to the Observance and Promotion of Humanitarian Principles and Norms. The participants pledged to ensure access to people in need of assistance and protection. On the understanding that assistance would be provided with impartiality, and with respect for national sovereignty and the traditional cultural values of the people, they committed themselves to establishing "corridors of tranquillity" in conflict zones to enable relief supplies to reach civilians. They also gave assurances about honouring the integrity of relief distribution resulting from negotiations and agreements with the parties involved.

The international community is becoming more insistent that states and other warring parties actually carry out their commitments to permit access. Although successes have to date been limited, tough negotiations have succeeded in opening up entry for relief supplies. With drought and famine threatening millions of people throughout Ethiopia and southern Sudan, relief supplies blocked and further massive population movements looming, sustained international pressure led to the opening of the Eritrean port of Massawa in late 1990. In other instances – in Sudan, Iraq and, more recently, Bosnia and Herzegovina – airlifts or land corridors have been used to gain access to isolated areas where displaced people have congregated or where civilian populations have been cut off from the outside world. Humanitarian cease-fires have also been negotiated to permit campaigns to immunize children, such as those undertaken by UNICEF in southern Sudan, or evacuations of the sick and wounded (see Box 4.3). The fragility of such arrangements, however, has continued to demonstrate the difficulty, despite repeated negotiations, in sustaining humanitarian agreements without the political will of the warring parties concerned. In Sudan, former Yugoslavia and elsewhere, relief flights and land routes have been subject to continual disruption.

Box 4.3

Children in War

Children are among the principal victims of war. They are killed, maimed and traumatized during indiscriminate attacks on civilian communities. They are frequently subjected to abhorrent practices, including torture, rape, detention and conscription into military service. They also suffer disproportionately from the side-effects of conflict, such as famine, malnutrition, disease and separation from their families. Those who survive are likely to be scarred for life.

There is nothing more natural than for desperate parents to wish to protect their children from the ravages of war. In April 1993, the media reported on a nine-year-old Bosnian boy, Almedin Borakovic, who had been evacuated from Srebrenica to Tuzla. His mother had been killed by a mortar shell in the besieged Muslim enclave. When his desperate father thrust him onto a truck packed with evacuees, he found himself in charge of four younger brothers and sisters, aged between 18 months and five years. The Borakovics were among the many unaccompanied children evacuated from Srebrenica. Their story echoes the fate of numerous children in other wars raging around the world today.

Children trapped in war zones are a highly emotional issue. The desire to shelter them from atrocities has led to many courageous and praiseworthy initiatives. Unfortunately it also sometimes results in inappropriate responses. In dire circumstances, there may well be no alternative to evacuation, but hasty, ill-thought-out actions that separate

children from their families often fail to take into account the best interests of the child. Such actions range from the misguided to the irresponsible or even criminal. The worst cases involve the removal of children for financial gain as part of international adoption rackets.

In 1992, as the situation in Bosnia and Herzegovina rapidly deteriorated, there was mounting pressure to evacuate children from its besieged capital, Sarajevo. One independent German initiative ended in tragedy when, on 2 August 1992, snipers opened fire on a convoy of evacuees, killing two children. It was subsequently discovered that the mother of one of them, supposedly an orphan, had not been informed that her child was being evacuated.

The war in Bosnia has produced other disturbing accounts. Newspapers described how private individuals visited conflict areas and "rescued" children by pretending to be their parents. They were lauded as heroes who had avoided red tape to save children's lives. Little attention was paid to the evacuated children themselves. Were they really orphans, as was often subsequently claimed? In times of war, it is hard to be sure. Past experience has shown that careless evacuation can easily lead to the permanent destruction of families.

In August 1992, in an effort to discourage such actions, UNHCR and UNICEF issued joint guidelines on the evacuation of children from war zones. They highlight two main principles. First, when possible, mother and siblings should also be evacuated to avoid splitting up families. Second, evacuated children must be thoroughly documented so that the

family can subsequently be reunited.

Ill-conceived attempts to shelter children from war stand in sharp contrast to the practice of forcing them to take an active part in the fighting. Angola, Cambodia, Mozambique, Somalia and Sudan are just a few of the conflicts that have produced child soldiers.

International humanitarian law and the UN Convention on the Right of the Child stipulate that children below the age of 15 shall not be conscripted into armed forces. Nevertheless, refugee and returnee children under 15 continue to be recruited, forcibly or voluntarily, both for active combat and equally unacceptable support functions such as carrying ammunition or scouting for military patrols.

The plight of child soldiers was all too clearly illustrated by the group of 12,500 unaccompanied Sudanese boys who crossed the border into Kenya in May 1992. Some of them began their odyssey as long ago as the mid-1980s when fighting in southern Sudan forced them to flee to Ethiopia. Having returned to Sudan following the collapse of the Mengistu regime in Ethiopia, they were forced to flee again, this time to Kenya. When fresh attempts were made to recruit them into armed forces, UNHCR arranged to relocate the camp 120 kilometers away from the border. Many of the boys have no idea whether their parents are alive or dead, and if alive where they are. In such circumstances, reuniting them with their families is immensely difficult. In the meantime, they remain vulnerable to the same violent forces that have dogged their seemingly endless ordeal.

"Protection and assistance efforts are more likely to succeed with the co-operation, or at least the consent, of affected governments"

Numerous declarations and resolutions from multilateral bodies call on states to facilitate the work of humanitarian agencies and ensure safe passage for humanitarian aid. However, the UN Security Council created an unusually clear precedent in resolution 688 of 5 April 1991 when it insisted that Iraq allow international humanitarian organizations immediate access to all those in need of assistance in all parts of Iraq. Focus on the issue of humanitarian access was somewhat blurred – though the impact may have been increased – by the association of the resolution with the creation of a safety zone in northern Iraq by means of military intervention, and the subsequent decision to establish and patrol a "no-fly zone". In a further step in December 1991, the General Assembly after protracted debate passed resolution 46/182, in which it asserted that humanitarian assistance could be provided with the *consent* of the affected country, rather than at its request as had been the case in the past. It is more difficult for states actively to refuse humanitarian assistance for their people than to neglect, passively, to *request* it. However, it remains to be seen how far the international community is prepared to go to gain access, particularly in situations which are marginal to the interests of powerful states.

Sovereignty and intervention: new approaches

The international community is divided and ambivalent in its stance on the limitations imposed by national sovereignty on humanitarian assistance to displaced people in times of war. Representatives of some states continue to insist that sovereignty overrides all other principles of international interaction, while others speak not only of a right but even a duty to intervene on humanitarian grounds. Whatever the eventual outcome of this debate, recurring humanitarian emergencies have undoubtedly focused attention on the question of how far the relief of human suffering can and should be subject to national boundaries and the consent of governments.

The United Nations Secretary-General, Boutros Boutros-Ghali, raised this question in a more general context in his *Agenda for Peace*. He wrote: "Respect for [the state's] fundamental sovereignty and integrity are crucial to any common international progress. The time of absolute and exclusive sovereignty, however, has passed; its theory was never matched by reality. It is the task of leaders of states today to understand this and to find a balance between the needs of good internal governance and the requirements of an ever more interdependent world."[19]

Protecting the victims of armed conflict increasingly means finding ways of protecting people inside their own countries, in spite of the constraints of sovereignty. Some of the recently-introduced practices designed to make humanitarian action more flexible – such as humanitarian cease-fires, corridors of tranquillity and open relief centres – remain within the bounds of sovereignty. And there are practical as well as legal reasons for continuing, when possible, to honour sovereignty. Protection and assistance efforts to the displaced are more likely to succeed if they have the co-operation, or at least the consent, of affected governments. "Humanitarian intervention", on the other hand, involves states acting unilaterally or collectively to assist people in another state without the consent of their government. It is likely to be less contentious – if not necessarily easier to enact – in situations, such as that in Somalia, where there is no functioning government. In the general situation of lawlessness that prevails there, assistance cannot be delivered effectively without substantial military protection.

One of the problems raised by the ambiguous status of sovereignty is whether, and under what circumstances, inter-governmental and bilateral institutions should deal with unrecognized political entities in the management of refugee problems. In situations of civil war or anarchy, humanitarian agencies are faced with a plethora of official or quasi-official authorities at national and local levels, as well as with liberation movements, self-proclaimed governments, tribal or clan leaders, war lords, bandits or irregular militias. Practical necessity dictates talking to whoever controls access to people in need, but such contacts may be interpreted (incorrectly) as implying recognition of these entities. It should be clearly understood that humanitarian assistance does not condone or give official status to a co-operating party.

States that have joined the United Nations, subscribed to the Universal Declaration of Human Rights, ratified the Geneva Conventions and their Protocols, and acceded to other international agreements, have in the process accepted certain legal obligations to permit and facilitate humanitarian aid. This is not an infringement of their sovereignty but an exercise of the responsibilities that go with it. Even in the case of northern Iraq, where access was initially established by force, subsequent humanitarian activities by UN agencies have been based on a memorandum of understanding with the Iraqi government, which enabled the UN to establish a massive presence in the north to provide assistance, monitor human rights and offer protection.

Recent, less restrictive, interpretations of sovereignty emphasize not only its form but also its content. The content includes a state's humanitarian obligations to its own citizens. Sovereignty involves a responsibility to meet the needs of the population or to allow the international community to assist. From this perspective, sovereignty and international humanitarian assistance are not mutually exclusive but complementary. But any government that systematically flouts its humanitarian obligations to its people, and refuses access to those in need, calls into question its own sovereign rights. In other words, the rights and responsibilities of sovereign states are inseparable.

"Sovereignty involves a responsibility to meet the population's needs or else allow the international community to assist"

For this reason, some observers argue that "humanitarian intervention" is a contradiction in terms. If states have given implicit prior consent, action without their consent cannot occur. As former UN Secretary-General Pérez de Cuéllar said, "What is involved is not the right of intervention but the collective obligation of states to bring relief and redress in human rights emergencies."[20]

An international consensus on humanitarian intervention is unlikely to emerge soon. Occasions when international assistance appears indispensable, in spite of the absence of a conventional appeal for help from the sovereign government, are always unique and must be judged in context. What is clear from recent experience is that some governments are taking a much more activist role in international institutions, with the aim of reaching those in need of international protection and assistance. This is less a matter of intervention than of a refusal to take "no" for an answer.

Protecting assistance

Lack of security is one of the major obstacles to protection and humanitarian assistance in conflict zones. Delivery of humanitarian assistance is frequently disrupted or halted because of threats to or actual attacks on the staff of relief organizations and their facilities and vehicles, not to mention on refugees themselves. The airlift that supplies the besieged city of Sarajevo, for example, had to be suspended three times in 1992 for a total of eight weeks and seven times

Box 4.4
Who Will Protect the Protectors?

Hundreds of people have been killed while working for international organizations, sometimes deliberately, sometimes caught in the cross-fire. Many others have been injured, tortured, abducted, detained or expelled. The following list includes only those UN staff members killed between 1973 and 1 June 1993 in the course of carrying out their duties. It does not include accidental deaths. Nor does it include peace-keeping troops killed in the service of the international community; nor the hundreds of relief workers employed by NGOs, the ICRC and other organizations, who have lost their lives over the years. It is, nevertheless, dedicated to all of them.

In Memoriam

OLIVARES-MORI, Fernando	ECLAC	Killed	Chile	06 Oct.	1973
SORIA-ESPINOSA, Carmelo	ECLAC	Killed	Chile	14 July	1976
KAMKAI, Bismillah	UNDP	Executed	Afghanistan	05 May	1979
SCHULTZ, Konrad	UNIDO	Killed	Guatemala	11 May	1982
EVNER, Ergun	UN	Assassinated	Austria	19 Nov.	1984
BREIR, Nabila	UNICEF	Killed	Lebanon	18 Dec.	1986
SHAH, Tawakal	UNICEF	Died in prison	Afghanistan	— May	1987
JAWAD, Abid	UNIFIL	Killed	Lebanon	21 May	
DARNISH, Jebreal Ibrahim	UNIFIL	Killed	Lebanon	26 May	
ZEIDAN, Sa'adi Mohammad	UNRWA	Died in detention	Syria	07 July	
HIGGINS, William R.	UNTSO	Executed	Lebanon	17 Feb.	1988
YASSIN, Zeidan Suleiman	UNRWA	Died in prison	Lebanon	17 Dec.	
NYIRENDA, Abel	FAO	Died after detention	Zambia	29 April	1989
HLASS, Gena	UNICEF	Killed	Lebanon	07 Dec.	
ARYAMBA, Frazer Fedit	WFP	Killed	Sudan	21 Dec.	
ARIKWANG, Angello	WFP	Killed	Uganda	15 March	1990
KAZMUZ, Yasir	UNRWA	Killed	Israel/West Bank	28 March	
DAROD, Issak Dhagan	UNHCR	Killed	Somalia	06 Dec.	
ABRAR FARAH, Adan Harun	UNHCR	Killed	Somalia	08 Dec.	
AINANSHE, Ahmed Liban	UNHCR	Killed	Somalia	04 Feb.	1991
OMAR, Abdillahi Sheikh	UNHCR	Killed	Somalia	02 July	
PUMPALOVA, Marta	UNICEF	Killed	Somalia	05 Jan.	1992
MUHE, Tekye	UNHCR	Killed	Ethiopia	10 March	
GARAD, Abdi Maalim	UN	Killed	Somalia	24 March	
MUTACA, Lourenço	UNHCR	Killed	Ethiopia	31 March	
AL-BUHAISI, Abdel Mu'ti	UNRWA	Killed	Israel/Gaza	11 May	
EL-FADI, Mamdouh Yousef	UNRWA	Killed	Israel/Gaza	21 May	
KASASHIMA, Kimio	WFP	Killed	Pakistan	14 June	
TAKIA, R.	UN	Killed	Iraq	17 July	
RAPPAPORT, Avinoam	ICAO	Assassinated	Kenya	20 July	
BEKERAN, Najibullah	UNCHS	Killed	Afghanistan	09 Aug.	
HUSINEC, Aram	UNESCO	Killed	Nigeria	12 Aug.	
MAUNG, Myint	UNICEF	Killed	Sudan	27 Sept.	
NGURE, Francis	UNICEF	Killed	Sudan	30 Sept.	
DEVEREUX, Sean	UNICEF	Killed	Somalia	02 Jan.	1993
SARY, Ty	UNTAC	Killed	Cambodia	12 Jan.	
HANG, Vicheth	UNTAC	Killed	Cambodia	12 Jan.	
BULLARD, Tony	UNCHS	Killed	Afghanistan	01 Feb.	
ZIA, Al Haq	UNCHS	Killed	Afghanistan	01 Feb.	
MATUKA, David Kabala	UNESCO	Assassinated	France	04 Feb.	
AWAD, Ali Soradi	UNRWA	Killed	Israel/Gaza	23 Feb.	
AFONSO, Alfredo	WFP	Killed	Angola	24 Feb.	
SHIVINDA, Pedro	WFP	Killed	Angola	24 Feb.	
AL GHARIB, Yusif	UNRWA	Killed	Israel/Gaza	18 March	
ROUF, Mohammad	JIU	Killed	Cambodia	29 March	
NAKATA, Atsuhito	UNV	Killed	Cambodia	08 April	

Principle source. ASIICS. With apologies to the relatives of any staff member whose name has inadvertently been omitted.

in the first six months of 1993 for a total of five weeks. Blockades of relief convoys and looting of relief supplies are, in some settings, more the rule than the exception.

The Secretary-General of the United Nations, in his 1992 Report on the Work of the Organization, observed that:

"The security and protection of staff and safe and effective delivery of relief materials are major concerns with regard to humanitarian efforts in conflict situations. Indeed, the situations in Somalia and the former Yugoslavia have demonstrated that it may not be a question of the capacity to deliver, but rather of the security conditions pertaining to distribution of relief supplies, which determine whether humanitarian assistance can be provided. Volatile security situations have led to the suspensions of operations. In other cases, relief operations have continued, but at a considerable hazard for those involved. United Nations and other humanitarian relief workers are often exposed to great dangers and many are risking their lives on a daily basis"[21] (see Box 4.4).

Methods of protecting humanitarian workers include the use of protective emblems such as the Red Cross and Red Crescent, the UN emblem and so forth. A more universal symbol, which could be used by NGOs working according to an agreed international code of conduct and with the agreement of parties to the conflict, might be useful.

Negotiations with the warring parties can result in guarantees of safe conduct, without which relief work might carry too great a risk. Almost all organizations that operate in war zones must use passive means of protection, such as stockades and shelters. In some settings, they may be forced to resort to locally hired, armed security guards. In others, the international community has decided to provide military escorts like those that accompany UNHCR convoys in the former Yugoslavia.

The use of armed forces to protect relief supplies and personnel is controversial. Some humanitarian organizations, including most prominently the ICRC, refuse military escort except in extreme circumstances such as those found in Lebanon during the 1980s and more recently in Somalia. They reason that military involvement in humanitarian work compromises its non-political nature, raises the temperature in a crisis and may turn humanitarian facilities and staff into targets. Other organizations conclude that the urgent need for relief and the intractability of some of the antagonists leave no choice but to proceed into conflict areas by any means possible.

"There has been growing acceptance of military involvement in emergency relief"

The military, in its turn, may have many reservations about working with relief agencies. Both military and civilian providers of assistance would agree that differences in professional ethos and management style make co-ordination between the two difficult. Nonetheless, productive relationships have been forged.

Acceptance of military involvement in emergency relief has grown with experience. A massive relief operation was undertaken by coalition forces on the Turkish border with Iraq in 1990, and undoubtedly saved many lives. In the former Yugoslavia, military forces have been involved directly in the provision of humanitarian assistance, through airdrops over eastern Bosnia and in the operation of the Sarajevo airlift. In addition, they have played a role in protecting the relief supplies and personnel of humanitarian agencies, notably by escorting land convoys (see Box 4.5). In a number of other operations, humanitarian agencies have come to rely on the military for the protection of convoys, for security at ports and airfields, and for their capacity to operate major airlifts. The difficulties of supplying an army in the field have much in common with the problems of assisting large numbers of displaced people affected by war. The logistical capabilities of military organizations and their ability to deploy rapidly, mobilizing transport and communications as well as supplies for immediate survival, can provide an indispensable lifeline in refugee emergencies taking place in the midst of armed conflict.[22]

"Humanitarian agencies have come to rely on the military for protection in a number of operations"

Of course, the traditional role of multilateral military forces is not to supply humanitarian relief. Peace-keeping or peace-making efforts are often the central elements of international political initiatives to contain and resolve conflicts. Where civil authority has broken down altogether, multi-national forces may also take part in the maintenance of law and order. In Cambodia, they were closely involved in preparing for the elections in May 1993.

The humanitarian role, which has recently gained more prominence, is not always clearly differentiated from these other tasks, at least in the eyes of intended beneficiaries. This sometimes causes confusion and resentment. Bosnian Muslims, for example, ask bitterly why the same soldiers who guard the convoys bringing food to keep them alive stand aloof from the battles that kill them. The restrictions on UNPRO-FOR's rules of engagement, mandated by the Security Council, are intended to keep it from becoming involved in the fighting on a partisan basis. But they are not always understood or welcomed by the people on the ground.

The co-ordination of humanitarian efforts with political and military actions in refugee-producing conflicts is not without its difficulties. It blurs traditionally distinct roles and, if mismanaged, could compromise the strictly neutral character of humanitarian aid, which is the best guarantee of access to people in need.

Nevertheless such co-ordination often provides an opportunity to advance the peace process, as relief efforts give rise to negotiations that can subsequently develop beyond humanitarian issues to conflict resolution. There is room for a variety of patterns and practices, as long as basic humanitarian principles are not compromised.

Part of protection is knowing how to recognize the limits of humanitarian action. Relief assistance can work at cross purposes with protection if it becomes an alibi for inaction in the political sphere. There may be circumstances in which it is proper to withhold humanitarian assistance, such as when warring parties are manipulating it to their own advantage in ways that promise to prolong a conflict, and are routinely violating international law in the process. The most difficult and controversial decisions that humanitarian organizations are called upon to make involve weighing the need for short-term help against the dangers of doing long-term harm. It would be naive to think, or to insist, that humanitarian assistance – alone of all the elements involved in a conflict – can be entirely free from calculations concerning ends and means.

Protection in armed conflict demands different techniques depending on the character of the conflict and the antagonists. If the refugees are a by-product of conventional war, forced to move in order to get out of the cross-fire or to find food, negotiations to arrange relief and protection for them have a good chance of success. Internal conflicts often pose much more complex problems. If the parties involved are motivated by a desire for international recognition and acceptance, however, they can often be persuaded to accede to humanitarian principles. The international community must insist, forcefully, that they do so.

Box 4.5

Protecting Assistance in Bosnia and Herzegovina

In November 1991, at the request of the Secretary-General, UNHCR assumed the role of "lead agency" responsible for co-ordinating United Nations humanitarian assistance in the former Yugoslavia. At that time, about 500,000 people had been displaced by the war in Croatia.

In April 1992, a second, more terrible war broke out in neighbouring Bosnia and Herzegovina – an ethnic mosaic of Muslims (44 per cent of the population), Serbs (31 per cent) and Croats (17 per cent). Within three months, the number of refugees, internally displaced people and others in need of assistance in the former Yugoslavia had soared to 2.6 million.

A year later, in July 1993, the total number of people requiring assistance and protection stood at 3.6 million, including 2.3 million in Bosnia and Herzegovina alone. If the hundreds of thousands of Bosnians who have fled to neighbouring countries are included, over two-thirds of the Bosnian population has been directly affected by the conflict,

The upheaval in the Balkans has prompted one of the largest relief operations in modern history. It has also drawn United Nations peace-keeping forces into close collaboration with humanitarian agencies in order to protect relief deliveries to civilian populations caught up in the war. Operations have taken place against a backdrop of intensive, vicious warfare and constant violations of human rights. The blockades of villages and towns,

the relentless shelling, and persecution and forcible expulsion of civilians have created a terrifying spiral of suffering, displacement and destruction.

With the land routes to the Bosnian capital of Sarajevo cut off, the UN Security Council adopted a resolution on 29 June 1992, charging UN peace-keeping troops with the security and management of the city's airport. Four days later, on 3 July, the humanitarian airlift to Sarajevo began – the largest operation of its kind since the Berlin blockade of 1948-49. During the first year of the airlift, over 46,000 metric tons of food and medical supplies were flown into the besieged capital, in more than 4,150 sorties by aircraft supplied by some 20 nations, providing the 380,000 inhabitants of Sarajevo with a vital lifeline to the outside world.

Meanwhile, a massive land operation involving the haulage of approximately 9,000 metric tons of emergency assistance each week was launched to provide relief to other areas of Bosnia and Herzegovina. Faced with the continuous harassment of relief convoys, the Security Council took an unprecedented initiative in September 1992 by extending the mandate of UNPROFOR peace-keeping forces to include the protection of humanitarian assistance. UNPROFOR's French, Spanish and British contingents – assisted by Dutch and Belgian transport units – have subsequently been providing military escorts to relief convoys.

Without these escorts, the humanitarian effort would almost certainly have ground to a halt.

However, the ruthless obstruction of the relief operation has continued, despite repeated assurances and commitments from the various parties to allow free passage of humanitarian aid. Relief convoys have frequently been blocked for days or even weeks on end. Because of the continuing denial of access to the besieged Muslim enclaves in eastern Bosnia, where hundreds of thousands of people have been subsisting under appalling conditions, airdrops of food and medical supplies were started in March 1993 by the air forces of the United States, France and Germany. Between March and July, well over 5,000 metric tons of supplies were parachuted into Srebrenica, Gorazde, Zepa and other locations. In some cases, and sometimes for long periods, the airdrops have provided their only lifeline while efforts continued to reach them by road.

In April, the conflict entered a new phase as fighting between Croat and Bosnian government forces escalated in central Bosnia and further south in the region around Mostar, Jablanica and Konjic. Tens of thousands of civilians fled or were trapped in besieged pockets, as "ethnic cleansing", once associated almost exclusively with the Bosnian Serbs, was practised by all sides.

On 4 June, the Security Council, acting under Chapter VII of the United Nations Charter, extended UNPROFOR's mandate to cover the protection of all the towns and besieged enclaves which the Council had earlier designated as "safe areas". The increased international presence probably saved Srebrenica from falling in April, and may have alleviated the pressure on one or two of the other "safe areas". However, Srebrenica, Gorazde and Zepa – all three completely encircled by Bosnian Serb forces – could not, under the almost intolerable conditions existing in July 1993, be described as truly safe, let alone economically viable in the long term.

By July, Sarajevo – another designated "safe area" – was also in an increasingly dire state. The city was without electricity for weeks on end, and critically short of all other forms of fuel. The water supply was deliberately sabotaged, and reports were received of people so desperate that they had resorted to boiling sewage. The sewage system had itself broken down, and there was an increasing danger of major epidemics. Meanwhile the shooting and shelling continued and Sarajevo seemed to be slowly but steadily dying.

In an increasingly precarious operational environment, UNHCR and UNPROFOR have been consistently forced to take part in protracted, and all too often inconclusive, negotiations to reach certain locations and guarantee the security of convoys. By early 1993, it had become clear that all three of the warring parties were seeking to manipulate humanitarian assistance to their own advantage and to prevent food and other supplies from reaching their enemies. UNHCR and UNPROFOR were accused either of taking sides, or of being too neutral. Food, shelter, water, fuel, electricity and even the evacuation of children and wounded were being employed as political and military weapons (see Chapter Five, Box 5.2).

Any excuse, ranging from military to bureaucratic, was being used to prevent, delay or divert the free flow of assistance. Frequent attempts were made to levy exorbitant tolls on convoy vehicles. As a result, by mid-1993, less than half of the total relief required was being delivered to its final destinations.

As early as the end of 1992, United Nations and other relief personnel were being deliberately targeted. The Sarajevo airlift has been repeatedly interrupted by serious security incidents, including the shooting down of an Italian transport plane on 3 September 1992 with the death of its four crewmen. By the first anniversary of the airlift, on 3 July 1993, at least 81 major incidents had been recorded, not counting the numerous occasions when small arms fire has been directed at planes, personnel and airport buildings.

The security situation has been particularly bad in the Mostar region in the south of the country, and in central Bosnia. In February 1993, an interpreter was killed and a Danish relief worker seriously wounded when a UNHCR convoy was attacked near Mostar. On 1 June, a convoy was ambushed just outside the besieged town of Maglaj in central Bosnia where 32,000 people were under fierce artillery attack by Bosnian Serb forces. Two of the Danish convoy drivers and one relief worker were killed and five others injured in the incident. In early July, the UNHCR office in Medugorje received bomb threats because of the ethnic origin of some staff members, and a fuel convoy trying to reach Sarajevo was hijacked. Supplies have frequently been seized at gunpoint. By mid-July, eight people involved in the UNHCR relief operation had lost their lives

and many more had been wounded. The ICRC and several NGOs had also suffered serious casualties, and 51 UNPROFOR soldiers had been killed in Bosnia and Herzegovina and in the United Nations Protected Areas (UNPAs) in Croatia.

The partnership between UNHCR and UNPROFOR has given rise to concern in some quarters that humanitarian aid may lose credibility or, worse, become politicized through association with a military presence. However, in circumstances such as those prevalent in Bosnia and Herzegovina, there has been no realistic alternative and it can be argued that drawing the military into playing an active humanitarian role – which, in certain situations only the military is equipped to perform – is an important and life-saving development.

There can be little doubt that the presence of UNPROFOR alongside UNHCR in Bosnia and Herzegovina has greatly helped the delivery of emergency relief. In spite of the relatively small number of troops involved – around 6,200 by mid-1993 – they have significantly improved delivery capacity. Even if the humanitarian aid has never reached the volume and consistency required, it nevertheless played a key part in averting a major humanitarian catastrophe during the winter of 1992-93. Whether that catastrophe has simply been postponed to the winter of 1993-94, will depend to a large extent on the international community's commitment to continue providing supplies, funding and sufficient numbers of peace-keeping troops equipped to protect an increasingly beleaguered humanitarian relief effort.

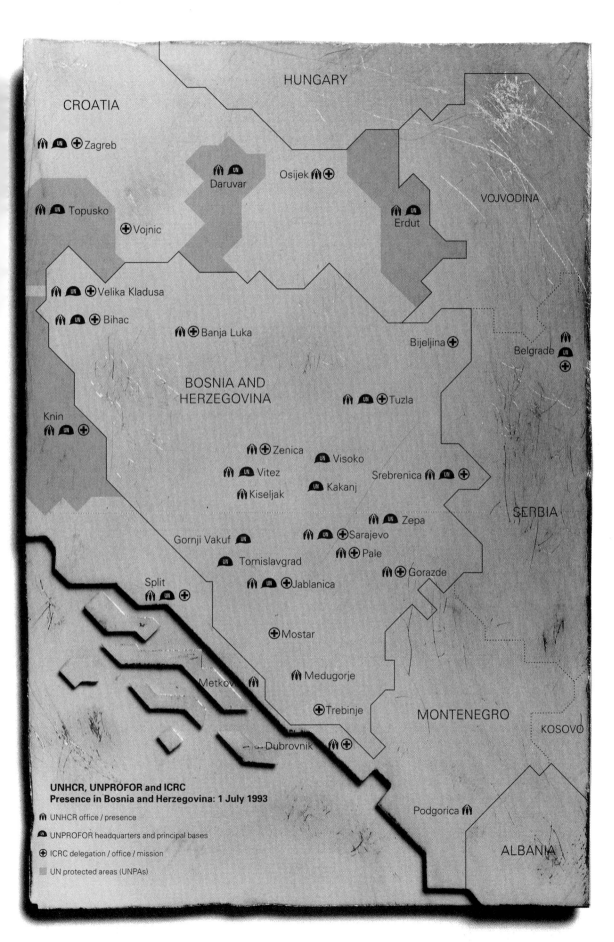

HUNGARY

CROATIA

UNHCR office / presence Zagreb

Daruvar

Osijek

VOJVODINA

Topusko

Erdut

Vojnic

Velika Kladusa

Bihac

Banja Luka

Bijeljina

Belgrade

BOSNIA AND
HERZEGOVINA

Tuzla

Knin

Zenica

Visoko

Vitez

Srebrenica

SERBIA

Kiseljak

Kakanj

Zepa

Gornji Vakuf

Sarajevo

Tomislavgrad

Pale

Split

Jablanica

Gorazde

Mostar

Medugorje

Metkovic

Trebinje

MONTENEGRO

KOSOVO

Dubrovnik

Podgorica

UNHCR, UNPROFOR and ICRC
Presence in Bosnia and Herzegovina: 1 July 1993

UNHCR office / presence

UNPROFOR headquarters and principal bases

ICRC delegation / office / mission

UN protected areas (UNPAs)

ALBANIA

Box 4.6

A Week in Bosnia and Herzegovina

Excerpts from UNHCR Situation Reports: 19-25 June 1993

Muslim enclaves in eastern Bosnia:
21 June: Bosnian Serb authorities finally allowed UNHCR to establish a presence in **Gorazde**, the last "safe area" to receive international presence [a team of 8 United Nations Military Observers (UNMOs) entered the town 5 days earlier]. On 22 June, after a 2-day hold-up, a 10-truck UNHCR convoy delivered 80 metric tons (MT) of food and medical supplies. A second convoy was repeatedly prevented from reaching Gorazde by crowds of Serb women. Two airdrops, during nights of 21 and 22 June, delivered additional 113.4 MT of supplies. 20 per cent of the town reported destroyed. Hospital overcrowded... no operating room... no anaesthetist. Scores of wounded forced to stay in their homes. Bread in short supply. Only valid currency is cigarettes: one pack worth DM100. Lack of footwear – inhabitants making sandals out of tyres and parachute cord.

Situation in **Srebrenica** continues to deteriorate, though cease-fire seems to be respected. Serbs only permit one UNHCR convoy per week. Sole water treatment plant irreparably damaged. Only solution appears to be rehabilitation of another treatment plant, abandoned 10 years ago.

Zepa remains calm. No injury or casualty since 8 May, partly due to UN presence. Road repairs have begun and elementary education has resumed.

Central Bosnia: Bosnian Croats refused entry to 60 trucks in 5 convoys. Only some 4,000 MT of relief supplies have reached central Bosnia this month. Reports of artillery and mortar fire in Turbe, Travnik and **Zenica**. Heavy fighting around Gornji Vakuf. Fighting and ethnic cleansing directed at Muslims erupted in Vares (a small Croat-held town 50 km north of Sarajevo), while Muslims continued the same practice with Croats in Kakanj. Vares flooded with 15,000 Croat refugees fleeing from Kakanj. Refugees accommodated in 2 schools, 2 sports halls and 2 disused factories. UNHCR delivered 90 MT of supplies.

UNHCR convoy destined for [Muslim-held] Tuzla thoroughly searched in Vares, where [Croat] HVO forces state they will continue to inspect all UNHCR vehicles travelling north. Attitude towards international agencies has deteriorated in Tuzla, due to sense of isolation. Latest news of huge Muslim "Convoy of Joy" is that, after being rescued by British UNPROFOR troops from HVO attack, 240 trucks finally made it to Zenica, 40 to Kladanj/Olovo area and 214 to Tuzla.

Western Herzegovina: HVO forces forcibly evicted 150 displaced Muslims – originally from Banja Luka – from Posusje. Local Croat officials sought UNHCR assistance in transporting the displaced, which was refused in light of their forced eviction.

Sarajevo: Heavy shelling of previous week gave way to relative calm. Lack of water and electricity becoming critical. On 22 June, 6 children and 10 family members evacuated to Paris for medical reasons.

Airlift [suspended on 15 June after gunfire erupted close to 2 incoming planes and destroyed windows of control tower] resumed 20 June. Between 20 June and 26 June, 1,077 MT of humanitarian aid were flown into Sarajevo in 93 separate sorties.

Bihac: Relatively calm. People are outdoors and free to be socially active for the first time since the beginning of the war.

Banja Luka: Leaders of both Croat and Muslim communities visited UNHCR offices. Muslim villagers report nightly attacks and incidents of murder. Croats report that houses have been burned, others looted and occupants beaten in one of their villages.

A few of the security incidents during the week: A Norwegian UNMO seriously wounded when hit in the chest by a .50 calibre round in Gorazde. Another UNMO team's armoured vehicle put out of action by the same weapon. Shots fired at an UNPROFOR driver in a patrol vehicle near Belgrade, narrowly missing his chest. A hand grenade missed the vehicle, but caused considerable damage to the road. Spanish UNPROFOR armoured vehicle surrounded by HVO soldiers in Mostar. In Sarajevo, four local Serbian interpreters travelling in an UNMO vehicle, were arrested by BiH [Bosnian government] forces, but later released. Canadian UNPROFOR troops at Pelimica threatened with a rocket-propelled grenade by HVO forces who accused them of delivering weapons to the BiH army. UNHCR convoy escorted by British UNPROFOR forces unable to enter Novi Travnik due to shelling by local Croats not wanting aid to reach BiH side. Negotiations failed and convoy returned to Zenica. A UNHCR convoy was stopped at a BiH checkpoint in Dabravine. BiH army demanded 50 per cent of load as price for letting it through to Vares. The convoy turned back and off-loaded at Breza.

Chapter five

Responding to Refugee Emergencies

In the autumn of 1990, United Nations agencies drew up contingency plans for an anticipated flow of refugees from Iraq into Turkey. Amidst some criticism that they were was being overly alarmist, and a consequent reluctance to contribute on the part of donors, preparations to receive up to 400,000 people were scaled back. In April and early May 1991, as government troops closed in, 1.8 million Kurds suddenly headed for the Turkish and Iranian borders (see Box 5.1).

Since then there has been a rapid succession of refugee crises. In 1992 alone, over 3.5 million people were forced to flee across an international border in search of safety. "Refugee emergencies" – large, sudden movements of desperate people in difficult conditions – have been a hallmark of the early 1990s.

In the 16 months between December 1991 and June 1993, the number of people dependent on international assistance in the former Yugoslavia rose from 500,000 to 3.6 million. In March 1992, some 3,000 refugees a day were arriving in Kenya to escape the fighting, famine and chaos in Somalia. At the peak of the crisis, the number of Somalis seeking sanctuary in neighbouring countries rose to more than a million, well over 10 per cent of Somalia's total population. At about the same time, a quarter of a million Muslim refugees from Myanmar fled into poverty-stricken Bangladesh, and up to 500 refugees a day were pouring into Nepal from Bhutan. By late 1992, the conflict between Azerbaijan and Armenia had created more than 800,000 refugees and internally displaced people, while the civil war in Tajikistan had uprooted another half a million. In February and March 1993, 280,000 refugees from Togo sought refuge in Benin and Ghana.

The scale, frequency and suddenness of the refugee crises of the 1990s have exerted enormous pressures on international emergency response capacities. Not all emergencies, however, fall into the same category. In some, large numbers of people have fled across international borders to escape persecution and oppression – as happened in the cases of Myanmar and Togo – creating traditional refugee emergencies

Box 5.1
Emergency Response in Iraq

Around four million people were displaced in the 12 months following Iraq's invasion of Kuwait on 2 August 1990. Between August and December, during the build-up to the Gulf War, more than a million migrant workers and other foreign nationals fled from Iraq and Kuwait into Jordan and other neighbouring countries, while some 850,000 Yemenis living in Saudi Arabia streamed back to their homeland.

It was not, however, until early April 1991, shortly after the war had ended, that armed conflict between the Iraqi government and disaffected groups within the country provoked one of the largest and fastest refugee movements in recent history. In a three-week period, over 400,000 Iraqis fled to the Turkish frontier. By mid-May a further 1.4 million had taken refuge either in the Islamic Republic of Iran or in the eastern border area of Iraq. With the exception of some 70,000 Shi'ites from the southern region around Basra, the overwhelming majority were Kurds.

The sudden, massive outflow prompted a humanitarian relief operation of unprecedented scope and intensity. On the Turkish border, providing assistance to so many refugees scattered across a dozen isolated and inhospitable mountain locations presented an immense logistical problem. Relief was provided by international agencies and also, on a much larger scale, by the 13-nation coalition force, around 30 bilateral donors

and over 50 NGOs. Employing more than 20,000 personnel and 200 aircraft, the allied operation provided dramatic and unprecedented evidence of the logistical and relief capacity of the industrialized states and their military establishments.

In the Islamic Republic of Iran, where the industrialized countries were considerably less forthcoming with assistance despite the much greater numbers of refugees, UNHCR mounted one of the most ambitious airlifts it had ever undertaken. Even so, deliveries could not keep pace with the speed of the emergency. By the end of April, only 12 per cent of the blankets, 9 per cent of the kitchen utensils and 11 per cent of the tents required had been delivered. Relief flights were consequently increased to ten a day throughout May. In all, the airlift delivered just under 6,100 metric tons of relief supplies during April and May 1991.

The speed with which the refugees fled Iraq was matched by that of their return. They started to trek home within six weeks of the start of the exodus. On 18 April 1991, the UN and Iraq signed an agreement allowing UN humanitarian centres to be established on Iraqi territory. Coalition forces extended their presence into the north of the country, creating a security zone near the Iraqi-Turkish border designed to encourage refugees back into more accessible areas of Iraq where they could be more easily fed and sheltered. In mid-July, when the coalition forces withdrew, responsibility for humanitarian assistance in the security zone was transferred to UNHCR.

The massive movement back down from the Turkish border region began in the second half of April, and the last of the mountain camps was closed in early June. Large-scale return from the Islamic Republic of Iran also began in April. By December, only 70,000 Iraqis from the 1991 refugee population were left in the Islamic Republic of Iran and some 10,000 in Turkey.

The refugees' return to a devastated landscape and continuing insecurity presented a number of serious problems. At the end of August, large numbers of people were still without adequate shelter in northern Iraq and in danger from the rigours of the oncoming winter. In a race against the clock, UNHCR launched one of its largest ever shelter programmes. Distribution of building materials was not started until 15 October, when the population movements were sufficiently stabilized. To be effective against winter, it had to be completed by mid-November. Although security considerations delayed the implementation of the programme, by 30 October some 1,600 trucks had crossed the border from Turkey to Iraq over dangerous mountain trails to deliver around 30,000 metric tons of winter construction material to half a million people. Between October and December 1991, reconstruction work was carried out in more than 1,500 of the 4,000 villages that had been destroyed.

With the emergency relief phase completed and rehabilitation and reconstruction under way, UNHCR handed over its operation to other United Nations agencies in June 1992.

The Iraqi refugee crisis, exceptional though it may have been in many ways – not least in the strategic interest that it held for the industrialized world – reflected the growing scale and complexity of humanitarian emergencies and revealed serious shortcomings in the ability of humanitarian organizations to respond swiftly and effectively. It provoked a radical reassessment of the UN emergency response systems.

Attempts to improve co-ordination, which lay at the heart of the debate, resulted in the establishment of the United Nations Emergency Co-ordinator and the creation of the Department of Humanitarian Affairs at the beginning of 1992. The crisis also resulted in an enhanced appreciation of the importance of early warning mechanisms and emergency response capacity in tackling major humanitarian crises.

In addition, difficult questions were raised concerning mandates and fundamental principles. How should the need for humanitarian intervention be balanced against national sovereignty? How can the unparalleled capacity of the military be used most effectively in humanitarian operations? Who should be responsible for the needs of mixed populations that include refugees? What is UNHCR's role in providing protection and assistance to internally displaced people? And what are the principles governing repatriation into situations of continuing conflict? Although definitive answers to these questions have yet to be found, they are of crucial importance if the international community is to respond effectively to future emergencies of this magnitude.

Winterization Programme in Northern Iraq: Aug.– Dec. 1991

- UNHCR office
- Refugee camp
- UNHCR operation area
- Winter materials supply line
- 4,000 or more shelters rebuilt
- Airport

that fall squarely under the responsibility of UNHCR.

In other, more complex, situations, armed conflict, political instability, drought, ethnic tensions, economic collapse and the deterioration of civil society have occurred in daunting combinations. Crisis conditions in one area may spill into others where they aggravate different problems – as, for example, when refugees from armed conflict pour into an area already suffering from acute food shortages. Multiple emergencies within a region, such as those in the Horn of Africa or the Balkans, interact with each other in unpredictable ways and at several levels. Such complex humanitarian emergencies involve not only refugees but also internally displaced people, as well as victims of war and famine. They require a different range of responses from the United Nations.

"A refugee emergency calls for extraordinary logistical and organizational feats"

Irrespective of whether it is a classical refugee influx or one occurring in the context of a wider humanitarian crisis, a refugee emergency calls for extraordinary logistical and organizational feats. People leave their homes with little or no means to sustain themselves. Their escape route often crosses inhospitable terrain and leads them to regions that lack the resources to support large concentrations of people (see Boxes 5.3 and 5.6). Food, water, sanitation, shelter and medical care have to be provided in inaccessible places under extremely difficult circumstances.

The death rate within the affected population traces a grim but accurate chart of how well emergency relief efforts are meeting the challenge. Among the Kurds fleeing to the Turkish border from Iraq in April 1991, the initial mortality rate was 18 times higher than that of non-refugee populations in both countries, though the situation improved relatively rapidly. By contrast, initially low mortality rates among

Somali refugees arriving in inhospitable areas of eastern Ethiopia in 1988-1989 increased sharply thereafter, reaching a peak nine months after they entered the refugee camps.[23]

Because of the extreme urgency involved, emergency operations are inevitably conducted under somewhat chaotic conditions. They are, moreover, frequently plagued by insecurity. The result may be inadequate assessment of needs and insufficient or inappropriate staffing. Other problem areas include the monitoring of aid supplies and the establishment of a clear division of labour among relief organizations, as well as the effective evaluation of operations.

The speed and efficiency of the initial response to a refugee emergency affect the welfare and in some cases the very survival of the people concerned; they may also influence the prospects for solutions. Strenuous attempts are therefore being made to overcome the weaknesses of past responses to emergencies in the light of experiences gained from recent crises, in particular those in northern Iraq, in Kenya and Somalia and in the former Yugoslavia. The new mechanisms, structures and procedures that are evolving have already been tested by events on a daily basis in countries such as Armenia, Azerbaijan, Benin and Tajikistan.

The quality of protection in an emergency depends, in the first instance, on an understanding of the refugees themselves and the circumstances surrounding their flight. The rather dry-sounding exercise known as "needs assessment" provides aid organizations with vital information about exactly who the people are, what physical condition they are in and, ideally, what kind of protection they need. The answers to these questions will not be uniform across a group of refugees, since it is essential, though often very difficult in an emergency, to distinguish the needs of particular groups such as women, unaccompanied children and members of ethnic minorities.

The profile of a refugee group is often distorted by their experiences. The age and sex composition of a group is revealing. There may, for example, be a conspicuous absence of young men. If so, have they been killed, imprisoned or conscripted for military service or forced labour? Are they fighting voluntarily with a rebel army? Or have they simply chosen to stay outside the formal assistance structure because they wish to protect their property or livelihoods?

Women and children account for roughly 70 per cent of a normal population in developing countries but make up about 80 per cent of refugees worldwide. The high incidence of female heads of family or unaccompanied women in many refugee groups gives rise to particular protection and assistance needs. Under-representation of young women in a refugee population, on the other hand, sends a particularly chilling signal and may indicate that they have been abducted or detained.

The capacities of the international humanitarian system have been severely strained by the recent succession of refugee emergencies. The problem is not simply the number and scale of emergencies. It has also stemmed from the fact that few of the displacements have been fully resolved. Consequently, resources deployed in reaction to one crisis have not been available for the next.

Protection: the first casualty in emergencies?

In the heat of a refugee emergency, the immediate priority is to save lives. Two factors, in particular, are crucial. One is to protect the displaced people from being forced back into the areas from which they have fled, and the other is to supply them with food, water, health care, shelter and sanitation. Meeting the physical needs of people in an emergency is the more tangible response of the two, and often seems to dominate the agenda of emergency assistance. But protection should be built into emergency management from the very beginning. The challenge is to provide aid in a way that shields people from further persecution and violence, while simultaneously laying the foundations for lasting solutions to their predicament.

One straightforward but vital element of protection is registration of the people coming forward for assistance in a crisis. Registration provides a picture of who is coming from where and for what reasons. This establishes a basis for monitoring conditions in the country of origin and deciding when it is safe to encourage refugees to return home. Other important protection measures include ensuring the civilian character of refugee camps, establishing a degree of mutual trust between the refugees and the authorities (whether of the host country or UNHCR), promoting efforts of the refugees to organize themselves and setting up procedures to deal smoothly with any protection problems that may arise.

"Households headed by women are particularly vulnerable"

The way assistance is provided affects the quality of protection afforded. For example, a refugee camp that is too close to the border of the country of origin may provoke military attack, be viewed as a convenient base by insurgent forces or inflame political tensions. Efforts to move refugee populations from volatile frontier areas may, however, run in to resistance either from a government anxious to keep open the possibility of rapid return to the country of origin, or from the refugees themselves.

Effective protection must also take account of the disruption of social structures that often characterizes refugee situations. Poorly laid-out camps may increase the vulnerability of certain groups, such as single women, minorities, or unaccompanied old people and children. In many societies, it is assumed that protection for women is provided mainly through the family. Yet family structures are likely to be severely weakened or destroyed altogether during a crisis. In such circumstances, households headed by women may become particularly vulnerable and be deprived of their fair share of rations or

Women and children crossing a dried-up lake. Mali, 1985.

services. Refugee women often face a threefold barrier to protection: their families have lost the power to protect; national protection has broken down or been withdrawn; and international organizations can encounter serious difficulties reaching women directly, or even recognizing their special needs. Specific guidelines on the protection of refugee women have been developed to help organizations working with refugees to ensure that women are protected against manipulation, exploitation and sexual and physical abuse, and that they are able to benefit from assistance and protection programmes without discrimination.[24]

"Protection is just as vital to survival in an emergency as food and shelter"

Refugees frequently find themselves living alongside other victims of upheaval – be they returnees, internally displaced people or affected local inhabitants. Since 1992, humanitarian agencies have experimented with a new approach to this type of complex situation, working increasingly closely to provide assistance to mixed populations. The practical benefits of this "cross-mandate" approach have quickly become apparent – notably in the Horn of Africa – but there are some concerns about how to ensure the quality of protection offered in such a framework. Some of the categories of people who require humanitarian assistance do not have a need for international protection as such, whereas others do. It is essential that the protection function is not lost or blurred during the rush to meet the urgent survival needs of mixed populations. For those who require it, protection is just as vital to survival in an emergency as are food and shelter.

One of the distinguishing characteristics of refugees is their need for international protection. Nevertheless, assistance and protection are often inextricably linked. An international presence established to provide assistance in countries of asylum or of origin is frequently the most effective protection tool available. By July 1993, UNHCR had some 590 staff members in the former Yugoslavia who were involved not only in distributing relief to the displaced and besieged populations, but also in monitoring the situation and trying, albeit in desperate circumstances, to restrain ethnic cleansing and defend human rights (see Box 5.2). In Somalia, UNHCR has established a presence near the Kenyan border and brought in food and assistance in an effort to stabilize the population movements and eventually create conditions conducive to the return of refugees (see Box 5.4). Open Relief Centres in Sri Lanka have become havens of safety, accepted and respected by both warring parties. In such cases, the international presence that accompanies the assistance is probably the best – though not necessarily wholly or even largely successful – form of protection possible.

Co-operation in emergencies

The United Nations system consists of various agencies, programmes and offices. Several of them, including UNHCR, WFP, UNICEF, UNDP, WHO and the Department of Humanitarian Affairs (which includes the Office of the United Nations Disaster Relief Co-ordinator) have emergency response as part of their mandate. Of these, UNHCR is the one with a specific responsibility for refugees, but the concerns of the others are obviously germane in refugee emergencies. Only the first three routinely carry out direct operations in the field during humanitarian emergencies using their own staff, equipment and management.

In addition to the UN agencies that may be present during an emergency, a great many local national organizations, both official and non-governmental, will be on the ground, ranging from military units to religious groups. International NGOs may also be active, along with the ICRC and the local Red Cross or Red Crescent (see Box 5.5). The International Organization for Migration (IOM) may also play an important part if people need transportation in an emergency. For example, almost one

Box 5.2
Evacuation from Srebrenica

In March 1993, the besieged town of Srebrenica in eastern Bosnia stood on the verge of catastrophe. Its original, mainly Muslim, population of 6,000 had swelled to over 50,000 as people fled from neighbouring towns and villages that had fallen to the advancing Bosnian Serb forces. Virtually cut off from outside assistance for almost a year, the people of Srebrenica were in a desperate condition. With no medicine or food apart from the limited supplies contained in airdrops, a large proportion of the population was close to starvation. Thousands were sleeping outside in the snow with little or no shelter, and there were many wounded and sick.

After sustained international pressure and a dramatic gesture of solidarity by the UNPROFOR commander, General Morillon, who entered Srebrenica on 11 March and refused to leave until UNHCR food convoys were allowed into the town, the first convoy for three months finally got through to Srebrenica on 19 March. The following day it returned to the Muslim-held town of Tuzla with 618 women, children and wounded on board.

Evacuation is a last resort, in that it acquiesces in the very displacement that preventive efforts aim to avoid. But in some circumstances it is the only way to save lives. There is a very fine line between refusing to facilitate ethnic cleansing and failing to prevent needless deaths. During the war in Bosnia and Herzegovina humanitarian agencies have been forced to confront this dilemma on a number of occasions.

In Srebrenica the line was clearly on the point of being crossed, and UNHCR and UNPROFOR decided to continue evacuating the most vulnerable members of the town's population. On 24 March, a helicopter airlift began – and was immediately suspended when Serb artillery shelled the landing zone, killing two people and wounding 14 others, including two Canadian soldiers, seconds after French helicopters had taken off with 24 evacuees.

A second food convoy reached Srebrenica on 28 March. Preparations had been made for it to evacuate 650 vulnerable cases. However, during the night thousands of frantic people began forcing their way on to the trucks. Among many heart-rending scenes, parents who were unable to get on board thrust their children into the arms of those who had succeeded. By the time the convoy left the following day, more than 1,600 old men, women and children – many of them unaccompanied – were packed into the 19 trucks. Six people had been killed in the scramble to get on board and a further seven deaths occurred during the arduous journey along snow-covered tracks to Tuzla.

A similar pattern of mass panic and tragedy took place when another convoy unloaded supplies in Srebrenica on 31 March. This time nearly 3,000 old men, women and children were evacuated on 14 trucks, with six deaths caused either by overcrowding or the freezing weather. The convoy was halted both at Serb checkpoints and, for five hours just short of Tuzla, by angry Muslim forces who believed the evacuations were helping the Serbs achieve their goal of taking over the whole of eastern Bosnia. Next day, the Muslim authorities in Srebrenica announced that no more evacuations would be permitted.

To avoid repetitions of the panic and overcrowding, it was decided that only half the trucks in future convoys would enter Srebrenica loaded with food. The other, empty trucks would wait outside the town, ready to take half the evacuees on board. After several convoys had failed to get through, a further evacuation took place on 8 April when 2,100 desperate people defied the local authorities and forced their way on to 14 trucks. The empty trucks waiting outside Srebrenica helped reduce the crush and avert casualties.

On 6 April, the Serbs had cut Srebrenica's water supply, and during the week of 12 April heavy shelling left dozens of dead and well over a hundred wounded. On 13 April, one more convoy evacuation, involving 800 people, took place. On 16 April, the Security Council designated Srebrenica a "safe area" under United Nations protection. Over the next ten days around 700 people, mostly wounded, were evacuated by helicopter.

By the time the evacuations ceased towards the end of April, a total of some 9,000 people had been rescued from Srebrenica. For those who stayed behind, the situation remained extremely bleak and precarious. As concern mounted about the long-term viability of the "safe areas" in eastern Bosnia and the plight of their trapped and traumatized populations, the possibility of further mass evacuations could not be discounted.

million people who fled from Iraq and Kuwait during the Gulf crisis were assisted to return home by the IOM.

"Co-ordination works best at field level"

A serious crisis is likely to involve dozens of relief agencies, while a protracted and highly visible one may attract literally hundreds of more-or-less independent participants. A monumental effort is required to assure that their actions are complementary, or at least do not work at cross-purposes. No single entity can exert authority over all the diverse actors, although co-operation is in the interest of all. The more urgent the needs on the ground, the greater the danger that questions of co-ordination will be neglected. This is an irony at best, and a tragedy at worst, for it is during emergencies that it is most important to ensure that no effort is wasted or counterproductive. However, co-ordination is costly in terms of time and staff – precisely the resources that are in shortest supply during a crisis.

In classic refugee emergencies, UNHCR has a clear mandatory responsibility within the United Nations system to provide protection and assistance. It performs this function in close collaboration with other UN agencies and NGOs that have expertise in particular sectors, such as food, health and water supply. When some 280,000 Togolese refugees flooded into Benin

and Ghana in early 1993, for example, UNHCR despatched an Emergency Response Team and mounted a $9.9 million programme on the basis of an appeal launched to the international community. In marshalling its response, it sought the support of the relevant UN agencies, primarily WFP and UNICEF, as well as a number of NGOs.

Not all humanitarian crises, however, fall so clearly under the mandate of any one UN organization. In complex humanitarian emergencies, a wide range of actors may have to be mobilized to respond to the needs of a multitude of affected people including refugees, internally displaced people and victims of war, drought and famine. In such situations, effective co-ordination is essential to ensure that responsibilities are clearly allocated and gaps in the relief response are covered. The disaster that has overtaken Somalia is a clear example of a multifaceted crisis requiring a co-ordinated, interagency approach.

Under such circumstances, the U N has adopted flexible patterns for co-ordinating the activities of its agencies and the private organizations that work with them. The Secretary-General has frequently designated a "lead agency" to take overall charge of humanitarian operations – a role entrusted to UNHCR, for example, in northern Iraq in 1991 and in the current humanitarian relief effort in former Yugoslavia. Alternatively, an individual may be appointed as an Emergency Co-ordinator or a Special Representative. In 1992, the United Nations took a new step aimed at improving the co-ordination of its responses to complex humanitarian emergencies with the

Box 5.3
Introduction to a Refugee Camp, Kenya, 28 September 1992

Refugees gather throughout the afternoon and into the night in a neutral strip of land between the Kenyan and Somali border posts near Liboi. By morning, there are

nearly 700 of them. A UNHCR team arrives at 8 a.m. to screen the new arrivals. They pick out those who are so sick or weak that they need immediate medical attention, issue ration tickets and try to prevent people who are not refugees (or who are already registered in a camp) from signing up for assistance.

The team separates the waiting crowd into three groups: the small farmers known as Bantu in Somalia, the cross-border tribes and people of urban origin. The Bantu, an ethnic group of Tanzanian origin, are in poor condition. They are dusty, footsore and exhausted. Apart from their ragged clothing they have no possessions except some containers for water and a few pouches that might once have held food. They have walked to the border from an area near Kismayu, a distance of almost 400 kilometres. They fled because of the drought, and because bandits had taken everything from them, including their stores of food.

Among them are some frail, elderly people and three orphaned brothers. The oldest looks about 13, the youngest eight. They think one of their uncles may be in Dagahaley refugee camp near Ifo. UNHCR will keep them in Liboi in a feeding centre for a few days to strengthen them while trying to locate the uncle.

The urban people, from Kismayu and Mogadishu, are better off but just as frightened of the violence that has engulfed their former homes. The cross-border tribes are nomadic; whether they are called Kenyan or Somali has never meant much to them until now. The UNHCR team questions them about traditional grazing lands and water points, trying to determine if they are indeed affected by the fighting in Somalia, or "merely" by the drought and general insecurity of north-eastern Kenya. One extended family has arrived with its animals – about 20 goats and five camels. The family is told it cannot take the animals to Ifo. There is not enough grazing and water for the livestock already at the camp.

People who are obviously ill or starving are not questioned too closely, but are sent on to a camp for at least temporary assistance. Some estimate that as many as a third of the people in the Kenyan camps are locals. No one doubts

that many of them are in serious need of assistance, though not of international protection. One family of nomads has lost a child – a three-year-old girl – in the night, probably from measles. They bury her as they wait to be screened.

By the end of the morning, 38 sick or badly malnourished people have been sent directly to the hospital in Liboi camp, with a relative to look after each one. Another 535 have been accepted for settlement at Ifo camp, one of three sprawling settlements near the town of Daddab, each of which shelters about 40,000 Somali refugees.

In groups of 50, carefully listed, they climb into open trucks for the dusty journey of about 90 kilometres. The group includes 311 children. Roughly 60 per cent of the 116 household groups are headed by women. On an empty stretch of highway, each head of household is given the precious slip of paper that will later be exchanged for a ration card.

The journey ends at Ifo camp. After they get off the trucks, the children are taken aside by Médecins sans Frontières and given a cup of milk, a measles vaccine and a vitamin A tablet. They are then screened for malnutrition. The mothers of those who need supplemental feeding are instructed to take them next day to a normal, intensive or super-intensive feeding centre. Meanwhile, the heads of family line up to register and receive their ration cards. More than 500 people are processed in little over an hour.

The refugees then get back on the trucks and are taken to the dis-

tribution centre run by CARE. They present their ration cards twice: first for "non-food items" including a tent or tarpaulin, blankets, a small stove and jerrycans for hauling water. Next they join the food line and receive flour, beans, oil, sugar, salt and a tin of fish. People struggle to lift the heavy loads back into the trucks.

One malnourished, unaccompanied boy of about 12 returns bereft. After being issued with his single ration card, he collected his food and joined up with a family who helped him load it into a truck. But then they pushed him out and threatened him. He doesn't protest. He is too exhausted; he has probably suffered worse. A Kenyan social worker takes him home for the night. The next day she will identify his clan and region, and try to find relatives in one of the camps. If there are none, an elder of his clan will find a family to take him in.

By the time the last groups are taken to their allotted sites, dusk is falling. They must erect their shelters and cook a meal before they settle down for the night. No fuel is provided; the refugees have to scavenge it from the bush, a demanding task in arid Ifo. Some, especially the nomads, have never encountered this kind of food. Used to meat and milk, they have to be taught how to make bread and cook the beans.

The first day as a refugee is untypical, but it introduces some of the central elements of camp life: boredom, bureaucracy and endless standing in line. The routine is like the diet: strange, distasteful and monotonous, but it is enough to sustain life and, perhaps, hope.

Box 5.4

The Cross-Border Operation into Somalia

Kenya was struck by one of the fastest growing refugee emergencies in 1992, with an average of 900 refugees entering the country each day. While significant numbers came from Ethiopia and the Sudan, the majority were Somalis fleeing one of the worst humanitarian disasters in recent history. By the end of the year, more than 400,000 refugees were in Kenya, including 285,619 Somalis. The influx required a massive emergency response: 11 new camps were established in Kenya during the year and assistance budgets soared.

In the turmoil that had befallen Somalia, the refugees were fleeing a combination of violence, anarchy and drought. The obvious dangers of a continuing exodus of epic proportions, and the difficulties of providing protection and assistance in the midst of the insecurity that plagues northern Kenya, were com-

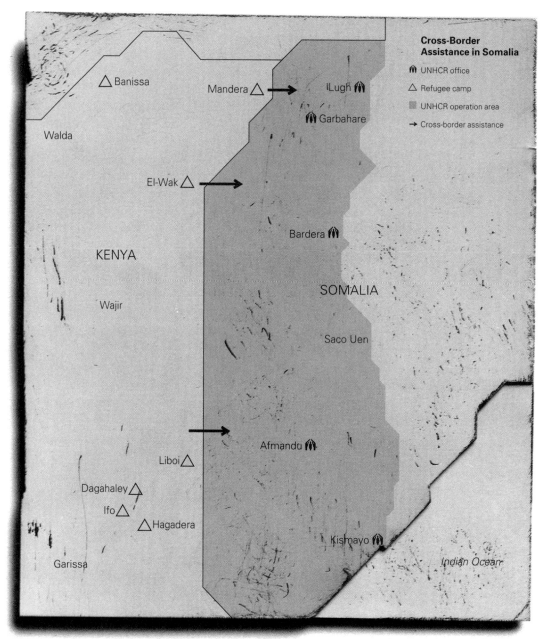

pelling arguments for looking beyond the traditional approach of delivering assistance only to the country of asylum. At the request of the UN Secretary-General, UNHCR therefore launched a crossborder operation in September 1992 with the initial aim of stabilizing population movements inside Somalia itself and stemming the momentum of refugee flows into neighbouring countries.

Initially constrained by the conspicuous lack of international political initiatives addressing the Somali crisis, the cross-border programme was given a new lease of life by the deployment of a US-led multinational force (UNITAF) in Somalia at the beginning of December 1992. This development meant that at last there was a realistic prospect of better security and improved control of relief distribution – essential pre-conditions for the return of Somali refugees. As a result, the cross-border operation stepped up a gear in January 1993, as UNHCR and other organizations began to expand their presence and programmes on the Somali side of the border.

The operation, which involves importing assistance from Kenya into "preventive zones" in southern Somalia, is intended to be both preventive and solution-oriented. At one level, it aims to mitigate at least one of the principal causes of displacement by providing assistance in specific areas that people might otherwise be forced to leave mainly for famine-related reasons. At another level, it seeks to create conditions conducive to the eventual voluntary repatriation of refugees from camps in Kenya. Indeed, some 3,200 Somali refugees returned home voluntarily, within the framework of the programme, as early as October and November 1992 .

In addition to providing food and other relief items, it is hoped that the cross-border operation will begin rehabilitating the social infrastructure, including schools and clinics, and encourage a return to self-sufficiency in agriculture and livestock. By June 1993, more than 160 Quick Impact Projects (see Chapter Six) were being implemented in co-operation with 20 NGO partners. By the same date, 188,000 Somali refugees had signed up for voluntary repatriation from the Kenyan camps. Around 30,000 had already returned home, 12,000 of them with the help of UNHCR. If security continues to improve, the UNHCR offices established in Somalia under the cross-border programme will be well placed to support the voluntary return of the 285,000 Somali refugees currently in Kenya.

The effectiveness of the cross-border programme in Somalia has still to be determined and is, to some extent, hostage to a political solution to the Somali crisis. It is, nevertheless, an interesting example of an innovative approach that aims to prevent and solve problems of displacement by extending assistance to all people in need in a given area, in the hope that some of them will be able to avoid becoming refugees, and that those who have fled their homes will be able to return.

Fig. 5.A

Quick Impact Projects in Kenya and Somalia: June 1993

Sector	Bardera	El-Wak	Garbahare	Lugh	Mandera	Nairobi	Total
Transport	0	0	0	0	3	0	3
Water	10	11	4	2	8	0	35
Infrastructure	2	1	0	4	1	0	8
Community Services	14	2	5	6	2	2	31
Education	2	3	1	2	9	0	17
Agriculture	9	1	2	0	13	0	25
Livestock	3	4	0	1	1	0	9
Forestry	0	1	0	0	0	0	1
Health	3	13	2	1	12	0	31
Total	43	36	14	16	49	2	160

establishment of a Department of Humanitarian Affairs. The experience of the past few years has led to improvements in co-ordination, not only within the United Nations system but also between UN and non-UN bodies such as the ICRC, IOM and NGOs.

"There is no daylight between crises; crisis has become the norm"

The "crisis-intensive" years of the early 1990s have taught some valuable lessons. One is that co-ordination works best at field level. Protection and assistance staff in the field have both a vivid appreciation of the nature of the problems that must be tackled and direct exposure to duplication or gaps in the work of the various agencies on the scene. This is a strong argument both for decentralization of decision-making concerning the conduct of operations and for the greatest possible responsiveness at headquarters to observations made in the field. If such an approach is to function smoothly, however, decisions taken at field level must proceed according to a clearly articulated division of labour.

Another important lesson that has been learned is that most of the support for refugees and displaced persons, particularly during the early stages of a crisis, is provided by the people and governments of the receiving communities. Even in this age of instantaneous communications and jet transportation, it takes time to mobilize and deliver assistance on the scale required when tens or even hundreds of thousands of people are suddenly forced to flee. International organizations should reinforce existing efforts to promote and support national preparedness by helping countries likely to receive refugees to develop relevant expertise, procedures and emergency response plans. Assistance of this nature undoubtedly strengthens protection. States which feel their concerns and burdens are understood and shared are less

likely to refuse to admit refugees or force them back across the border.

A third lesson – though one which still raises as many questions as it answers – stems from the relationship between the new generation of peace-making or peace-keeping initiatives and humanitarian assistance. At the operational level this has led to the growing involvement of armed forces in humanitarian activities – a pattern likely to be repeated in future crises.

Since 1991, multinational military forces deployed under the auspices, or with the blessings, of the United Nations have been used in four major humanitarian relief operations: in "Operation Provide Comfort" in northern Iraq, in the UN Transitional Authority in Cambodia, as the UN Protection Force (UNPROFOR) in Croatia and Bosnia and in "Operation Restore Hope" in Somalia. Three of the four directly involved aid and protection for refugees or returnees. The fourth, in Somalia, involved internally displaced people and, along with other efforts such as the cross-border assistance programme run by UNHCR from neighbouring Kenya, has slowed the outflow of Somali refugees to surrounding countries.

Despite the effectiveness demonstrated by military forces in these humanitarian operations, questions remain about how extensive a role they should play. Some of the reservations are that military support is too expensive, and that the self-contained nature of military operations tends to retard the building of local capacities essential for long-term solutions to take hold. There are also fears, discussed in the previous chapter, that a military presence may politicize humanitarian relief. Clear criteria need to be established for humanitarian activities undertaken in association with peace-keeping efforts.

Preparedness

A refugee emergency, by its very nature, demands immediate action. Delay may cost lives. Initial responses to both the huge Kurdish movement toward Turkey in 1991 and the first mass arrivals of Somali refugees in Kenya in 1992 were woefully inadequate. Preparedness is the key to emergency response. Maintaining a capacity to respond to emergencies at full readiness would, however, be immensely expensive. It would involve keeping a great many resources waiting idly for a crisis to occur. The materials and expertise needed for a relief effort in the tropics would be next to useless in a winter emergency in the mountains of Central Asia. Only national defence establishments and local fire departments routinely maintain so much idle capacity. For other institutions, including humanitarian ones, careful planning and standby arrangements can help to compensate for the lack of excess capacity.

The elements of preparedness are staff, supplies, appropriate management skills, logistics and communications. Of course, emergency funds must also be available to support the mobilization of human and material resources. As refugee emergencies increase in number and frequency, the opportunity for agencies to return to "normal" patterns of staffing and operations after an emergency has virtually disappeared. There is no daylight between crises; crisis has become the norm. As a result, institutions that work with refugees have had to revamp their emergency arrangements. UN agencies such as WHO and UNICEF have created new emergency response units. UNHCR has increased its emergency fund to $25 million and created new structures within the organization to allow it to respond quickly when mass displacements occur.

At UNHCR, emergency preparedness is one of the three main programme strategies for the early 1990s, along with prevention and repatriation. Emergency preparedness and response officers have been appointed and teams designated to cover each region where crises are likely to develop. Beyond the finite resources of regular staff, UNHCR has established standby arrangements with the Norwegian and Danish Refugee Councils, under which people with the necessary skills can be loaned to UNHCR on very short notice. Similarly, the Swedish Rescue Board maintains standby logistical and technical support for UNHCR, which can be deployed in as many as three emergency operations at any one time. These arrangements allow a field station to be set up, completely operational and self-sufficient, at 72 hours' notice.

UNHCR and its national partners such as the Nordic agencies have built up limited stockpiles of supplies and equipment. While it is often less expensive to buy basic commodities on the open market at the time of an emergency than to store them in advance, other items are more difficult to procure at such short notice. Therefore small stocks of vehicles, field survival kits, telecommunications equipment and portable computers have been set aside for use in a crisis. Basic relief supplies such as tents, blankets and water tanks are maintained in centrally controlled (but not centrally located) warehouses maintained by the suppliers or by NGO partners. This kind of standby capacity is the most effective way of breaking the impasse between the need to be prepared and funding limitations.

"There has been a much higher proportion of winter emergencies in the 1990s"

The refugee emergencies of the 1960s, 1970s and 1980s took place mostly in tropical or semi-tropical locations. Emergency procedures and supplies were largely geared to warm climates. In the 1990s, there has been a much higher proportion of winter emergencies: the former Yugoslavia, Azerbaijan, Armenia, northern Iraq and Tajikistan, to name just a few. Winter emergencies are more demanding in terms of fuel, clothing, shelter and food requirements, and pose a distinctive set of threats to health. They place additional demands on standby arrangements.

Preparations for a crisis are not complete when people, supplies and equipment are lined up. Staff must be exhaustively trained in conducting emergency operations, for they will often be setting up the equivalent of medium-sized cities in places where there is nothing – no infrastructure,

Box 5.5
The Role of NGOs in the Field

Non-governmental organizations perform an indispensable, though varying, role at every stage as a refugee situation develops. They are involved in preventive efforts from the very first signs of crisis; once an emergency is under way, they are instrumental in saving lives and meeting the basic needs of the victims; and, finally, they play a key role in the identification and implementation of solutions, including voluntary repatriation.

Where prevention is concerned, those NGOs already well established on the ground can provide invaluable information about unfolding crises, alerting the world to the imminence of refugee flows and other population movements. Repeated violations of human rights, impending crop failure and

rising ethnic tensions are all examples of early warning signals that are often first detected by NGOs.

In the emergency phase of refugee crises, rapid intervention by NGOs frequently saves innumerable lives. Because of their size and flexibility, they can react quickly to provide essential relief such as health care, food, water supplies and shelter. Once survival is assured, NGOs help refugees look forward to a better future by providing education and social services.

NGOs also have a role to play in solutions to refugee problems. The resettlement of millions of refugees could not have taken place without their active collaboration. Their involvement is also crucial during voluntary repatriations, when their contributions include accompanying refugees back to their places of origin, designing and implementing quick impact rehabilitation projects and monitoring

human rights. In carrying out these and other activities, more than a few NGO staff have lost their lives.

Since its establishment in 1951, UNHCR has collaborated with NGOs in all its fields of activity. Over 200 NGOs co-operate in UNHCR's relief or legal assistance programmes. In all, UNHCR maintains regular contact with close to 1,000 NGOs involved with refugees in one way or another.

Recent, large-scale refugee outflows have led to a new stage in the development of UNHCR-NGO relations. The needs to improve emergency response systems, establish preventive networks, strengthen indigenous NGOs, and ensure continuity between relief and solutions are some of the challenges currently facing UNHCR and NGOs alike. A strong spirit of partnership and a willingness to complement each other's work by means of close consultation are essential to both.

Fig. 5.B
Non-Governmental Organizations: UNHCR's Operational Partners, 1991-1992

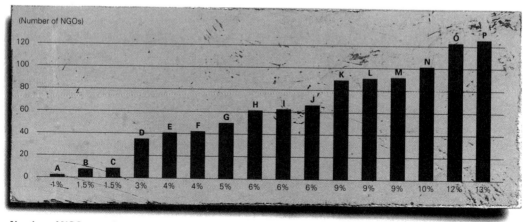

Number of NGO operational partners in each sector of activity

A Fish – 3 NGOs
B Livestock – 8 NGOs
C Forestry – 9 NGOs
D Crop Production – 35 NGOs
E Water – 41 NGOs
F Sanitation – 43 NGOs

G Food – 51 NGOs
H Protection – 62 NGOs
I Income Generation – 63 NGOs
J Shelter – 66 NGOs
K Community Services – 89 NGOs
L Transport – 91 NGOs

M Domestic Needs – 92 NGOs
N Education – 102 NGOs
O Agency Operational Support – 124 NGOs
P Health and Nutrition – 126 NGOs

no economic base and in some cases virtually no natural resources. Certain tools have to be prepared in advance if such a daunting task is to be manageable: these include country profiles, detailed maps and carefully worked-out contingency plans for disaster-prone areas.

Prolonged emergencies

When does an emergency cease to be an emergency? When death rates stabilize? When international assistance and protection agencies are able to hand over responsibility to local authorities? When a reasonable degree of self-sufficiency has been attained? Self-sufficiency for refugees in the country of asylum is an increasingly elusive goal. In earlier periods it was quite common: for example, UNHCR helped to establish 144 rural settlements for refugees in Africa between 1962 and 1986, on land made available by host governments. Such courses of action are a rarity today.

Although African countries have seldom closed their borders, the legendary African hospitality toward refugees appeared to be wearing thin when, in 1992, the government of Malawi announced plans to introduce restrictive measures, including the fencing of refugee settlements, aimed at the more than one million Mozambican refugees on its territory.

The same kind of frustration was evident in the Kenyan authorities' sudden decision the same year to demand the immediate repatriation of all refugees on its soil – a demand it subsequently retracted. Such reactions occur either because the pressure of population growth on natural resources makes additional cultivators appear to be more of a burden than a benefit. They may also happen because governments fear that refugees might bring social or political instability. In either situation (and the two often co-exist), refugees often end up living in closed or isolated camps where they have little scope for economic self-reliance and where humanitarian emergencies can fester at varying levels of intensity.

To help avoid this happening, maximum use has to be made of available resources. The most abundant, wasted resources in a refugee camp are the time and skills of the refugees themselves – especially the men. Women continue to fulfil their responsibilities to perform household labour and child care, which are always time-consuming and may be more laborious away from a familiar setting. However, separated from their field, flocks or other means of livelihood, many male refugees spend idle days in enormous frustration. In a prolonged emergency, both the welfare of the displaced people themselves and the budgets of aid agencies can benefit if this human resource is put to productive use.

The impact of refugee emergencies is by no means confined to the refugees themselves. It is the least developed countries that have been host to the great majority of refugees over the past two decades. Refugee influxes often impose heavy short- and longer-term burdens on such countries and may aggravate the social, economic and environmental crises that they already face.

"The least developed countries host the great majority of refugees"

The nature of a refugee emergency does not allow for proper environmental planning to take account of the ecological impact of a sudden large-scale increase of population. In many receiving countries, the influx of people has destabilized the local environment and depleted already scarce vegetation in semi-arid areas. Cutting of wood for fuel and construction results in deforestation while refugees' livestock aggravate over-grazing. When an emergency is prolonged by failure to achieve a political settlement, the circles of land degradation around refugee settlements grow ever wider. A refugee crisis can turn into an environmental crisis that is capable of generating further displacements if remedial action is not taken. Somalia, Sudan, Kenya,

Malawi and Pakistan have all experienced environmental devastation as a result of mass arrivals from neighbouring countries (see Box 5.6). Environmental measures should be incorporated into refugee programmes at the earliest stages of planning to minimize the damage.

Poor planning can exacerbate the situation. For example, the contractor asked to prepare the site of the Ifo refugee camp in Kenya, at very short notice and at great speed, simply scraped away all the vegetation from a huge square of land. Once installed, the refugees were left to

Box 5.6

Shouldering the Burden: The Case of Malawi

Malawi is a small, densely populated country in southern Africa. Its economy is predominantly agricultural. More than 85 per cent of its 10.3 million people live in rural areas. With a GNP of $230 per capita in 1991, Malawi ranks among the world's least developed countries.

A massive influx of refugees from the devastating war in neighbouring Mozambique began in 1986. By 1993, Malawi was host to a million Mozambican refugees – equivalent to 10 per cent of its own total population.

Refugees live in 13 of Malawi's 24 administrative districts and, in some cases, they outnumber the local inhabitants. They live either in so-called open settlements alongside Malawian villages, or else in large, organized camps. As the shortage of arable land prevents their involvement in agriculture, they are almost entirely dependent on outside relief for food, water and essential services. Their presence has been a tremendous burden on local economies. It has also had a negative effect on the development efforts of the country as a whole.

The country's road system, particularly the network of dirt tracks that link rural areas to main roads,

was not designed to carry more than 180,000 metric tons of relief a year. Road surfaces, bridges and culverts have all been severely damaged by the frequent passage of heavy vehicles. As a result, it is more difficult for Malawian farmers to transport their agricultural products, and this has affected food distribution throughout the entire country. Access to refugee centres has also deteriorated.

Even more devastating has been the impact of the refugee presence on Malawi's forests. Refugees have felled large numbers of trees in order to acquire wood for fuel and building materials. The refugees' settlements, located in some of the most ecologically vulnerable areas of the country, have exacerbated deforestation and led to subsequent land degradation. Malawi is currently losing about 3.5 per cent of its forest cover each year.

In addition to these problems, the steadily increasing demand for already scarce goods and services has led to tension. Refugees are in direct competition with Malawians for access to severely stretched government services, including health facilities, schools, water supplies, informal employment opportunities and welfare programmes. Despite the provision of large-scale foreign aid to support the refugees, the Malawi government has had to divert a significant proportion of its

own revenues to the refugee programme, thus reducing resources available for national development.

Sustainable development will only be possible in Malawi if the impact of refugees on the country's resources is significantly reduced. UNHCR has become involved in reforestation, the construction and maintenance of roads and water supplies, and the distribution of locally produced, fuel-efficient stoves. However, the scale of these activities falls well short of compensating for the strains caused by the refugee presence, let alone meeting wider national needs.

For this to be achieved, UN development agencies and bilateral aid donors will have to provide substantial support. Development projects specifically designed to tackle problems in refugee-hosting areas are already at the advanced planning stage. Even if the recent momentum in repatriation to Mozambique is maintained (see Chapter Six, Box 6.2), Malawi will undoubtedly feel the consequences of the refugees' presence for years to come. It remains to be seen, however, if the international community is prepared to fund development and rehabilitation projects which compensate Malawi for the generous asylum it has provided to the Mozambican refugees.

struggle with dust storms in the midst of a man-made desert without a scrap of shade or windbreak, and had to walk long distances to reach the meagre resources of the bush. The mistake was not repeated at other sites, but Ifo may never recover. It was typical of the kind of mistake made in emergencies, when speed is of the essence and attention is focused on immediate needs.

Repatriation and the end of the refugee phase of an emergency do not necessarily signal the end of a crisis. UNHCR was able to withdraw from northern Iraq in mid-1992 after helping some 1.7 million displaced people reintegrate into their communities. The crisis of displacement was over, but the political and economic crisis, and responsibility for averting continuing threats to the security of the population, remain in the hands of other UN agencies and member states. In 1991 and 1992, up to half a million Ethiopian refugees fleeing conflict in Somalia spilled back into their home country, triggering a "returnee emergency" of daunting proportions.

The reinforcement of co-ordination within the United Nations system in general, and of emergency response capacity in particular, has undoubtedly increased efficiency in the face of refugee crises. This has been demonstrated in the humanitarian operations in the former Yugoslavia, Kenya, Bangladesh and elsewhere. There is, however, a pressing need to look beyond emergencies towards solutions. Rather than being seen as isolated events, refugee crises need to be approached as the first stage of a continuum that links emergency response, mediation, repatriation, rehabilitation and development. To be effective in this respect, the United Nations must continue its efforts to improve co-ordination both among its different agencies and between its political processes and the activities of its humanitarian and development organizations. Approached otherwise, emergency response may only succeed in converting a death sentence to one of life imprisonment in dependence, alienation and confrontation.

New arrivals from Mozambique.
Nyamithutu, Malawi, July 1991.

© Agence Vu/John Vink

Chapter six

Going Home: Voluntary Repatriation

In 1992, UNHCR helped some 2.4 million refugees to return home – including over 1.5 million Afghans. Repatriation of the first of the 50,000 Guatemalan refugees in Mexico began in January 1993; in the rest of Central America, the process had almost been completed. By the end of April, 365,000 Cambodians had returned, and in June 1993, plans to assist 1.3 million refugees to return to Mozambique began to be implemented. Throughout 1992, an average of 46,000 refugees went back to their home countries every week – a rate unprecedented in previous years (see Annex I.8). There have been setbacks as well. In October, for example, repatriation to Angola was abruptly halted by renewed fighting.

The easing of political tensions and the winding down of a number of civil conflicts have made large-scale voluntary repatriations possible. In several countries, the return of refugees is an essential part of the transition to peace, rather than simply a result of it. In Central America, long the theatre of seemingly intractable conflicts, the repatriation of Salvadorians and Nicaraguans was a key element of the political settlement that brought an end to the civil wars in both countries. Cambodian refugees in Thailand returned to their war-torn country in time to participate in the national elections held in May 1993. The repatriation of Namibian refugees in 1989 was not only one of the fruits of the political settlement that resulted in independence, but also played a role in the process of national consolidation.

Although every repatriation movement is unique, they all share some common characteristics. One of the most striking is that, rather than following the resolution of conflict, repatriation now often takes place in the midst of it – or at least in a context of continuing instability or insecurity. This poses formidable problems for the protection of returning refugees. The international community has accepted that the need for international protection does not end the moment someone crosses the border back into his or her homeland.

The ideal environment for the return of

refugees is one in which the causes of flight have been definitively and permanently removed – for example, the end of a civil war or a change of government which brings an end to violence or persecution. This ideal is rarely achieved. Instead, refugees return to places where political disputes still simmer and occasionally boil over; where fragile cease-fires break down, are repaired and then break down again; where agreements are broken and trust is minimal. The great majority of returnees in the early 1990s have been going back to situations of just this kind – for example in Angola, Mozambique, Somalia, Cambodia, Sri Lanka and Afghanistan.

It is often difficult for external observers to understand why people choose to return in such uncertain conditions. While the emotional pull of the homeland is not to be underestimated, the motivation is usually a mixture of positive and negative. In ideal circumstances, voluntary repatriation is the best solution for most refugees. It restores citizenship and ends the pain of exile. For the many refugees whose prospects at home are far from certain, however, it is only the best of a shrinking range of choices. Opportunities for permanent settlement in

countries of first asylum are narrowing. Resettlement in third countries is offered to no more than 0.5 per cent of the world's refugees. Even temporary asylum is being granted less often. A life of exile is for many a life of misery – of poverty, dependency and frustration.

Many refugees have seen security in their country of asylum deteriorate so suddenly and dramatically that the dangers at home become the lesser of two evils. Over 80,000 Ugandan refugees returned from southern Sudan after being attacked by Sudanese rebel forces in 1989; Angolans in Zaire and Ethiopians in Somalia fled back to their home countries when fighting broke out around them in 1991–92. Elsewhere, the protection and assistance available is so inadequate that refugees have preferred to return to continuing insecurity at home. In such circumstances, they can hardly be said to have exercised a free choice.

For UNHCR, charged with protecting refugees and finding durable solutions for their problems, the standard criteria for return are "voluntary repatriation in safety and dignity", preferably in an organized fashion and with the co-operation of the governments of both the host country and the country of origin. But refugees often decide

Box 6.1
Repatriation to Cambodia

Between 30 March 1992 and 30 April 1993, more than 365,000 Cambodians returned home – a rate of nearly 1,000 a day. Most of them had spent between 10 and 14 years in refugee camps in Thailand. About 2,000 of those who returned came from other countries in South East Asia.

The repatriation was one of the largest logistical operations ever undertaken by UNHCR, and was carried out under particularly difficult circumstances: the Cambodian

infrastructure had been devastated by 22 years of war, and the situation in the country as a whole was far from secure. Yet despite the question marks that still hang over the future of Cambodia, many observers consider the repatriation programme a success.

In Thailand, Cambodian refugees were housed in seven camps. Three of these – Site 8, O'Trao and Site K – were controlled by the Democratic Party of Kampuchea (DPK), better known as the Khmer Rouge; a further two – Site 2 and Sok Sann – were affiliated to the Khmer People's National Liberation Front (KPNLF); Site B was under

the control of the Sihanoukist faction, FUNCINPEC; and finally, there was the UNHCR camp at Khao-I-Dang which had, since the early 1980s, served as the staging post for resettlement overseas.

Preparations for repatriation began with the Paris Peace Accords of 23 October 1991. Shortly afterwards, UNHCR commissioned the French organization, Spot Image, to carry out satellite surveys of arable land in Cambodia. These appeared to show large, uncultivated areas. As the great majority of returnees were of peasant stock, it was decided to offer them between one and two hectares of arable land each. However, it soon became clear that this was impractical. Land had been redistributed after the war and much of that which remained unoccupied had either been mined or was inaccessible as a result of frequent cease-fire violations.

From 20 May 1992, less than two months after repatriation began, UNHCR started to diversify the options available to those returning. While continuing to offer them arable land as Option A, it added Option B (a smaller plot of land and a house) and Option C (a $50 cash grant for each adult and $25 for each child under 12). In addition, each repatriating family received a 400-day supply of food, as well as household utensils and agricultural tools.

This vast operation reached full momentum in the late summer of 1992, when the average monthly rate of return exceeded 30,000, despite difficulties caused by the monsoon season. More than 450 convoys of buses and trucks crossed the frontier, ferrying returnees to the six temporary reception centres that had been built in Cambodia. Those wishing to head east or south travelled by train. Between 30 April 1992 and 24 March 1993, the so-called Sisophon Express made 71 journeys, carrying 90,000 returnees in all, from Sisophon to the Phnom Penh reception centre. From there, they proceeded by truck, bullock cart, boat or even helicopter, depending on their destination and the state of the roads.

The great majority (87 per cent) of the returnees chose to take a cash grant because it offered

greater freedom, notably the possibility to change their minds about where they wished to live after they returned to Cambodia. Contrary to expectations, most repatriates managed to find relatives whom they had believed dead or lost, and decided to settle down with them.

In accordance with the terms of the Paris Peace Accords, returnees were completely free to choose where they settled. Despite UNHCR warnings, some even opted for insecure areas. More than 77,000 refugees from the Khmer Rouge camps in Thailand spread out all over Cambodia without, initially at least, any serious signs of friction. Many others chose to settle in areas held by factions other than the State of Cambodia. Approximately 36,000 returned to KPNLF areas, some 4,000 to the FUNCINPEC zone and a similar number to areas controlled by the Khmer Rouge, all with the assistance of UNHCR.

The top priority following repatriation has been to promote the successful reintegration of returnees. In addition to negotiating the allocation of land by local authorities, UNHCR had by June 1993 committed $7.8 million for some 50 quick impact development projects (QUIPs), which are being implemented in collaboration with UNDP. These are designed to help returnees reintegrate and reach self-sufficiency, while simultaneously benefiting the local population. Projects include the repair of 220 kilometres of roads and the construction of 355 schools, 1,300 water points and 32 health centres. Agricultural programmes have also

been launched to rehabilitate 8,000 hectares of land and provide seeds for 60,000 families.

Since becoming involved in Cambodia, UNHCR has, for the first time in its history, tried to organize mine clearance in areas receiving large numbers of returnees. De-mining operations have been carried out in collaboration with military personnel from UNTAC and an NGO called Handicap International.

In accordance with its traditional protection role, UNHCR, together with UNTAC's civilian police contingent and all its other partners, is closely monitoring the situation inside Cambodia to try and ensure that returnees do not suffer political reprisals.

The repatriation operation itself may have contributed to the process of national reconciliation in Cambodia. As it drew to a close, "refugees" and "returnees" were increasingly referred to simply as "Cambodians": citizens who, like the others, would soon exercise their right to vote. Nevertheless, the run-up to the national elections in June 1993 was fraught with tension: peace-keeping troops, election monitors and civilians were murdered; bomb blasts rocked Phnom Penh; and important provisions of the Peace Accords continued to be violated by more than one party. The elections themselves were an unexpected success, with Cambodians turning out massively to vote. However, the ensuing difficult negotiations, which aimed to persuade all the parties to live with the results of the elections, indicate that the future of Cambodia still hangs very much in the balance.

to return independently, according to their own pace and criteria. UNHCR is then left with the choice of refusing to assist in the process, which would undermine the refugees' autonomy and jeopardize their chances of successful return, or of facilitating it despite reservations. In practice, the only forms of refugee repatriation that UNHCR refuses to assist are those that are enforced.

Organized repatriations

When refugees return home under the terms of a plan that is worked out well in advance and has the support of both home and asylum governments, as well as that of UNHCR and the refugees themselves, some problems of protection and assistance can be avoided. Such plans commonly include amnesties for political offences, assurances of safe passage for returning refugees, material assistance to help them re-establish themselves and provisions for international presence of some kind to monitor their safety. Organized plans are also likely to have greater resources behind them, though rarely at the level desired.

"Repatriation plans are not just about the return of refugees"

One of the most painstakingly organized repatriation plans ever to have been implemented has been taking place in Cambodia (see Box 6.1). The physical return of refugees from the Thai border camps was completed in April 1993, 13 months after it began. The repatriation operation is far from over, however. The economic and political situation in Cambodia is fragile. Urgent tasks of protection and assistance remain and are being carried out to try to ensure that this solution is indeed durable.

Arguably the single most important part of an organized repatriation takes place before it begins. Planning is crucial. Where the refugees will go,

how they will survive the first hard months while they re-establish their livelihoods, what dangers they may face and who will protect them – such questions must be answered in advance.

A repatriation plan is not just about the return of refugees; it should also be closely connected to the processes of peace-making, peace-keeping, political reconciliation and economic reconstruction. Plans should allow room for flexibility, and the people who implement them must be ready to improvise as necessary. But a solid foundation, in the form of a comprehensive plan, increases the likelihood of success. The peace agreement for Mozambique, signed in October 1992, opened the way for a repatriation plan that was being prepared while the peace negotiations were still taking place (see Box 6.2).

Planned repatriations are not always initiated by governments or international organizations. Refugees themselves often take the lead. The organized movement of Guatemalan refugees back to their home country is an example. Although the violence and extensive violations of human rights that prompted their departure were still occurring, the 50,000 or so Guatemalan refugees resident in Mexico began preparing for their return several years ago.[25] Since mid-1991, the government of Guatemala has taken part in a dialogue with representatives of the refugees on issues surrounding repatriation.

Both sides established negotiating bodies in 1991. Shortly afterwards, a group was set up to mediate between the refugees and the government. It was composed of the Human Rights Ombudsman from Guatemala (who subsequently became President on 5 June 1993), a representative of the Bishops' Conference, a member of the Guatemalan Human Rights Commission in Mexico, and UNHCR. A Tripartite Commission, consisting of UNHCR and the governments of Guatemala and Mexico was also established. In early 1992, these separate negotiating bodies were joined by a fifth: the International Returnees Support Group, which included representatives of four foreign embassies in Guatemala and two international NGOs.

Two years of negotiations preceded the first repatriations. On 20 January 1993, nearly 2,500 refugees crossed the border into Guatemala. The return took place on the basis of an agreement between the government and the refugees' negotiating bodies. The agreement covered the following points:

• Return should be voluntary on the part of each person involved, and be carried out collectively in an organized fashion in conditions of safety and dignity.
• The government recognized the returnees' rights to free association and organization.
• Returnees were exempted from military service and participation in self-defence groups for three years.
• Return must be accompanied by UNHCR, the Guatemalan Human Rights Ombudsman, the Catholic church and the Returnees Support Group.
• Returnees and their representatives should have freedom of movement within Guatemala.
• The rights to life and personal and communal integrity should be respected.
• Returnees should have access to land.
• International mediation, monitoring and verification of the terms of the agreement should be permitted.

A verification group was set up to perform the role outlined in this last point.

The first convoy of returning refugees was accompanied by some 240 foreign observers and health workers. It was escorted by Guatemalan government officials and highway police, UNHCR, the Red Cross and members of the refugees' negotiating team. Every aspect, including the route, the timing and the public visibility of the return journey were politically charged subjects of negotiation in which the views of the refugees usually prevailed.

The elaborate planning and implementation of the Guatemalan repatriation agreement is testimony to the high levels of mistrust and anxiety surrounding it. Despite numerous allegations of bad faith from both sides, the refugees submitted a plan for the repatriation of over 12,000 people in seven organized return movements scheduled between May and December 1993. Collective returns were, however, suspended following political upheaval in Guatemala in May and are expected to resume after consolidation of the new government. UNHCR has established a presence in the main areas of return, with the agreement of all parties, and will assist the reintegration process through grants to individuals as well as community-oriented aid. The latter consists mainly of short-term, high-impact projects designed to boost local incomes, as well as investments in education, water, sanitation and health.

"Returnees everywhere know they will encounter hardship and possible dangers when they go back home"

The refugees who have returned to Cambodia under UN auspices, or to Guatemala under the multi-party accords, know – like returnees everywhere – that they will encounter hardship and possibly danger in their reclaimed homelands. Planning and organization are fragile defences against such uncertainties. But the international community's involvement in their return does at least assure them that the outside world is not ignorant of, or indifferent to, their fate.

Spontaneous repatriation

The great majority of refugees who return to their home countries do so on their own initiative, rather than by agreeing to join a formal repatriation plan devised under international auspices after a "fundamental change of circumstances" has made possible a return "in safety and dignity". In 1992, for example, of the estimated 2.4 million refugees who repatriated, around 1.7 million did so spontaneously.

Spontaneous repatriation poses a dilemma for the organizations involved in protecting refugees – namely governments, NGOs and

Box 6.2
Planning a Repatriation Programme: Mozambique

The signing of a peace accord between the Mozambican government and the armed opposition movement, RENAMO, in Rome on 4 October 1992 opened the way for the largest organized repatriation ever undertaken in Africa. Repatriating the 1.3 million Mozambican refugees scattered across five southern African countries – Malawi, Zimbabwe, Tanzania, Zambia and Swaziland – poses an enormous challenge. Indeed, the number of returnees could rise as high as 1.7 million, if an additional 400,000 unregistered Mozambicans in the region join the repatriation programme.

Fifteen years of conflict in Mozambique left as many as three million dead, a similar number internally displaced and most of the country in ruins. It caused an estimated $15 billion in damage to the economy. Clinics, schools and government buildings were destroyed; basic community services were wiped out; and major roads were heavily mined or rendered unusable by years of neglect.

The devastation and economic chaos caused by the civil war, the fragile political situation and delays in various aspects of the peace process have made the repatriation programme especially difficult to plan. In an attempt to tackle the formidable obstacles to successful repatriation and reintegration, a regional plan of operation was drawn up in early 1993 by UNHCR

in consultation with a number of other UN agencies and NGOs. The plan divided the operation into three principal phases: pre-departure, movement and reintegration. It is scheduled to be implemented over a three-year period, starting at the end of June 1993, at a cost of $203.4 million. Half a million Mozambicans are expected to repatriate in 1993 alone, most of them from Malawi.

A major priority in the "pre-departure phase" of the plan was to establish a legal framework for the repatriation. An agreement was signed between UNHCR and the Mozambican authorities in March 1993. This stipulates that the voluntary character of repatriation must be strictly observed and that UNHCR will be allowed to monitor the situation of returnees, who will not be punished or discriminated against. The Mozambican government has agreed to make land available for cultivation and settlement. Separate tripartite agreements are also being negotiated between the governments of each of the asylum countries, Mozambique and UNHCR.

The pre-departure phase of the plan has also included practical measures such as the registration of those wishing to return, vaccination and health screening programmes and the provision of information to refugees about the situation in Mozambique. As the estimated two million mines scattered around the country pose a particular danger to returnees, great emphasis has been placed on the development of an effective mine awareness campaign. In Mozambique itself, surveys are being undertaken in districts likely

to receive large numbers of returnees, and steps have been taken to repair roads, rehabilitate water supplies and health facilities and stockpile a limited quantity of relief supplies.

To organize transportation for 1.3 million people would be a mammoth and indeed unnecessary task. In planning the "movement phase" of the operation, emphasis was placed on assisting refugees to organize their own return. UNHCR will only provide transport for refugees in areas where commercial transport is unavailable, as well as for vulnerable groups including invalids, unaccompanied minors, the elderly and single parents with dependent children.

The success of this repatriation, like many others, will depend on the creation of sufficiently stable conditions for the refugees to re-establish themselves in their home country. In the "reintegration phase" of the plan, therefore, the emphasis is on food production, the restoration of basic water supplies, health care, education, the repair of basic infrastructure such as roads and bridges and the promotion of income-generating activities.

Quick Impact Projects (QUIPs) are expected to play a key role. Along the lines of those pioneered in Central America and Cambodia (see Box 6.4), the Mozambican QUIPs are being designed to create basic infrastructure capable of absorbing the returning refugees, and to help them become self-sufficient. The projects are also intended to benefit other groups in returnee areas, such as internally displaced people and demobilized soldiers and their families.

The overall rehabilitation of returnee areas will require far more than immediate reintegration assistance for returning refugees. Further political initiatives are needed to consolidate the peace process; and the destruction caused by the years of war will only be remedied by substantial development aid. The repatriation plan underlines the need to dovetail reintegration assistance provided by UNHCR with United Nations peace-building efforts, as well as with long-term reconstruction and development programmes by agencies such as UNDP, FAO and the World Bank. Without a concerted and sustained effort by the international community to provide the urgent and comprehensive aid needed by Mozambique, the fragile process of reconciliation could easily be jeopardized and with it the resolution of one of Africa's largest and longest-standing refugee problems.

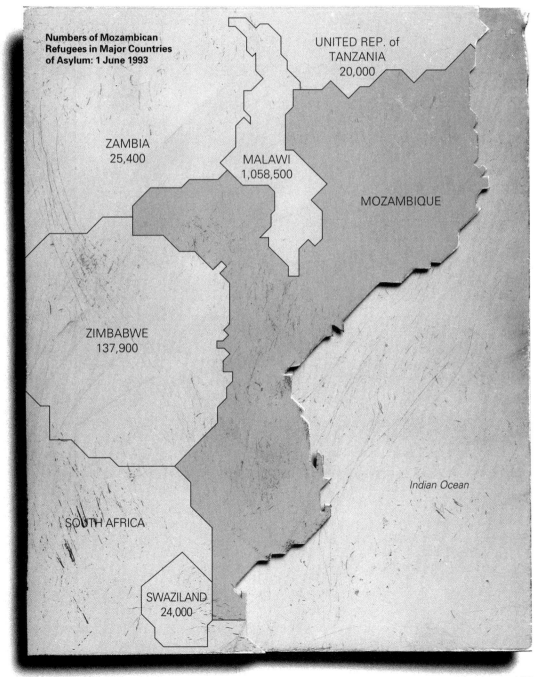

Numbers of Mozambican Refugees in Major Countries of Asylum: 1 June 1993

UNITED REP. of TANZANIA
20,000

ZAMBIA
25,400

MALAWI
1,058,500

MOZAMBIQUE

ZIMBABWE
137,900

SOUTH AFRICA

Indian Ocean

SWAZILAND
24,000

UNHCR. Their duty to protect does not allow them to encourage repatriation into situations they consider unsafe; but they also have a responsibility to assist refugees who decide to exercise their right to return to their own country.

If UNHCR believes repatriation to be premature, it usually attempts to tread the fine line between facilitating return and actively encouraging or promoting it. It will not advise people to go back – it may advise them not to – but it will, nonetheless, give repatriation assistance to those who decide they wish to do so. It will also go on trying to promote the conditions for a safe return and to negotiate guarantees for the protection of returnees, including access for international monitors.

"It is important to ensure that repatriation is truly voluntary"

This has been the pattern of the largest repatriation that has taken place in recent years: the return to Afghanistan of refugees in Pakistan and the Islamic Republic of Iran. Despite continued fighting in the capital, Kabul, and other areas, Afghan refugees began to repatriate in increasing numbers following the fall of the Najibullah regime in April 1992. By the end of that year, well over 1.5 million people had gone back. The return movement has continued in 1993, though at a somewhat slower rate. By June 1993, a total of around 1.7 million Afghans had returned home with UNHCR assistance.

The divisions created by 15 years of war persist, and are not likely to disappear in the immediate future. A fragmented ethnic composition has been compounded by external intervention and various conflicting ideologies which threaten to tear the country apart. The major ethnic groups (Pushtun, Uzbek, Tajik, Baluch, Hazara and Turkmen) as well as the two major religious groups, Sunni and Shi'ite, are all represented in neighbouring countries and maintain close ties

across borders.

The complex political and humanitarian crisis has been accompanied by economic devastation. Afghanistan was one of the world's least developed countries even before it plunged into war in 1979. Today, the country's infrastructure has been destroyed, food is scarce, health care overburdened and water and sanitation services are severely degraded. On top of all this, the countryside is infested with mines (see Box 6.3). Nonetheless, a total of 1.3 million people are expected to return to Afghanistan during 1993, taking the overall number to almost three million.

As the return movement got under way, UNHCR allowed refugees leaving camps in Pakistan to trade in their ration cards for 300 kilograms of wheat and $130 in cash. In the ensuing months, it established a presence within Afghanistan to monitor the safety of the returnees, help reconstruct destroyed houses and irrigation systems and provide humanitarian assistance during the harsh winter of 1992-93. Because of the precarious conditions, however, repatriation continued to be facilitated rather than formally encouraged.

Some spontaneous returns result from decisions by individuals or single family groups to go back. Others are planned and orchestrated by the refugees collectively, often through their own leaders, as happened in the case of the Afghans. One protection concern in these circumstances is to ensure that repatriation is truly voluntary for all of those involved.

A common image of refugees is one of passivity and dependence. Spontaneous repatriation shows the refugee in a different light – as a decision-maker, willing to undergo risks to take control of his or her own fate. People decide to go home for a variety of reasons: because they are confident that circumstances have changed, because they are afraid of missing the chance to reclaim property or rights of usage or because the conditions of exile have become too difficult or dangerous. Repatriation may also be motivated by a desire to take part in the reconstruction and reconciliation process at home.

De-mining Afghanistan

In Afghanistan – as in many other parts of the world, such as Angola, Cambodia and Mozambique – refugees are returning to a devastated country littered with land mines. It is thought that about two million Afghans are disabled, an average of one person in every family. Twenty per cent of them are believed to have been victims of mines or other explosive devices. Ordinary Afghans going about their daily lives in the affected areas are in constant danger.

No one knows how many mines there are. According to widely varying estimates, between two and ten million mines of different types have been scattered individually, dropped at random from the air or sown in concentrated minefields. The vast majority have not been recorded nor are they laid in predictable patterns. They are virtually ubiquitous in places which have seen heavy fighting, lying in deadly ambush in fields, villages, roads, tracks, creeks and canals.

De-mining is a slow, laborious and costly process. Most mine-clearance is carried out manually. UNOCHA, the UN agency responsible for co-ordinating humanitarian assistance to Afghanistan, employs nearly 2,000 Afghans who have been trained by international experts in de-mining. With the present capacity, about 10 square kilometres can be cleared per year. By early 1993, more than 60,000 explosive devices had been removed from 25 square kilometres of land. UNOCHA estimates that priority areas (such as roads, canals and agricultural land) covering a total of about 60 square kilometres could be cleared within three to five years if adequate financial resources are made available.

The dangers involved in de-mining are acute. In 1992, nine Afghan and two international mine-clearers died from injuries after de-mining accidents, 16 had to undergo amputations, six were blinded and a further 43 suffered minor injuries.

Under the UNOCHA programme, refugees returning from Pakistan receive mine-awareness training before going home. Even so, the numbers of mine-related casualties treated in ICRC clinics in Kabul and the border area of Pakistan have increased dramatically since April 1992. Many other victims die before reaching a clinic.

In order to limit the number of casualties, UNOCHA was planning to provide mine-awareness training for 330,000 Afghans in 1993, particularly in provinces expecting large numbers of returnees. There is clearly an urgent need for the training of refugees repatriating from Pakistan to be reinforced, and for it to be introduced for those returning from the Islamic Republic of Iran. Otherwise people will continue to be maimed and killed needlessly, perhaps for many years to come.

Repatriation emergencies

A special category of repatriation concerns movements caused by people fleeing from danger in their countries of asylum. Hundreds of thousands of refugees have returned to Angola, Ethiopia, Liberia and Sudan, among other countries, because fighting broke out in the place where they had sought refuge. Repatriation under emergency conditions is at the extreme end of the spectrum of unplanned and unorganized movements. As such, it produces acute humanitarian problems.

Some 500,000 Ethiopian refugees in Somalia were forced back into eastern Ethiopia when armed conflict in Somalia reached a climax in 1991. To begin with, many of the returning refugees, rather than proceed to their home villages, remained in crowded, dangerous border camps where the food supply was somewhat more reliable. However assistance to the returnees was severely hampered by the remoteness, extreme poverty and insecurity of the region, and the initial mortality rate was high.

Returnees were eventually dispersed to their home villages with the aid of travel grants provided by UNHCR. Nevertheless, conditions in areas affected by large concentrations of returnees, refugees and displaced people remained precarious as a result of a deadly combination of drought, famine and inter-clan fighting. In the face of such generalized deprivation, the government of Ethiopia, UNHCR and other UN agencies agreed to pool their resources to assist all those in need, regardless of whether they were local or displaced people. The programme carried out under this "cross-mandate approach" involves relief, rehabilitation and small-scale development aid, as well as repatriation assistance.

"Most refugees go back to areas devastated by war"

Repatriation emergencies are sometimes provoked more directly, by attacks on refugee camps. When refugee camps housing Sudanese in western Ethiopia were engulfed by fighting in May 1991, some 380,000 refugees fled back to the border area and into Sudan itself. UNHCR had no access to the war zone into which they repatriated, and was unable to offer protection directly, despite recognizing a responsibility for people compelled to return to their home countries.

From repatriation to reintegration: the "development gap"

Most refugees go back to areas that are among the least developed in the world, and have been devastated by war. Habitability and productive capacity have been reduced; social and communal bonds unravelled. The potential scale of the problem is immense. Afghanistan, Angola, Burundi, Cambodia, Chad, Eritrea, Ethiopia, the Lao People's Democratic Republic, Mozambique, Rwanda, Somalia and Western Sahara have all either already experienced sizeable returns or are expected to do so soon. During recent months many thousands have returned without assistance, and millions more may do so over the next few years.

There is a yawning gap between the repatriation assistance made available to returning refugees and the enormous development needs of the areas to which they return. The durability of voluntary repatriation as a solution for refugees may hinge on an effective response to these longer-term requirements.

Unless return is accompanied by development programmes that address people's immediate needs as well as longer-term goals, it may undermine rather than reinforce the prospects for reconciliation and recovery. The lengthy timetables and planning processes typical of traditional development projects respond neither to the returnees' own particular need for early self-sufficiency, nor to the wider requirements of the community into which they must reintegrate. An effort is being made to bridge this gap through development projects that can be formulated and implemented quickly, and that benefit the community as a whole.

In the past, repatriating refugees were provided with seeds, tools, a modest amount of food and equipment or perhaps a small cash grant. Occasionally, short-term projects were established in the areas to which they were returning to strengthen infrastructure and provide both the refugees and the local population with new economic opportunities. But in many cases, repatriation assistance stopped at the border.

It is now more widely recognized that the traditional approach is no longer adequate. It is not simply that individual returnees may need more assistance in order to survive or that, if they fail to get it, they may again head for the border. Instead, there is a growing realization that extreme deprivation and competition for resources can re-ignite conflict and undermine the achievements of a fragile peace. Some governments are reluctant to encourage their citizens to return because they know how difficult it will be to feed and shelter them once they are back. If repatriation is not linked to the rehabilitation of productive capacity, a vicious circle of renewed disintegration and displacement is likely to emerge. The development gap, for this reason, represents a problem of protection as well as assistance.

One factor that contributes to the development gap is the poor fit between the mandates of the institutions that deal with refugees and those responsible for promoting development. Like most governmental and non-governmental organizations that deal with refugees, UNHCR

Guatemalans returning from Mexico.
Huehuetenango, Guatemala, February 1989.

UNHCR/Liba Taylor

is not a development agency. And yet development institutions have no mandate to give priority to areas that are having to absorb large numbers of returning refugees. Caught in this gap, the needs of returnees are often overlooked or addressed inadequately. Greater attention is being paid to this problem, but a more systematic linkage between repatriation assistance and development aid is needed to help returnees and their communities cope with the difficult and often prolonged period of transition that follows mass repatriation.

"It makes sense for humanitarian agencies and development institutions to work together"

Refugees often return to areas inhabited by internally displaced people, as well as by other residents who never moved but were nonetheless affected by the same factors that drove away the refugees. Demobilized soldiers and their families also sometimes require help to re-establish their homes and livelihoods. The mixture of people in need of assistance provides a strong argument for community-based programmes. Projects that focus on individuals or even single categories of people can be divisive, rendering the reconciliation process even more complex.

Returning refugees are often resented by people who stayed behind. Land, buildings or implements abandoned by those that flee may have been taken over by others, posing problems when returning refugees want to reclaim them. In such circumstances, assistance programmes that single out returnees can very easily aggravate simmering resentments, whereas aid that benefits an entire community may subdue potential conflicts.

The approach to returnee assistance developed by UNHCR in Nicaragua, known as the Quick Impact Project (QUIP) initiative, is now widely used as a model for reintegration programmes in countries that have been devastated by years of armed conflict and economic decline (see Box 6.4). QUIPs are small projects which attempt to address specific, often urgent, requirements affecting entire communities. They can be completed within a few months at relatively low cost (about $30,000 on average). Having demonstrated their value in Central America, QUIPs are now being implemented in other settings, including Somalia and Cambodia.

It makes sense for humanitarian agencies and development institutions to work together to bridge the gap between short-term repatriation assistance and long-term development. Each has an interest in assuring that the momentum of development is not lost in the communities to which refugees return. On their own, QUIPs are limited and local in their effect. They cannot rebuild shattered economies, but they can play a useful role as part of a larger plan that aims to do so. They can help to meet urgent needs and promote social reconciliation during the delicate period before the benefits of longer-term development become apparent.

Progress has been made, in conjunction with UNDP and other agencies, in laying the foundation of a more comprehensive approach to repatriation. Nevertheless, the roles and responsibilities of agencies involved at various stages of the continuum that stretches from relief to development still require further clarification. Co-operative efforts undertaken within the framework established at the May 1989 International Conference on Central American Refugees, usually known as CIREFCA (see Box 6.5), and plans for the reintegration of returnees in Cambodia and Afghanistan are encouraging examples of increased inter-agency co-operation in the process of reintegration. The coming years will present many more such challenges. They will be an important test of the capacity of the UN system to provide genuine and lasting solutions for refugees.

Obstacles to repatriation

The most acute obstacle to repatriation is obvious: continuing violence and persecution. In the

Box 6.4
Quick Impact Projects

Traditionally, returning refugees were provided with a modest package of food and relief items, sometimes dismissively referred to as "a cooking pot and a handshake". Occasionally, short-term projects were implemented in returnee areas, but often returnees and the resident population were left largely to fend for themselves.

The assistance programme developed by UNHCR, known as the Quick Impact Project (QUIP) initiative, was first applied in Nicaragua. QUIPs are simple, small-scale projects located in areas where returnees and displaced people are concentrated. They can be implemented rapidly and at low cost, making maximum use of local resources. Wherever possible, QUIPs are based on proposals drawn up by the communities concerned, and actively involve the returnees themselves and other local residents.

Although QUIPs aim to address the immediate reintegration needs of returnees, they also aim to be sustainable. By filling the gap which has traditionally existed between returnee relief operations and longer-term reconstruction efforts, QUIPS have become known as a "bridge to development".

There is no such thing as a typical QUIP. In Nicaragua, UNHCR's two-year $12 million reintegration programme has been used for a wide variety of purposes: repairing and reconstructing facilities such as schools, health centres, roads and bridges; boosting the agricultural sector through the provision of livestock, seeds, processing machinery and transport; and establishing co-operatives and small businesses, in both rural and urban areas. A number of QUIPs were tailored to meet the specific needs of women and other special groups.

On the Tuapi river in north-eastern Nicaragua, a bridge has been constructed with UNHCR funding. Under the management of a local NGO, members of the community provided the labour required to erect the bridge, and they now maintain it on a voluntary basis. Costing just $16,000 to complete, the bridge saves local farmers and traders a 20-kilometre walk to the next river crossing, thereby stimulating agricultural production and boosting the local economy.

In some areas of Nicaragua, QUIPs have been planned and implemented in clusters, in order to maximize their effect. In the Rio Coco region for example, rice production has been constrained by the inability of farmers to transport, process and market their harvest. QUIPs have been used to open up a disused jungle path, provide local communities with oxen, boats, trucks and threshing machinery and establish training courses designed to help the beneficiaries maintain and manage these resources.

According to a recent evaluation of the programme, the 300 QUIPs implemented in Nicaragua have produced valuable results. As well as expanding economic production and providing amenities that the government was unable to finance, the QUIPs have encouraged returnees, displaced people and the resident population to work together, promoting reconciliation in divided communities At the same time the projects have strengthened the capacity of local organizations and enterprises, and have made it easier for returnees to make a living in rural areas instead of drifting into the towns in search of work.

While the Nicaraguan QUIPs have proved effective, it may not be easy to replicate this type of programme elsewhere. The repatriation to Nicaragua involved only 70,000 refugees – a small number compared to countries such as Afghanistan and Mozambique, where the numbers will run into millions. The Nicaraguan repatriation followed a definitive peace settlement and change of government, and was organized by UNHCR. In other countries, repatriation is likely to take place in less stable circumstances. Although Nicaragua has been severely affected by a decade of war, the country remains more developed, both in institutional and economic terms, than most of the other states where large-scale repatriations are anticipated. Moreover, the commitment of aid donors to the Nicaraguan peace process has provided much greater financial support than may be available in other parts of the world.

Despite these potential limitations, QUIPs provide an important link between the returnee relief operations implemented by UNHCR and the longer-term reconstruction efforts of national governments and development agencies. QUIPs cannot, by themselves, rebuild countries and economies seriously damaged by long periods of armed conflict. They can, however, become an important component of a broader rehabilitation strategy.

former Yugoslavia and Liberia, to name only two examples, tensions have yet to subside to anything approaching a level that would permit the serious consideration of return. Outbreaks of fighting disrupted planned repatriations to Angola and Somalia, while the threat of renewed hostilities has raised questions about the wisdom or durability of others. Continuing violence is a major concern in South Africa, where returnees have been arrested and detained, often for the same reasons that caused them to flee in the first place, despite the amnesty agreed for the repatriation. In June 1992, UNHCR made a strongly worded protest to the South African government, expressing its concern at excessive use of police power, instances of brutality and torture and, above all, at the reported deaths of 15 returnees.

"There may be more mines in Cambodia than there are Cambodians"

Formal repatriation operations sometimes stall because of failure to arrive at an agreement with the refugees' home government. In June 1993, an estimated half-million Eritrean refugees were still marooned in Sudan, many months after the EPLF victory brought *de facto* independence, owing to lack of agreement between the government of Eritrea and the international community over the level of external financial support for the repatriation effort. Some 50,000 people have returned spontaneously without international assistance, but many others who are ready and willing to repatriate have been unable to do so. The government of Rwanda refused to accept the return of refugees from Uganda, citing the acute shortage of land in the densely populated country – a stance that led to an armed attack by refugee forces in October 1990. Hundreds of thousands more people were displaced by the fighting that followed. Concern on the part of the Ethiopian government to ensure that adequate resources were made available for the reintegration of

returnees also delayed organized repatriation of Tigrayan refugees from the Sudan. Following the conclusion of a Tripartite Agreement between UNHCR and the governments of Ethiopia and Sudan, UNHCR launched a $10 million funding appeal and in June 1993 12,000 of the remaining 50,000 Tigrayan refugees returned home.

Land mines are a major obstacle to repatriation in a number of areas where armed conflict has raged. Cambodia and Afghanistan already have the world's highest proportions of people disabled by loss of limbs. It is estimated that there are between four and ten million mines in Cambodia. If the higher estimate is correct, there are more mines than Cambodians. The presence of mines in northern Somalia has hindered the return of refugees from Ethiopia. Similar problems cloud the prospects for repatriation to Mozambique. Modern plastic anti-personnel mines are difficult to detect and delicate to handle. Clearance is a lengthy and highly dangerous job that tends to be performed on an *ad hoc* basis, as no single international organization has a mandate or the capacity to carry it out systematically on a global scale.

Conflicts over the ownership of land are common after people return home. When 5,000 internally displaced people moved back from the capital of Tajikistan to their homes in the south of the country their path was blocked by local people, apparently because of disputes over land ownership and rights to water. Where exile has been prolonged, customary rights of usage may translate into *de facto* ownership. In other situations, land belonging to people affiliated with rebel movements is allocated to government supporters. Mechanisms for resolving land disputes need to be established in a manner that gains the trust of all parties, as they are a necessary part of the process of reconciliation and reintegration.

Monitoring the safety of returnees

Protecting refugees during the process of repatriation and reintegration involves, first and foremost, overseeing the guarantees or assurances that have made return feasible. Arrangements that permit international monitoring of the safety of returnees are an integral part of most formal repatriation agreements. Sometimes they are even negotiated during or after spontaneous repatriation movements.

Monitoring the safety of returnees is part of the repatriation component of the UN Transitional Authority in Cambodia (UNTAC). Similarly, in Afghanistan, UNHCR officials have maintained a presence along major routes of return, at border crossings and in returnees' communities to keep an eye on safety and security. Monitoring is also taking place in Guatemala and El Salvador. Under the terms of an accord with the government of Guatemala, UNHCR is providing information and training about protection issues to returnees, NGOs, the government and the military. It is also allowed to obtain information about any Guatemalan refugee who is detained after returning home.

A crucial, if unglamorous, element of protection for returnees is documentation. Becoming a refugee often results in the effective loss of a legal identity in the home country. From the time of the League of Nations onwards, protecting refugees has meant supplying them with identity papers and travel documents when necessary, and negotiating the right to full national registration and recognition upon repatriation. Measures of this sort have been a particularly important aspect of the protection of returnees in Central American countries. Without this form of protection, the returnee may remain a virtual non-person, or become the target of discrimination or retaliation.

Arrangements for monitoring and protecting the safety of returning refugees is one of the most important advantages of international involvement in planning repatriation. Transitional in nature, such arrangements – if successful – should lead to their own demise. In the interval between repatriation and full reintegration, however, they can make a vital contribution to rebuilding both the confidence and the safety of returnees.

Box 6.5

Central America at the Crossroads

Central America has seen a marked reduction in conflict and tension over the past few years. From being a virtual synonym for violence and instability, it has become something of a model for future efforts by the international community to consolidate peace, development and democracy by means of a comprehensive regional approach. In 1989, it was estimated that as many as two million people had been uprooted over the previous decade, of whom 165,000 were recognized as refugees.

By June 1993, more than half of these had returned home, while local integration schemes were well under way for the approximately 40,000 Nicaraguan and Salvadorian refugees remaining outside their home countries. The only significant refugee population in the region for whom a firm solution has still to be found is the 43,000 Guatemalans in Mexico.

Throughout most of the 1980s, Nicaragua, El Salvador and Guatemala were caught in a web of guerrilla warfare, sweeping counter-insurgency operations, widespread political and social unrest and sharp economic decline. Individual and collective persecution was rife. Atrocities and massacres took place in Guatemala and El Salvador. In Nicaragua, indigenous peoples were forcibly relocated. By the mid-1980s, with the stakes raised by superpower involvement, the hostilities in Central America were threatening to engulf the entire region.

While some 80 per cent of those fleeing Central American countries during this period headed north to the United States, large numbers of impoverished refugees from rural areas fled across the nearest border. Salvadorians sought refuge in Belize, Costa Rica, Guatemala, Honduras and Mexico. While some Guatemalans also entered Belize, most crossed into Mexico. Indigenous Nicaraguans from the north flooded across the Rio Coco to Honduras, while those from the south of the country fled to Costa Rica.

One of the most remarkable aspects of the Central American crisis has been the way that humanitarian initiatives have helped stimulate political processes which have in turn led to a widespread, though by no means complete, restoration of peace and democracy. Another notable feature has been the decisive role the refugees themselves have played at both political and humanitarian levels.

Attempts to restore peace and stem the refugee flows started early, although several years passed before they began to make an impact. The critical problems of protection arising from the conduct of the wars led UNHCR to mount a

major campaign to promote awareness of refugee law and fundamental human rights. This resulted in the Cartagena Declaration of November 1984 which recommended that the refugee definition in Central America be broadened explicitly to include victims of conflict and of massive violations of human rights.

Intensified efforts by the Central American presidents to reach a peaceful, negotiated settlement culminated in the Esquipulas II Accords of August 1987. The peace plan included a range of principles and commitments which provided the foundation for future refugee-related diplomatic efforts, among them

the conviction that peace and development were inseparable and that there could be no lasting peace unless the plight of refugees and displaced people was resolved.

As the peace process gathered momentum, the impetus gradually changed from flight to repatriation, but people were often returning to fragile or dangerous circumstances. The decision of many Central American refugees to return home during continuing conflict, and at great physical risk, was an extremely complex phenomenon.

The conclusion of a 1987 agreement granting limited autonomy for indigenous peoples in Nicaragua resulted in the return of several

Fig. 6.A
Evolution of Assisted Refugee Caseloads in Central America, Mexico and Belize: 1979 – 1991

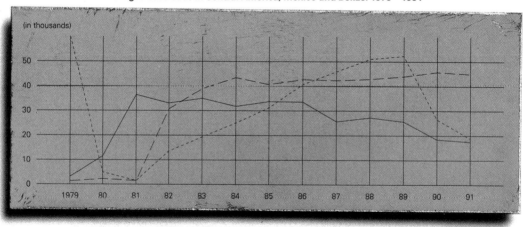

Salvadorians: (———)

1979: 3,000	1982: 33,166	1985: 34,330	1988: 27,068	1991: 16,979
1980: 12,000	1983: 35,256	1986: 33,913	1989: 25,798	
1981: 37,381	1984: 32,273	1987: 25,737	1990: 18,537	

Nicaraguans: (- - - - -)

1979: 60,000	1982: 13,900	1985: 31,813	1988: 51,358	1991: 18,995
1980: 5,000	1983: 19,402	1986: 40,710	1989: 52,890	
1981. 1,760	1984: 25,228	1987: 45,816	1990: 26,819	

Guatemalans: (— —)

1979: 1,000	1982: 30,600	1985: 40,656	1988: 42,831	1991: 45,007
1980: 2,000	1983: 39,071	1986: 42,732	1989: 44,047	
1981: 1,475	1984: 43,623	1987: 42,276	1990: 45,354	

thousand refugees from Honduras that year. During the same period, opposition forces in El Salvador initiated a policy of re-populating areas of conflict in order to broaden their base of popular support. Both internally displaced people and refugees from camps in Honduras became involved in this strategy. Despite the highly confrontational and controversial nature of their return, their stated objective, inspired by the regional peace agreement, was to "build peace".

As the United Nations launched an ambitious plan of economic and social development in support of the Esquipulas Accords, it became clear that greatly increased international assistance would be required to resolve the problem of uprooted populations. To this end, the International Conference on Central American Refugees (CIREFCA) was convened by the UN Secretary-General in May 1989 in Guatemala City.

Of the estimated two million people uprooted since 1979, only a fraction – some 150,000 – were benefiting from UNHCR protection and assistance. An additional 900,000 undocumented Central Americans were scattered throughout the region, living in permanent fear of expulsion. An even greater number were displaced inside their own countries without any form of international protection or assistance.

To respond to this challenge, the CIREFCA Conference adopted a "Concerted Plan of Action" with an initial time-frame of three years. The plan embodied a set of commitments based on fundamental principles of humanitarian and refugee law. It outlined specific strategies to achieve durable solutions, either through voluntary repatriation or local integration for all four categories of people displaced

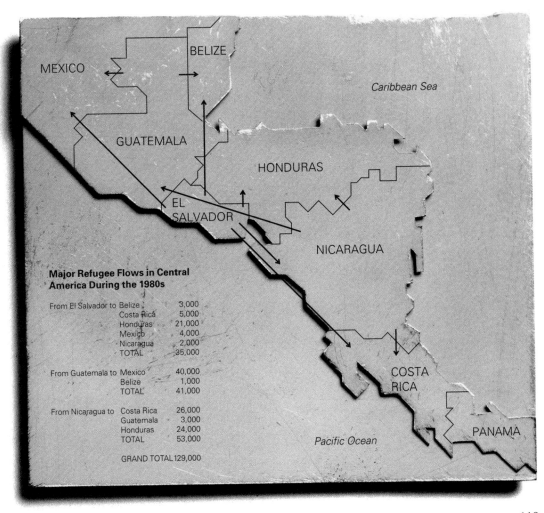

Major Refugee Flows in Central America During the 1980s

From El Salvador to	Belize	3,000
	Costa Rica	5,000
	Honduras	21,000
	Mexico	4,000
	Nicaragua	2,000
	TOTAL	35,000
From Guatemala to	Mexico	40,000
	Belize	1,000
	TOTAL	41,000
From Nicaragua to	Costa Rica	26,000
	Guatemala	3,000
	Honduras	24,000
	TOTAL	53,000
GRAND TOTAL		129,000

during the years of conflict: refugees, returnees, internally displaced and "externally displaced" (a category of people who were outside their countries but had not registered as refugees, and were therefore undocumented). UNHCR and UNDP were given a joint mandate to implement CIREFCA's decision to link humanitarian activities with broader development programmes.

At two international follow-up meetings of CIREFCA, in June 1990 and April 1992, the international community continued to give strong political and financial support for the process. By 31 January 1993, over $240 million had been allocated to CIREFCA projects in seven countries. The flexibility of the CIREFCA process was demonstrated as funding priorities were adjusted in the light of experience on the ground. At the 1992 meeting in San Salvador, the Plan of Action was extended for an additional two years, by which time it is hoped that the refugee crisis will have been largely resolved.

Since the first CIREFCA Conference in 1989, the situation of Central American refugees has changed considerably. The 1990 change of government in Nicaragua led to a mass repatriation of 70,000 Nicaraguan refugees and former combatants from Honduras and Costa Rica. Greater emphasis was placed on returnee programmes thereafter. The socio-economic devastation which faced the return-ing refugees spurred UNHCR to go beyond its traditionally limited returnee assistance "package" and launch an ambitious programme of Quick Impact Projects (QUIPs) in an attempt to turn the voluntary repatriation into a truly durable solution.

The repatriation of Nicaraguans and, later, of Salvadorians made it possible to close all the refugee camps in Costa Rica and Honduras by the end of 1991. Attempts to consolidate the local integration of those refugees not wishing to repatriate are progressing, especially in Belize and Costa Rica. Some 25,000 Nicaraguans, for example, will probably remain in Costa Rica where they are expected to achieve complete social, economic and legal integration with the help of an ambitious programme of CIREFCA projects and parallel legal measures that are being taken to regularize their status.

On 20 January 1993, the first mass repatriation of Guatemalan refugees – the largest refugee group remaining in Central America – took place after lengthy and sometimes heated negotiations between the Guatemalan government and refugee representatives. In a scenario remarkably similar to that surrounding the earlier Salvadorian repatriation from Honduras, 2,473 refugees seized the initiative and staged a mass return to a conflict zone, in spite of serious concerns about security and a lack of available land. If successful, their reintegration could pave the way for the return of the remaining 43,000 Guatemalan refugees in Mexico. The difficult task of ensuring safe conditions for the returnees has once again led to UNHCR involvement in monitoring protection and security within the country of origin.

The positive evolution of the refugee situation in Central America has taken place against the background of profound political changes, hastened by the end of the Cold-War era. Civilian governments are now in place throughout the region. In El Salvador, verification of compliance with the UN-sponsored peace agreement has done much to reinforce the peace process which, despite setbacks, has held firm. In Guatemala, peace negotiations between opposing sides are scheduled to resume, raising hopes that this 30-year internal conflict – the oldest in Latin America – may finally be resolved.

The major challenge now facing the international community is to consolidate the region's fragile peace. This will involve strengthening respect for fundamental human rights, and establishing effective development programmes to rebuild national economies as well as to provide basic services to areas devastated by war. As former UN Secretary-General Javier Pérez de Cuéllar said, in May 1989, "CIREFCA is not an end in itself but merely a milestone along the way to development, stability and peace in Central America".

Chapter seven

Prevention

Prevention – if it can be accomplished – is the most effective form of protection for people in danger of becoming refugees. As recent events have shown all too clearly, the international community must take earlier and more effective action if it is to prevent potential refugee-generating situations from deteriorating to the point where flight becomes the only option. The crises in the Horn of Africa, the former Yugoslavia, the Caucasus and elsewhere have followed a broadly similar pattern of evolution, albeit under very different circumstances: in each case, tensions arising from unresolved political, ethnic, religious or nationality disputes led to human rights abuses which became increasingly violent. Left unchecked, this process frequently develops into armed conflicts that force people to flee their homes, and often their countries, in search of safety. By then, it has proved too late to avert widespread suffering, and far more difficult to assist and protect people or to achieve lasting solutions.

The types of mass displacement that have occurred over the past decade or so cannot be handled solely by providing protection in countries of asylum. Of the three conventional forms of solution for refugees – local integration in the country of first asylum, resettlement in another country or voluntary repatriation – the first two are under severe pressure because of the sheer magnitude of the outflow. The developing countries that provide sanctuary for the vast majority of the world's refugees face economic, environmental and political problems which make it increasingly difficult for them to shelter masses of people for long periods. Wealthier countries also face political, social and economic pressures to adopt more restrictive policies toward asylum-seekers. Many traditional countries of resettlement are showing greater reluctance to accept new refugees. In some, there is an indiscriminate social backlash against all forms of immigration.

While very few people would argue with the truism that prevention is better than cure, in the refugee context prevention is a controversial issue. The concept itself is open to misinterpretation, and even to misuse. Preventive action can take a constructive form. It can be aimed at protecting potential victims, forestalling an increase in the numbers of those already affected and promoting solutions to their problems before they are forced to flee. Less positively, it can simply involve throwing up barriers to stop victims of persecution and violence from entering a country. Constructive prevention aims to reduce or remove the conditions that cause people to flee, while the negative version – which should more properly be called obstruction – makes escape from persecution and danger more difficult, or impossible.

"The cost of failure to take preventive action can be very high"

Unfortunately, obstructive prevention does take place, in a number of different forms. These range from the forcible turning back of refugees at frontiers, to interdiction on the high seas followed by direct return, to bureaucratic requirements for exacting documentation in advance of entry. Milder forms of obstructive prevention go under the name of deterrence, a tactic that erects barriers to all immigrants and imposes harsh conditions upon reception, on the questionable assumption that economically motivated migrants will be discouraged while refugees will not. In reality, practices that raise barriers for one group raise them for all.

Prevention of refugee flows can be initiated long before, immediately before, or at various stages during the development of a crisis. Measures to prevent the recurrence of a crisis are, moreover, a crucial element in implementing enduring solutions.

At the most general level, prevention is – or should be – directed at root causes, and goes far beyond the scope of humanitarian concerns alone. Displacement is the symptom of a host of social ailments. Preventing the accumulation of social and economic strains that produce refugee-generating conflict and persecution is a many-faceted undertaking. It involves promotion of human rights, economic development, conflict resolution, the establishment of accountable political institutions, environmental protection and so forth. It encompasses, in other words, virtually the whole of the human agenda, with particular emphasis on the responsibilities of states to care for all their people without discrimination. At this level, successes in prevention are impossible to measure while failures to prevent the occurrence or recurrence of refugee-producing crises are all too easy to quantify.

Far-sighted, all-embracing prevention has rarely been attempted, and generally only on a remedial basis in order to prevent the recurrence of major disaster. Perhaps the most spectacular examples are the post-World War II reconstruction of West Germany and Japan, designed to avoid repeating the mistakes made in the aftermath of World War I, and the Marshall Plan for Western European recovery. Of a lesser magnitude, but still important, are current programmes to consolidate the peace-making processes in Cambodia and Central America.

Rather than addressing root causes well before people are obliged to flee, most preventive efforts focus on immediate causes, when flight is imminent or has already started. Typically, they involve attempts to repair relations between people and their government before it is too late and to provide supplementary or substitute protection until this can be accomplished. In this respect, prevention is closely linked to the promotion of solutions. Efforts to stabilize internal population movements and to provide protection and humanitarian relief for internally displaced and other civilian victims within their home country are, in many instances, inseparable from measures to foster conditions conducive to the voluntary return of those who have already left. Finally, prevention involves helping states set up effective institutions, laws and procedures that enshrine the principles of national protection and guarantee the rights of minorities. The cost of failure to take preventive action can be very high, as illustrated by the situation of the Kurds

Box 7.1
The Former Soviet Union: A Prevention Test Case

The end of the Cold War and the dissolution of the former Eastern Bloc have opened up a Pandora's box of ethnic and regional tensions. In parts of the former Soviet Union, minority groups have either been expelled or have fled discrimination and conflict. Some 25 million Russians live outside the Russian Federation in the independent republics, while 72 million people live beyond the boundaries of the republics of their ethnic origin.[26] The 1989 census reported 128 ethnic groups in the former Soviet Union, 22 of which consist of more than one million people (see Box 7.2). Just before the Soviet Union was dissolved, a Moscow periodical reported 76 clearly defined territorial disputes involving ethnic groups.[27]

Over the last three years, major conflicts in Azerbaijan, Georgia, Moldova and Tajikistan have produced more than a million refugees. The conflict over Nagorno-Karabakh, a region inside Azerbaijan populated mainly by Armenians, has caused the largest haemorrhage of refugees in the former USSR. By June 1993, almost 200,000 Azeris had fled from Armenia to Azerbaijan, while some 300,000 Armenians had escaped in the opposite direction. Within Azerbaijan, a further 300,000 people had been uprooted. In neighbouring Georgia, secessionist struggles in Abkhazia and Ossetia have caused numerous civilian casualties and large-scale population displacement. Elsewhere, the tensions in Moldova between ethnic Romanians and Slavs have caused extensive population movements, while in Central Asia, a power struggle in Tajikistan has led to massive displacement (see Box 7.5).

Tensions continue to rise elsewhere as nationalism in all of the 15 newly independent republics encourages secessionist tendencies and widespread discrimination against minorities. In the Baltic States, for example, new laws threaten more than a million ethnic Russians with statelessness. Similar problems are occurring elsewhere as new states adopt legislation that often fails to provide safeguards for minority rights. Within the Russian Federation, separatist sentiment in some of its 21 "Autonomous Republics", have raised fears that the process of fission may not yet be over. If ethnic conflict spreads throughout the former Soviet Union, the resulting population movements could be immense.

There is therefore an obvious need to pre-empt forced population movements by tackling their causes or, failing that, to contain and manage them. As many instances of mass displacement are caused by problems involving minorities, these must be a key focus of preventive measures. Advice on drafting laws and institutions based on respect for human rights, backed up with effective human rights monitoring, is one field in which international assistance may make a difference. Constitutional guarantees for minority rights and non-discriminatory nationality laws, in particular, need to be developed. Where tensions threaten to degenerate into violence, programmes are needed to encourage coexistence among diverse groups. Republics where fighting has already erupted may require help in setting up effective institutions for negotiation and conflict resolution. Such republics may also welcome assistance to increase their capacity to respond to refugees' needs and other problems of displacement, to prevent these from spreading and causing further destabilization.

The absence of appropriate national legislation has been a handicap in tackling problems of displacement, as has the fact that, until recently, none of the republics of the former USSR had ratified the 1951 Convention relating to the Status of Refugees or its 1967 Protocol.[28] In late 1991, therefore, UNHCR began a programme of institution building and training, covering topics such as refugee law, human rights, immigration, nationality and statelessness.

As has been so dramatically demonstrated in the former Yugoslavia, prevention, mediation and conflict resolution cannot succeed without the political will of the parties directly involved. Preventing escalation of conflict and displacement in the former Soviet Union will require not only a more effective response from the international community as a whole, but also the willingness of the governments and people concerned to guarantee the rights of minorities and to commit themselves to conflict resolution. Their readiness to accept and indeed welcome assistance in building legal structures and political institutions to achieve these ends is grounds for some encouragement.

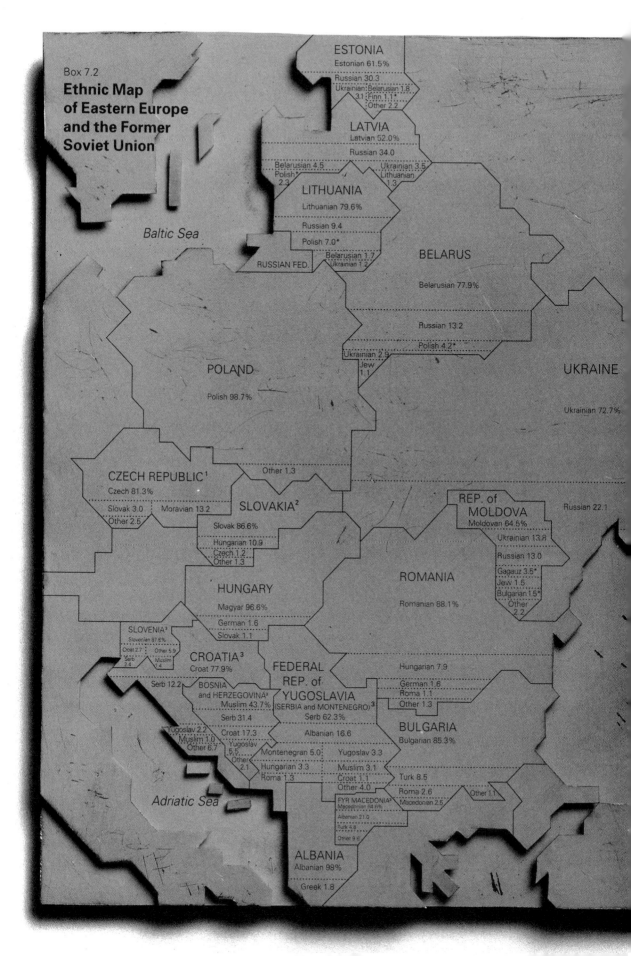

Box 7.2

**Ethnic Map
of Eastern Europe
and the Former
Soviet Union**

Baltic Sea

ESTONIA
Estonian 61.5%
Russian 30.3
Ukrainian 3.1 Belarusian 1.8
Finn 1.1*
Other 2.2

LATVIA
Latvian 52.0%
Russian 34.0
Belarusian 4.5 Ukrainian 3.5
Polish 2.3 Lithuanian 1.3

LITHUANIA
Lithuanian 79.6%
Russian 9.4
Polish 7.0*

RUSSIAN FED.
Belarusian 1.7
Ukrainian 1.2

BELARUS
Belarusian 77.9%
Russian 13.2
Polish 4.2*

POLAND
Polish 98.7%
Ukrainian 2.9
Jew 1.1

UKRAINE
Ukrainian 72.7%
Russian 22.1

CZECH REPUBLIC [1]
Czech 81.3%
Slovak 3.0 Moravian 13.2
Other 2.5

Other 1.3

SLOVAKIA [2]
Slovak 86.6%
Hungarian 10.9
Czech 1.2
Other 1.3

REP. of MOLDOVA
Moldovan 64.5%
Ukrainian 13.8
Russian 13.0
Gagauz 3.5*
Jew 1.5
Bulgarian 1.5*
Other 2.2

HUNGARY
Magyar 96.6%
German 1.6
Slovak 1.1

ROMANIA
Romanian 88.1%

SLOVENIA [3]
Slovenian 87.6%
Croat 2.7 Other 5.9
Serb 2.4 Muslim 1.4

CROATIA [3]
Croat 77.9%
Serb 12.2

Hungarian 7.9
German 1.6
Roma 1.1
Other 1.3

**BOSNIA
and HERZEGOVINA** [3]
Muslim 43.7%
Serb 31.4
Croat 17.3
Yugoslav 2.2
Muslim 1.0
Other 6.7

**FEDERAL
REP. of
YUGOSLAVIA**
(SERBIA and MONTENEGRO) [3]
Serb 62.3%
Albanian 16.6
Yugoslav 5.5
Montenegran 5.0 Yugoslav 3.3
Hungarian 3.3 Muslim 3.1
Roma 1.3 Croat 1.1
Other 2.1 Other 4.0

BULGARIA
Bulgarian 85.3%
Turk 8.5
Roma 2.6 Other 1.1
Macedonian 2.5

Adriatic Sea

FYR MACEDONIA
Macedonian 64.6%
Albanian 21.0
Turk 4.8
Other 9.6

ALBANIA
Albanian 98%
Greek 1.8

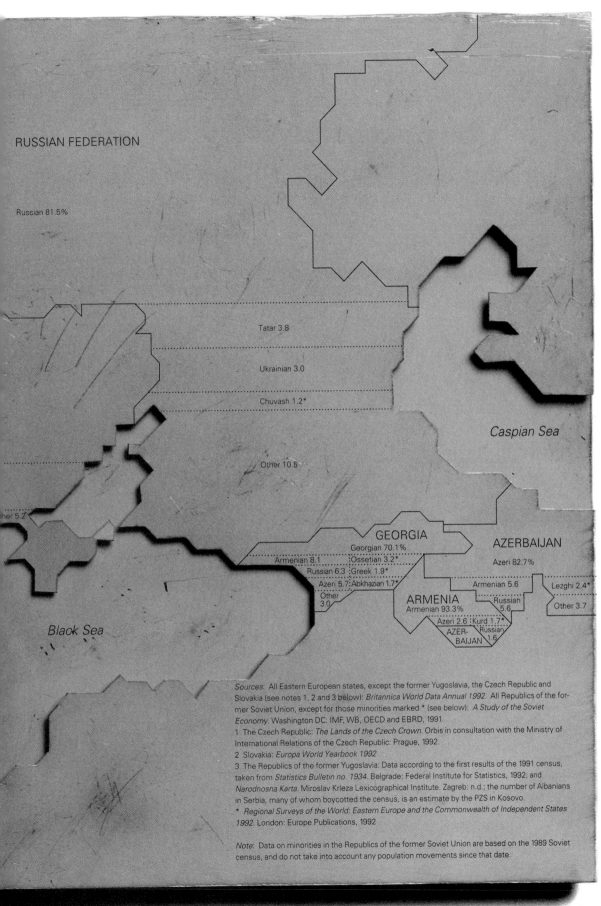

RUSSIAN FEDERATION

Russian 81.5%

Tatar 3.8

Ukrainian 3.0

Chuvash 1.2*

Other 10.5

Caspian Sea

...ner 5.2

GEORGIA
Georgian 70.1%
Armenian 8.1   Ossetian 3.2*
Russian 6.3   Greek 1.9*
Azeri 5.7   Abkhazian 1.7*
Other
3.0

AZERBAIJAN

Azeri 82.7%

Armenian 5.6   Lezghi 2.4*

Russian
5.6   Other 3.7

ARMENIA
Armenian 93.3%

Azeri 2.6   Kurd 1.7*
AZER-
BAIJAN   Russian
1.6

Black Sea

Sources: All Eastern European states, except the former Yugoslavia, the Czech Republic and Slovakia (see notes 1, 2 and 3 below): *Britannica World Data Annual 1992*. All Republics of the former Soviet Union, except for those minorities marked * (see below): *A Study of the Soviet Economy*. Washington DC: IMF, WB, OECD and EBRD, 1991.
1 The Czech Republic: *The Lands of the Czech Crown*. Orbis in consultation with the Ministry of International Relations of the Czech Republic: Prague, 1992.
2 Slovakia: *Europa World Yearbook 1992*
3 The Republics of the former Yugoslavia: Data according to the first results of the 1991 census, taken from *Statistics Bulletin no. 1934*. Belgrade: Federal Institute for Statistics, 1992; and *Narodnosna Karta*. Miroslav Krleza Lexicographical Institute. Zagreb: n.d.; the number of Albanians in Serbia, many of whom boycotted the census, is an estimate by the PZS in Kosovo.
* *Regional Surveys of the World: Eastern Europe and the Commonwealth of Independent States 1992*. London: Europe Publications, 1992

Note: Data on minorities in the Republics of the former Soviet Union are based on the 1989 Soviet census, and do not take into account any population movements since that date.

continued overleaf →

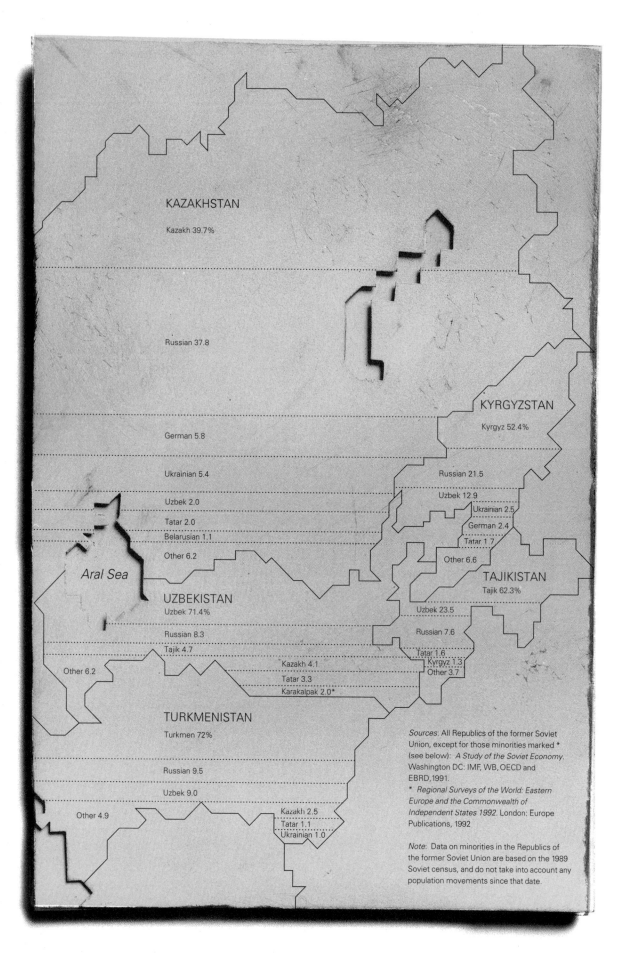

KAZAKHSTAN

Kazakh 39.7%

Russian 37.8

German 5.8

Ukrainian 5.4

Uzbek 2.0

Tatar 2.0

Belarusian 1.1

Other 6.2

Aral Sea

UZBEKISTAN

Uzbek 71.4%

Russian 8.3

Tajik 4.7

Other 6.2

Kazakh 4.1

Tatar 3.3

Karakalpak 2.0*

TURKMENISTAN

Turkmen 72%

Russian 9.5

Uzbek 9.0

Other 4.9

Kazakh 2.5

Tatar 1.1

Ukrainian 1.0

KYRGYZSTAN

Kyrgyz 52.4%

Russian 21.5

Uzbek 12.9

Ukrainian 2.5

German 2.4

Tatar 1.7

Other 6.6

TAJIKISTAN

Tajik 62.3%

Uzbek 23.5

Russian 7.6

Tatar 1.6

Kyrgyz 1.3

Other 3.7

Sources: All Republics of the former Soviet Union, except for those minorities marked * (see below): *A Study of the Soviet Economy*. Washington DC: IMF, WB, OECD and EBRD, 1991.
* *Regional Surveys of the World: Eastern Europe and the Commonwealth of Independent States 1992*. London: Europe Publications, 1992

Note: Data on minorities in the Republics of the former Soviet Union are based on the 1989 Soviet census, and do not take into account any population movements since that date.

and Shi'ites in Iraq and that of the Muslim population in Bosnia and Herzegovina.

Early warning, monitoring and reporting

The success of prevention depends on effective early warning of impending displacements. Early warning, in turn, relies on the systematic collection and analysis of observations from potential refugee-producing areas. Because the causes of forced population movements are so broad and complex, the task of monitoring is enormous. Even when it is founded on the best information, however, early warning is only useful if it sets in motion a policy response. It is not preventive in itself (although monitoring may be, to a limited extent). At most, it can provide a sound basis that may help policy-makers to make informed and timely decisions. But its value depends entirely on whether or not it leads to effective preventive action.

Among the danger signals that early warning can pick up are human rights violations, the manipulation of communal tensions in political campaigns and increased numbers of stateless people. Violations of rights, particularly if systematically directed at the members of one ethnic, religious or national group, are a direct cause of flight. They also contribute to the development of armed conflict, which is the single biggest cause of displacement. In many countries, the contest for political power is waged in divisive terms, with benefits distributed to supporters from a particular region, clan or ethnic group while rival groups are repressed. The formation of new states (and sometimes radical changes of regimes in existing states) may result in the withdrawal of nationality rights from substantial numbers of people resident in the territory of the new state. This is a particular concern for the millions of Russians who have long resided in former Soviet republics other than Russia (see Boxes 7.1 and 7.2)).

Early warning systems are intended to identify risk factors and bring them to the attention of the international community, prompting positive action to avert potential or emerging refugee flows. The reports of humanitarian and development workers, journalists, citizens' groups and scholars may all feed into such systems (see Box 7.3). However, the most reliable method for anticipating problems is through direct monitoring. Stationing observers in the field is costly, but it serves a valuable purpose in addition to early warning. Monitoring and reporting raise the potential stakes for those conducting a policy of displacement, or persisting in actions that cause it. Potential perpetrators of violence or persecution sometimes exercise restraint in the presence of external witnesses.

"Alarms raised by NGOs and others have all too frequently fallen on deaf ears"

To date, systematic monitoring and reporting arrangements have usually only been established when a crisis is already under way. They have rarely been employed before displacement occurs. For example, monitoring by the Conference on Security and Co-operation in Europe (CSCE) and NGOs of the situation affecting the ethnic Albanian majority in the Kosovo region of Yugoslavia has had mixed results. The region has already seen a substantial exodus of people, but armed conflict – which would generate a much greater one – has not yet broken out. Serious violations of human rights nonetheless continue to occur even in the presence of monitors and despite publicity and widespread international condemnation. Discriminatory laws have been progressively introduced since Kosovo lost its status as an autonomous republic in July 1990, while continuous and unprovoked violence against non-Serbs has become a feature of daily life. Almost all Albanian-language schools above the elementary level have been closed; employees are required to swear an oath in support of the Serb government (elected in a poll boycotted by the majority of the ethnic Albanian population), and there have been mass dismissals of ethnic Albanians from public sector jobs. Repeated warnings to the Serbian authorities not to initiate ethnic cleansing in Kosovo have done little to improve the human rights standing of the Albanians.[29]

In marked contrast to the situation in Kosovo, the Former Yugoslav Republic of Macedonia, for all its problems, illustrates the potential benefit of preventive initiatives that are underpinned by the policies of the government concerned. The republic is an ethnic mosaic – made more fragile by the effects of refugee inflows and the economic boycott of neighbouring Serbia – in

Box 7.3

The Advocacy Role of NGOs

Since time immemorial, men and women of good will have joined forces to campaign for humanitarian causes. The stand taken against slavery by the Quakers in the 17th century is an early example of the commitment of a group of people to improving the lot of humankind. Today, thousands of non-governmental organizations (NGOs) exist, both religious and secular, and more than 1,000 are involved directly or indirectly with refugees. Of these, some focus primarily on working with refugees in the field (see Chapter Five, Box 5.5), while others devote most of their energies to playing an equally vital advocacy role.

Modern NGOs seek to influence the policy decisions of the international community by sensitizing public opinion, the news media and politicians to important issues, by recommending actions and by exposing failures and abuses. Advocacy groups are especially active in matters concerning human rights, sustainable development and the environment – all areas that have a direct impact on population movements.

NGOs also make important contributions to the promotion, preparation, ratification and implementation of international legal norms. The Convention on the Rights of the Child and the Conventions adopted at the Earth Summit in Rio de Janeiro are recent examples of the creation of ground-breaking international legal structures that have been heavily influenced by NGO participation. NGOs played a similarly crucial role by helping in the preparation of the 1951 Refugee Convention. In fact, their contribution to international refugee protection can be traced right back to the beginning: it was a group of NGOs which, in 1921, pressed the newly-formed League of Nations to appoint the first High Commissioner for refugees.

It is by monitoring the implementation of laws and conventions, at both the national and international levels, that NGOs make perhaps their greatest impact. Through their presence on the ground, and with the help of extensive networks they have built up over the years, they are the primary, and often the only, independent witnesses of human rights violations. They are thus indispensable partners in any strategy that aims to pre-empt refugee flows, as their testimony can provide early warning of potential movements and activate human rights mechanisms before refugees are forced to flee and seek international protection. NGO staff also frequently take direct action to halt flagrant human rights abuses – often at considerable personal risk. Their public denunciations of such violations can put considerable pressure on governments to take corrective action.

Current vital refugee issues in which NGOs have adopted a combative stance include the battle against racism and xenophobia in industrialized countries, the accompanying erosion of the right to asylum, and the widening gap between the industrialized countries of the North and the impoverished lands of the South. They are also the most vociferous campaigners on behalf of minority rights everywhere.

Many NGOs can operate unencumbered by the political constraints which sometimes hamper the policies and actions of inter-governmental organizations and national governments. Taking as their constituency those who are least able to present their own cases, they are at once the strongest supporters and most vocal critics of international programmes to protect and assist refugees. Both their support and their criticism strengthen international protection.

which nearly 40 per cent of the population is made up of ethnic groups other than Macedonians. Despite the continuation of certain forms of discrimination against the Albanian minority, the government has welcomed international monitoring of human rights. The permanent presence of a CSCE mission has helped prevent the exacerbation of tensions and has also fostered positive developments. At another level, the preventive deployment of an UNPROFOR peace-keeping contingent to the Former Yugoslav Republic of Macedonia, in response to warning signals that the Yugoslav conflagration might easily spread there, appears to have reduced the likelihood of that happening.

Monitoring and reporting do not become redundant when refugees begin to move. They are still necessary to warn of further displacements, identify opportunities for mediation and build confidence for repatriation. Monitoring is often an important component of UN peace plans, for example in Cambodia and El Salvador (see Box 7.4). In situations such as these, monitors are needed to verify whether or not the parties to agreements honour their undertakings to respect human rights.

However, in many refugee-producing situations, clear and repeated early warnings of deteriorating human rights or dangers to the food supply have either been ignored by the international community or have elicited inadequate or sluggish responses. This was the case during the build-up to the Ethiopian famines of 1984-85 and 1989-90, the exodus from Iraq in 1991 and the upsurge of violence in Yugoslavia in 1990-91. It has also been evident in connection with existing and potential conflicts in the former Soviet Union today. Alarms raised by NGOs and others have all too frequently fallen on deaf ears. Although improved methods of collection, coordination and analysis of information may solve part of the problem, such measures will have little impact if the international community remains unable or unwilling to translate information into prompt and effective action on a scale commensurate with the problem concerned.

Preventive action

In the context of refugee flows, preventive action includes both political and humanitarian initiatives. Their combined aim is to avoid the breakdown of national protection, while meeting the material needs of people at risk of displacement, so that they do not have to cross borders in order to find food, medical care and other necessities. These two objectives are, of course, very closely related.

"Humanitarian assistance can play an important role in prevention"

At its most general, preventive action encompasses the entire range of contacts and negotiations that encourage respect for human rights, protection of minorities, observance of humanitarian law and good governance. When refugee flows seem imminent, however, the focus narrows to the specific conditions that put people at risk. At the diplomatic level, the means for addressing them include direct consultations with the governments concerned; appeals to the parties to the conflict (who may include insurgent groups or irregular forces) to observe humanitarian norms; and the convening of international conferences to focus concern on a particular problem. Personal visits by special envoys and high officials are often used to initiate direct contacts. For example, the UN Secretary-General has sent special envoys to Haiti and the former Yugoslavia in the recent past, as well as naming a special representative to report on the problems of internally displaced people.

Humanitarian assistance itself can play an important role in prevention. The negotiations involved in delivering assistance may create an opening for dialogue, drawing antagonists into discourse with external observers in a way that allows the international community to exercise some restraint on refugee-producing behaviour. In Central America and the Horn of Africa, assistance has helped to open up negotiations which, in time, moved on from initial questions of assistance to address the wider political disputes underlying the conflict. In some situations, however, the balance sheet is more mixed. There is concern, for example, that humanitarian assistance in the former Yugoslavia may, for all its compelling urgency, have masked the inability of the international community to solve the conflict and that it has, moreover, been manipulated by the warring parties for their own political ends.

"Legal systems need to be established or strengthened to provide better protection for minorities"

Direct intervention with governments is often the most productive form of prevention. Representatives of inter-governmental bodies can urge national authorities to discipline human rights abusers. For example, the political settlement in El Salvador made provision for a Truth Commission that investigated human rights abuses and extra-judicial killings perpetrated during the civil war. It recommended decommissioning some military officers and barring certain rebel leaders from running for public office. These proposals have been largely carried out despite reluctance from both parties. Similarly, international observers may intervene directly with local authorities to halt the maltreatment of particular groups – a form of action that may be particularly important in areas where local authorities such as mayors, village elders or tribal leaders have significant autonomy, or where central authority is contested, weakened or destroyed altogether.

International assistance to help states avoid creating conditions that lead to refugee flows constitutes another form of prevention. When a new government comes to power, or a new state is created, the lack of familiarity with the norms of both national and international humanitarian law may inadvertently contribute to a build-up of tensions among groups within the state. Training and technical assistance are needed for drafting human rights legislation and laws concerning nationality, statelessness, migration and so forth. Legal systems need to be established or strengthened to provide better protection for minorities, just and consistent settlement of grievances and a constitutional framework for the avoidance and resolution of conflicts. Legal training and advice offered at an early stage can pay handsome dividends later on. Such measures hold a prominent place in UNHCR's strategy in Eastern Europe and the republics of the former USSR. On their own, however, they are unlikely to have a noticeable impact. Much more comprehensive – and expensive – political and economic packages are required to address the immense problems facing, for example, various African countries and former Soviet republics.

The close interlinking of social, economic and political factors has given rise to debate on the role of development assistance as a means of resolving the problems that produce refugees. In so far as economic deprivation forms part of the concatenation of causes that produce flows of refugees and migrants, economic assistance can be of help.

The scale and priorities of development aid, however, restrict its impact on the economic conditions that encourage displacement. Current bilateral and multilateral development assistance is of limited scope when compared with net capital transfers from the developing to the industrialized world in the form, for example, of debt servicing or unfavourable terms of trade. A recent estimate from UNDP indicates that trade barriers are costing developing countries ten times the amount they receive in aid.[30] Furthermore, a lot of aid is concentrated on the macro-economic level and thus works very slowly and indirectly, if at all, to promote the kind of human development that is of immediate benefit to the disadvantaged and marginalized groups who often become refugees. The beneficial effects of development assistance are, moreover, dangerously offset by the significant military component of many bilateral aid packages. Besides diverting scarce resources from economic development, this has undoubtedly increased the intensity of local and regional conflicts and exacerbated refugee flows in situations as diverse as Central America, the Horn of Africa, Afghanistan and Iraq.

Although better targeted development assistance with an emphasis on human needs – including job creation, education, health and the alleviation of poverty – has an indirect role to play in preventing the emergence of refugee situations, it is unlikely to be effective unless it is accompanied by political initiatives to resolve conflicts, manage underlying antagonisms and build institutions that effectively protect human

Box 7.4
Monitoring Human Rights in El Salvador

The United Nations Observer Mission in El Salvador (ONUSAL), set up by the Security Council in May 1991, is an integral part of the UN effort to end a 12-year civil war that cost as many as 75,000 lives. As part of a pioneering peace-building initiative launched in response to an internal conflict, ONUSAL has demonstrated the important role human rights monitoring can play in creating the confidence necessary to achieve and maintain peace.

In early 1989, the UN Secretary-General began the protracted and complex process of brokering a political agreement between the government of El Salvador and the Frente Farabundo Martí para la Liberación Nacional (FMLN), the guerrilla force that had been opposing the government since 1980. ONUSAL was born during, and became an important part of, that process.

The first major step towards a resolution of the conflict came with the conclusion of the San José Human Rights Agreement in July 1990 – almost two years before the final peace settlement was signed on 16 June 1992. The San José

Agreement set out minimum standards for the protection of human rights in El Salvador, including an end to arbitrary arrests, detention and torture. Equally importantly, it established a framework for verification, which subsequently led to the deployment of more than 100 ONUSAL observers to monitor respect for human rights by both parties to the conflict.

ONUSAL was not originally intended to begin work until a cease-fire had come into force. However, it was soon realized that large-scale human rights monitoring could actively help pave the way to a negotiated settlement. As a result, ONUSAL's operations were launched in July 1991 while the conflict was still in progress.

The San José Agreement created an important precedent by stipulating that ONUSAL be allowed unhindered access to any person or location in the country without prior notice. Its mandate thus extended to all areas, including conflict zones where, for four years, UNHCR had been providing protection and assistance to voluntary returnees from Honduras in extremely difficult – and at times dangerous – circumstances.

The size of the ONUSAL operation, as well as the external political support and media attention it

received, allowed it a breadth of coverage that UNHCR and the ICRC had struggled for years to obtain. Its presence had a significant restraining effect on combatants, and helped foster a climate of security and confidence which facilitated negotiations. It also helped to reduce the level of violence directed against non-combatants.

When peace was established on a provisional basis in early 1992, ONUSAL's mandate was expanded by the Security Council to include military, police and political divisions. It is scheduled to continue its operations in El Salvador until it has verified the presidential elections due in March 1994.

Despite the effectiveness of its human rights activities, ONUSAL has faced a number of problems and constraints. It still has much work to do to strengthen and improve vital national institutions such as the judiciary and the police; and there have been delays in implementing some of the institutional and economic reforms foreseen in the peace accords. However, no serious outbreaks of hostilities have occurred for a year and a half, and – despite the scars of the past – El Salvador appears to be continuing its progress towards national reconciliation.

rights. Indeed, aid provided without the prior establishment of favourable political conditions can simply reinforce oppressive regimes and accentuate inequalities. Economic development is itself a source of tension, as there are always relative winners and losers in the process. There are persuasive arguments for linking aid to the establishment of representative forms of government and respect for human rights, not least the rights of minorities.

"There is a growing recognition that human rights are a legitimate international concern"

Assistance and protection in countries of origin

To be effective, prevention must involve an active international presence at the grass-roots level. This is necessary in order to alleviate the pressures that threaten to uproot people and, when displacement has already occurred, to promote conditions that allow refugees and displaced people to return home.

There is thus a compelling need for far-sighted assistance and protection strategies, that pay special attention to people who have already become displaced within their countries and are therefore in particular danger of becoming refugees. Naturally, the scope for such strategies depends on access and is, therefore, virtually nil in cases where the door remains firmly closed to international presence. Although presence is a vitally important element of prevention, its effectiveness depends on its scale, among other factors. Presence does not in itself guarantee success, as the shameless proliferation of ethnic cleansing in the former Yugoslavia has all too graphically demonstrated.

The question of access raises a number of concerns about the general principles that guide international decision-making as well as actual practice on the ground. Operating within the territory of a state to assist and protect people in fear of their own government is at odds with the notion that national sovereignty is inviolable. United Nations resolutions on this question make it clear that humanitarian assistance should be rendered with the consent of the government concerned. At the same time, there is growing insistence within the international community that consent for purely humanitarian actions should be given as a matter of course. That insistence, however, may sometimes be motivated by concerns which go beyond the humanitarian and tends to be more vocal when the interests of powerful states are directly involved – as in the case of Iraq or the former Yugoslavia – than when the problem is more peripheral to their concerns.

There are practical as well as legal reasons for requiring the consent of governments. Their opposition can endanger the effectiveness as well as the durability of any improvements brought about by in-country assistance, whereas their participation can enhance and extend the benefits.

These concerns are particularly relevant to the situation of the internally displaced. Although there are no precise statistics for the numbers of internally displaced around the world, 24 million is probably a fairly conservative estimate.[31] Many are victims of the same upheavals that have produced refugees, for example in Afghanistan, Guatemala, the Horn of Africa, Sri Lanka and the former Yugoslavia. Most are potential refugees. Like refugees, they are particularly vulnerable. They need protection, assistance and a solution to their plight. And in many instances they, like refugees, cannot rely on the protection of their own governments. Yet there are substantial constraints on providing assistance to internally displaced people, and even more sub-stantial problems in protecting them. The international community is reluctant to take action within the territory of a sovereign state without the consent of the government. Obtaining such consent often entails difficult and laborious negotiation and substantial political pressure.

When the territory in which people are displaced is not under the control of a recognized government, the question of consent is doubly difficult. As the case of Somalia demonstrates, protection of the internally displaced is constrained not only by state sovereignty but also by the decline or collapse of state authority. As countries break up into self-proclaimed republics, and republics fragment into territories ruled by warlords, it is difficult to know who bears responsibility for protecting people, and to find someone with whom to negotiate access to people in need. Warlords, unlike even the most maverick of governments, are particularly resistant to reasonable persuasion. In some cases – such as Liberia, Iraq and Somalia – armed intervention may be the only effective option.

There is a growing realization that it is senseless to insist that people in flight must cross an international border before they can be offered assistance, particularly if it is the need for assistance that is propelling them toward the border. Yet only by crossing a border does a person fleeing from persecution or violence come under the protection of existing international refugee law. Provisions in international law for assistance to people displaced within the borders of their own country are limited.

International humanitarian law provides for the protection of civilians in internal armed conflicts, in particular through Additional Protocol II to the Geneva Conventions. However, Protocol II only comes into full operation when the party opposing the government has an organized armed force, which it is using to exert control over a significant slice of territory. Consequently it does not apply in cases of internal disturbance and tension, even though violence and violations of human rights may be widespread. The Protocol does not, for example, apply to either Haiti or Kosovo at present.

Human rights law does apply to these and similar situations. However, it is considerably weakened by the fact that governments are allowed to excuse themselves from many human rights guarantees during a state of emergency – precisely the time when the need for protection is likely to be greatest. There is no effective international mechanism to question the need for governments to resort to such emergency powers, nor any means to prevent human rights violations when a state abuses its powers.

Similarly, there are no specific legal instruments addressing the protection needs of internally displaced people, nor any internationally mandated body with overall responsibility for them. Securing observance of the norms of human rights and humanitarian law for this group is one of the most important challenges facing the international community. Meeting it will require the development of institutional and practical mechanisms to protect the human rights of the displaced and to ensure their access to humanitarian assistance. The growing recognition that human rights are a legitimate international concern is gradually allowing international bodies greater scope for attending to the needs of the internally displaced.

"The international community is gradually acquiring greater scope for attending to the needs of the internally displaced"

Protecting and assisting people inside their own countries is sometimes desirable in its own right. It may help people to avoid having to move at all. Those who have moved may be able to remain closer to home, and consequently find it easier to return when conditions permit. In other situations, in-country assistance is merely the least unsatisfactory of a limited range of choices when other countries are unwilling to provide asylum even on a temporary basis, or when endangered people are themselves unable or unwilling to move across an international border. The Kurds of northern Iraq faced this kind of situation in early 1991; many Bosnian Muslims remain trapped in areas of great danger today.

Box 7.5

Tajikistan: An Integrated Approach

Following the break-up of the USSR in 1991, the five Central Asian countries (Kazakhstan, Kyrgyzstan, Tajikistan, Turkmenistan and Uzbekistan) faced a vacuum of authority and, in some respects, of identity. The ethnic diversity of these newly independent states was accentuated under Soviet rule, in part by the questionable way in which their borders were redrawn in the 1930s and in part because of arrival of ethnic groups from other Soviet Republics (see Box 7.1).

The current displacement in Central Asia dates back to before the break-up of the Soviet Union. In 1989, over 100,000 Meshketi Turks were uprooted from Uzbekistan to the Russian Federation and Azerbaijan. In June of the following year, escalating tensions led to killings in the Osh Valley of Kyrgyzstan, causing thousands of Uzbeks to flee the area.

The most conspicuous example of regional instability, however, has been in Tajikistan, a country of some 5.4 million people, of whom only 62 per cent are ethnic Tajiks. Since June 1992, a civil war has pitted former communist leaders against a coalition of self-declared parliamentary democrats and Islamic radicals. By June 1993, opposition forces had lost the initiative but fighting continued in parts of the country and insecurity was still rife in many areas.

As many as 30,000 Tajiks are thought to have been killed in the war. Up to half a million were driven from their homes, some 356,000 of them in the southern part of the country including 60,000 refugees who poured into northern Afghanistan in December 1992. To the north, smaller numbers of refugees have also fled to Kyrgyzstan and Kazakhstan.

The conflict in Tajikistan has been viewed with acute anxiety by neighbouring states. Given the convoluted ethnic composition of the region – there are some four million Tajiks in Afghanistan, 800,000 in Uzbekistan and 20,000 in the Xinjiang region of north-western China – they fear that an influx of refugees could spark off ethnic conflicts within their own borders. The problems of Central Asia in general and of Tajikistan in particular have raised the urgent question of how regional and UN initiatives can best prevent, contain and, where necessary, reverse explosive situations which if left to fester may lead to conflagrations similar to those raging in Azerbaijan and Bosnia and Herzegovina.

The presidents of the Central Asian States and the Russian Foreign Minister, meeting in Alma Ata on 2 November 1992, laid the basis of a regional approach to the crisis. They agreed to work towards the re-establishment of legitimate government in Tajikistan and entrusted a peace-keeping function to CIS troops. This consensus provided a foundation upon which the UN could, in turn, bring to bear a co-ordinated approach, combining peace-keeping and peace-making efforts with the humanitarian relief provided by UNHCR and the ICRC.

In early 1993, after months of intensive diplomatic activity, the main actors in the Tajikistan conflict began to implement the measures necessary for the return of refugees and internally displaced people. One of the most difficult problems was the hostility of local populations towards returnees. On 18 March 1993, internally displaced Tajiks began returning to their war-ravaged province in southern Tajikistan, after receiving assurances that they would be well received. But at least 15 of them perished from exposure and hunger when, for seven long days, the local inhabitants blocked them from entering their home town of Kabadian. Only after intensive negotiations involving the UN Department of Political Affairs, ICRC and UNHCR were they at last allowed back into the town. The UN presence has played an important role in progressively allaying such hostile attitudes. By June 1993, 240,000 internally displaced people had returned to their home regions. The repatriation of refugees from Afghanistan had also begun, with the first convoy returning on 22 May.

Despite these successes in organizing the return of those displaced by the war, memories of the human rights abuses that have been perpetrated by both sides will not vanish overnight. Addressing the root causes of problems which are compounded by the traditional clan alignments and rivalries so rife in Central Asia will be a long-term undertaking. If peace is to be fully restored, continued mediation and monitoring will be necessary along with substantial rehabilitation and development aid.

Tajikistan has emerged as something of a test case. Failure to stop the conflict, or to consolidate the peace process, could have dire consequences for the entire region.

Innovative responses

The challenge of protecting people within their own countries – whether from violence, persecution or the effects of serious deprivation resulting from conflict – requires innovative responses. One of its effects has been to draw the United Nations into approaches that increasingly combine political and humanitarian initiatives in an effort to prevent further displacement, restore peace and achieve solutions for people who have been uprooted. In Tajikistan, the civil war that erupted in May 1992 drove up to half a million people from their homes, including 60,000 refugees who fled to neighbouring Afghanistan. United Nations efforts to prevent escalation of the numbers of those displaced have gone hand in hand with action to promote the safe return of those already uprooted. Peace-making, peace-keeping and humanitarian initiatives have been drawn together into an integrated approach that attempts to embrace prevention, relief and solutions (see Box 7.5).

Two other new approaches have been pioneered by UNHCR in Sri Lanka and Somalia. In Sri Lanka, Open Relief Centres were set up to provide shelter to returning refugees and internally displaced people who might otherwise seek refuge abroad (see Box 7.6). In Somalia, an attempt is being made to create "preventive zones" that will obviate the need for people to leave the country to obtain food and, at the same time, help create conditions conducive to the return of refugees from Kenya (see Chapter Five, Box 5.4). In both cases, a clear link exists between prevention on the one hand and the pursuit of solutions on the other.

Reception centres were first established in Sri Lanka in 1987 to ease the repatriation of ethnic Tamil refugees from India. They were designed as a sort of half-way house between exile and the reintegration of the returnees into their home communities. As repatriation got under way, a new outbreak of fierce fighting in northern Sri Lanka threatened to displace the returnees again, along with other residents of the areas. Even as the fighting continued, both sides agreed to an expansion of the relief centres to provide safety and sustenance to the local population so that they could stay in the country if they wished to do so.

The establishment of the Open Relief Centres in 1990 was somewhat controversial. Some argued that their existence might encourage the major asylum country for the refugees, India, to force people to return to Sri Lanka against their will. However, an agreement reached with the Indian government in July 1992, allowing UNHCR to monitor return movements from India so as to ensure that they are voluntary, allayed that concern. There has also been anxiety that the concentration of people in the centres creates easy targets. But the neutrality of the Open Relief Centres has been largely respected by the parties to the conflict, and thousands of people have sought shelter in them at one time or other. While providing an alternative to seeking safety abroad, the arrangement does not create obstacles for those who still wish to escape further afield.

"In complex situations, no response is unequivocal in its effects"

The establishment of "preventive zones" in Somalia in late 1992 arose from three principal concerns. One was the tremendous pressure on the refugee camps for Somalis in Kenya, which were housing more people than the fragile local environment and infrastructure could accommodate. Another was the deteriorating situation in border areas of Somalia and Kenya, where large numbers of people were gathering in extremely precarious conditions. And the third arose from the fact that the journey to Kenya was becoming more hazardous because of armed conflict and banditry in border areas, as well as land mines on the roads.

The preventive zones are partly created by the movement of supplies across the border from Kenya into areas of Somalia badly affected by conflict-related famine. The operation has three main objectives: to stabilize the remaining populations in the preventive zones; to bring relief supplies to people at risk of becoming refugees mainly because they lack food; and to create conditions conducive to the voluntary return of refugees residing in the Kenyan camps. The assistance taken across the border includes food, seeds, agricultural equipment and livestock. Small projects to rehabilitate schools, clinics and sanitation systems are also under way.

The protection role of preventive zones is indirect. The idea is based on the assumption that the chief cause of population movements in the targeted area is the search for food. Conflict and insecurity are also major factors, however, and it is often difficult to state categorically that one reason predominates. It is important to ensure that the effort to reduce one source of pressure to move does not deter people from attempting to escape from other equally or even more dangerous pressures.

In complex situations, no response is unequiv-

Box 7.6

Open Relief Centres in Sri Lanka

Since independence in 1948, Sri Lanka has been plagued by escalating violence between the majority Sinhalese community and the Tamils, who make up 25 per cent of the population. By the mid-1980s, political violence and the increasing polarization of the two communities had led to full-scale civil war in the north and east of the country.

After bloody massacres by government troops in the north in 1983, the exodus of Tamil refugees leaving Sri Lanka grew to a flood. By 1992, the numbers worldwide had risen to half a million, with 200,000 asylum-seekers in Europe and 230,000 across the Palk Strait in the Tamil-populated regions of southern India.

UNHCR established a presence in Sri Lanka in 1987 to provide assistance to returnees following an agreement between India and Sri Lanka that many hoped would bring an end to the conflict. But the fighting continued and indeed escalated. In 1990, an upsurge of internal displacement, fuelled a new exodus of asylum-seekers. In an effort both to help returnees affected by the fight-

ing and to mitigate the immediate causes of departure, UNHCR set up two Open Relief Centres (ORCs) in Mannar district, the main point of departure from Sri Lanka to India.

One of these is at Pesalai, a fishing village on the northern coast of government-controlled Mannar Island. The other is on the mainland at Madhu shrine, a traditional Catholic sanctuary in the heart of dense forest, located at a junction of jungle tracks leading to the coast in an area largely dominated by insurgent forces.

The ORCs are not, properly speaking, safe havens – indeed, earlier efforts to establish a safe haven had to be abandoned for lack of agreement on a demilitarized zone. Instead, they are temporary sanctuaries where displaced people can obtain essential relief assistance in a relatively safe environment, pending stabilization of conditions in their home area. Through them, UNHCR staff are able to monitor the situation and help shield the civilian population from some of the consequences of conflict. Perhaps as a result, during the period of conflict in 1990, there were no large-scale atrocities in the area where the ORCs are located, in stark contrast

to the eastern districts where UNHCR was not present.

The ORCs were supplemented by decentralized sub-centres that helped provide a measure of safety even in remote areas, as well as a network for the distribution of relief. As a result of these arrangements, many of those in danger of displacement felt able to remain at or near their homes and continue their livelihoods.

The ORC network responded to different degrees of displacement, allowing people an element of choice. In a volatile situation of military offensive and withdrawal, people could leave and return to their homes with relative ease and speed. Following the establishment of the centres, the outflow to southern India was reduced from 100,000 during the initial disturbances of June and July 1990 to a trickle in later months despite the continuing violence. As one Tamil commented, "We came to Madhu so that we could go to India from here. But then we heard that UNHCR had plans to establish a camp. We decided to remain here because we felt this camp gave us protection from the army attacks and aerial bombing that forced us to leave our homes."[32]

ocal in its effects. Concerns surrounding the preventive zone approach include the possibility that the initial assumption is incorrect. If the people leaving the targeted zones are fleeing primarily because of violence and persecution rather than food shortages, they are unlikely to be induced to stay by assistance programmes. But if they are, they may be exposed to greater risks than those which the assistance programmes are intended to alleviate. Preventive zones could also serve as magnets for people beyond the target area, thereby actually contributing to displacement rather than preventing it. Problems of sovereignty may arise in connection with cross-border operations, although in the case of Somalia the absence of effective central authority meant that sovereignty had ceased to be a real issue.

Because each refugee problem is unique, the possibility of providing protection in the country of origin must be judged case by case. In Sri Lanka, the Open Relief Centres were established with the consent of the government and the acquiescence of opposition groups. In Somalia, there was no central government to object or consent. The Allied military effort to provide a safe haven for the Kurds in northern Iraq illustrates the very high cost, in terms of finance, military commitment and continuing insecurity, when external protection is imposed without the co-operation of the government.

The idea of creating islands of safety within dangerous settings, so that people are not compelled to flee their countries, is an attractive one. Yet it is fraught with practical difficulties. Even an effective "safety zone" might have disturbing ramifications. It could serve as a pretext for other states to refuse sanctuary to people who still feel compelled to flee their country altogether. It might also dilute the sense of urgency about taking political initiatives to end the violence and persecution that drives people from their homes. And it could, in effect, ratify the creation of ghettos for beleaguered populations and even encourage mass expulsion. Despite the potential pitfalls, the search for innovative strategies to provide people with alternatives to exile must continue. As experience accumulates, the conditions for effective protection in countries of origin become clearer. Any innovation will have to meet three basic requirements: it must be fully consonant with human rights standards; it must not interfere with the fundamental right to seek asylum in another country; and it must not result in people being compelled to remain in territory where they are in serious danger.

High hopes are invested in the notion of prevention. While exploiting its potential to the fullest, it is also important to retain an awareness of its limitations. The situation in the former Yugoslavia provides a sobering lesson in the extent of those limitations. Massive humanitarian assistance to well over two million internally displaced people and war victims in Bosnia and Herzegovina has undoubtedly limited the scale of refugee movements into neighbouring European countries. Nevertheless, attempts to tackle the causes of displacement have so far failed. International pressure has been repeatedly ignored; humanitarian assistance has been blocked and manipulated; civilians have been under constant attack; and negotiations at all levels have been obstructed. The pattern of gross violations of human rights known as "ethnic cleansing" has continued, even in the UN Protected Areas of Croatia. To be successful, prevention requires a modicum of local will to co-operate or at least a responsiveness to external pressure. In situations where uprooting is a primary aim rather than the by-product of conflict, there may be little scope for positive prevention beyond the deployment of international military force.

Prevention is not a substitute for asylum, for the very simple reason that it does not always work. Despite concerted efforts to attenuate the causes of forced departure and reduce the need for movement across borders, the fundamental right to seek asylum in other countries must be preserved.

Cambodians returning from Thailand on the "Sisophon Express".
Cambodia, May 1992.

© H.J. Davies

Chapter eight

Broadening the Focus of Protection

The world of refugees is a violent and uncertain one. Action to protect them is beset with political upheavals, ethnic clashes, ideological struggles, wars and persecution. Access to asylum and material relief are their most immediate requirements. In the longer term, they need a return to peace and the means to start rebuilding their livelihoods. Both humanitarian assistance and political efforts to resolve the underlying causes of displacement are therefore crucial to the welfare and security of today's refugees. Nevertheless, although humanitarian action must take place in parallel with political activity, it must not become politicized.

Humanitarian and political initiatives have very different starting points: international political negotiations proceed from the interests and priorities of states; humanitarian actions proceed from the needs of individual human beings. The overlap between the two is, however, considerable, and so, therefore, is the scope and need for co-operation between humanitarian and political organizations.

Although the core of the traditional response to refugee problems is humanitarian, it is increasingly clear that action to deal with such problems must extend into broader realms if it is to be successful. More effective ways – and, above all, greater international will – have to be found to address the dire poverty and economic decline which is swelling the tide of migrants from many parts of the world. At the same time, political and economic initiatives are necessary to prevent and resolve the causes of refugee flows. If solutions are to be durable, humanitarian assistance must be linked to long-term development, and protection for the displaced allied to reconciliation efforts.

Strategies to solve refugee problems must take into account all the various factors that compel people to leave their homes. Protecting people against forced displacement requires a comprehensive and integrated response that deals with such problems in their entirety. It is likely to begin by tackling the immediate humanitarian needs of the people affected, including the need for asylum, at least on a temporary basis. It continues with an array of actions designed to enhance respect for human rights and humanitarian law, to prevent further displacement, to resolve armed conflict and to create conditions conducive to voluntary repatriation. It must also make provision for protection and assistance during re-integration, and link these with broader development and reconciliation plans.

Implementation of a comprehensive response to a refugee problem requires the co-operation of a broad range of actors: the governments of the country of origin and the countries of asylum, donor states, international agencies, NGOs and opposition forces. While being tailored to fit particular regions and specific situations, such a response would be likely to include co-ordinated action in the fields of foreign policy, international law, economic co-operation, immigration and asylum policy, as well as official development assistance. This is obviously beyond the scope of humanitarian organizations alone.

Humanitarianism may not be enough on its own, but it is essential. Political initiatives to address causes, obtain peace agreements and negotiate solutions are necessary, but often move forward slowly and uncertainly. Humanitarian, non-political action on behalf of refugees must not be held hostage to politics. Just as humanitarian action cannot substitute for political initiative, neither can the political replace the humanitarian. The needs of people have an independent priority. No matter what political mêlée surrounds it, protection and material assistance must be provided as quickly, efficiently and neutrally as possible. Close co-ordination between political bodies and human-itarian agencies is therefore needed to ensure that the capabilities, as well as the limitations, of humanitarian work are taken into account.

One situation which demands close co-ordination is when economic sanctions are imposed. Sanctions are important instruments for containing and punishing aggression. However, unless clear exemptions are provided for humanitarian activities and for relief supplies

such as food and medicine, the first to suffer are vulnerable people. The UN sanctions imposed on rump Yugoslavia (Serbia and Montenegro) for its role in supporting the Bosnian Serb militias have directly affected refugees and other vulnerable groups in that country. On occasion, they have also hindered UNHCR deliveries to besieged Muslim enclaves in eastern Bosnia, which have been supplied by convoys that cross Serbian territory. Convoys have not only been held up by Bosnian Serb obstruction but also because they are obliged to await clearance from the Sanctions Committee in New York.

As humanitarian action becomes dynamically linked to peace-keeping and peace-making in the 1990s, humanitarian organizations have to strive to keep the issues of refugees and displacement on the political agenda while preserving a non-political approach. Meanwhile, the challenge for political bodies is to support humanitarian action while resisting the temptation to use it as a bargaining chip in negotiations.

The emerging strategy of comprehensive response to refugee crises emphasizes the need to strengthen the state's responsibility for its own citizens, within an international framework and according to internationally accepted standards. The link between state responsibility and the international agenda is human rights.

The international community's willingness to see people exiled from their own countries and thrown into dependence on international assistance and protection is being stretched to breaking point. This is manifesting itself in a more active international insistence that states meet their obligations towards their own people.

The international community does not insist on a right of intervention but it does, increasingly, insist on a right of regard. It is now clear that internal policies and practices which cause large numbers of people to flee are a threat to international peace and security. The inter-national community is consequently more willing to act collectively to assert a concrete interest in human rights, the treatment of minorities and other matters that were previously shielded from view by the screen of national sovereignty. Today, that screen is becoming more transparent. Authorities who persist in actions likely to generate mass displacements across, or even within, their borders can expect to find themselves subject to international pressures ranging from urgent diplomatic representations, to sanctions, and, in extreme cases, to full-blown military intervention.

In 1991, the United Nations Security Council set a precedent by emphasizing that violations of human rights in Iraq threatened international peace and security. It went on to pass resolution 688, which authorized member states to deliver assistance to the Kurds by whatever means necessary – paving the way for military intervention. The importance of human rights has been subsequently stressed in peace agreements in El Salvador and Cambodia.

Long paralyzed by ideological confrontation, the various mechanisms that the United Nations has established to monitor human rights should now be used to greater effect. Special attention must be given to ethnic and minority rights as the recent conflict in former Yugoslavia has shown. Moreover, to take full advantage of the more universal approach that has become possible, the industrialized world needs to move beyond its traditional emphasis on political and civil rights and also acknowledge the economic and social rights and aspirations of citizens in the developing world.

Recently, many welcome changes have occurred that increase respect for human rights. Dictatorships have given way to more democratic forms of government in many parts of the world. Unprecedented cuts have been made in military arsenals. Equally importantly, there is a growing acceptance that the human rights of citizens within a state are not the exclusive business of the government of that state and that the international community has a legitimate interest in seeing that rights are respected.

Protection of refugees has in the past focused on their fundamental right to asylum. Asylum, however, can be seen as a single point on a spectrum of the human rights that relate to movement. Those rights begin with the right to remain safely at home. Forcible displacement violates this right and gives rise to the need for asylum. Action on behalf of refugees should focus on preventing the development of conditions that impel people to flee. Failing that, it should aim to restore the normal state of national protection, in which states accept and fulfil their responsibilities towards their own citizens and receive help, if they need it, to carry out those responsibilities.

The concept of protection, therefore, needs to be broadened to include notions of prevention and solution. Human rights and refugee law need to elaborate more fully standards on the right to remain and the right to return home, and to emphasize that those who have been forced to move, or who are in imminent danger of displacement have a right to humanitarian assistance and protection.

International protection is being extended to more and more refugees, and special arrangements are being made to protect considerable numbers of internally displaced people. Concerted efforts are needed to strengthen the structures of international protection to keep pace with the growing needs.

The challenge of protection in the 1990s is a twin challenge. The first element is indeed to provide international protection to those who are forced to flee violence and persecution, through the offer of asylum and the pledge of *non-refoulement*. The second is to insist vigorously that national protection of fundamental human rights be maintained and restored so that people do not have to seek protection outside their own countries.

Safeguarding human rights is a domestic responsibility of sovereign states, and one of the primary objectives of the United Nations. It is a goal in its own right, and a necessary condition for the attainment of international peace and security. For both these reasons, it is here that the solution to the refugee problem must begin.

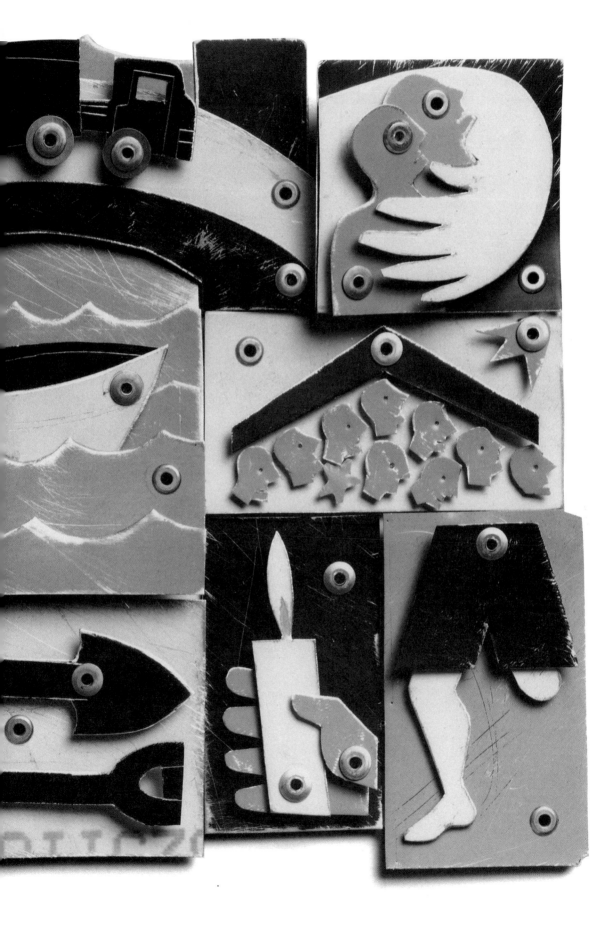

Refugee Statistics

I.1 Refugee Populations by Country or Territory of Asylum and by Origin: 1991 and 1992

I.2 Top 50 Countries and Territories Ranked According to the Ratio of Refugee Population to Total Population

I.3 Top 50 Countries Ranked According to the Ratio of Refugee Population to Gross National Product per Capita (GNP)

I.4 Major Refugee Flows by Country or Territory of Asylum and by Origin: 1991 and 1992

I.5 Indicative Numbers of Asylum Applicants in 26 Industrialized Countries: 1983-1992

I.6 Leading Nationalities of Asylum Applicants in Ten European Countries (by year of asylum application): 1988-1992

I.7 Leading Nationalities of Asylum Applicants in Ten European Countries (by country of asylum application): 1988-1992

I.8 Indicative Numbers of Returnees During 1992

The Problems With Refugee Statistics

The collection of accurate statistical data on refugees and asylum-seekers is one of the most problematic issues confronting UNHCR. Precise refugee statistics are required constantly within the agency for planning, budgeting and fund-raising purposes. Governments and other organizations – the press and media, NGOs and research bodies – also make constant demands on UNHCR for facts and figures, especially when major refugee movements or repatriation operations are taking place. All too often, however, UNHCR finds it difficult to answer such queries with any real degree of accuracy. Moreover, the figures collected by UNHCR frequently diverge from those reported by journalists, voluntary agencies, host governments and donor states.

These problems derive from a number of different factors. The word 'refugee' is itself subject to quite different interpretations. Under international law, the concept has a very specific meaning, and is used to describe people who have left their own country because they have a well-founded fear of persecution, or because their safety is threatened by events seriously disturbing public order. The figures used by UNHCR for public information and fund-raising purposes have traditionally been based on this definition.

Other organizations use a different approach. Some base their refugee statistics on a more restrictive definition. The US Committee for Refugees (USCR), for example, which publishes an influential annual refugee survey, lists only those refugees "in need of protection and/or assistance". The distinguishing characteristic of such refugees, the survey explains, is "their inability to repatriate due to continued fear of persecution in their homelands and the absence of permanent settlement opportunities in their countries of asylum or elsewhere". Under this definition, some sizeable refugee groups which have settled in places such as Western Europe, Canada, the US and Australia are excluded altogether.

Other commentators, especially those in the media, use a much broader approach. Rather than employ a narrow, legalistic definition of the refugee concept, they consider a refugee to be anyone who has been forced to leave their usual place of residence by circumstances beyond their control. Press reports about countries such as Afghanistan, Mozambique and Sudan, for example, often refer to the large number of refugees living within those countries. More often than not, the refugees referred to are actually internally displaced people – those who have been uprooted, but who remain within the borders of their own country. In the developed countries, statistics referring to recognized refugees, and those relating to asylum-seekers whose claims to refugee status have not yet been adjudicated, are often confused and combined.

UNHCR's own approach to refugee statistics has been affected by the growing complexity of humanitarian emergencies. In a number of recent operations – most notably in Ethiopia, former Yugoslavia and Iraq – UNHCR has been requested to provide assistance to populations composed of refugees, returnees and internally displaced people, as well as the resident population. In such circumstances, it makes sense for UNHCR to collect statistical data on needy people or beneficiaries, rather than refugees as conventionally defined.

Conceptual problems apart, there are many practical obstacles to the collection of accurate refugee statistics. In several recent emergencies, UNHCR field staff have been faced with movements of more than a million people, over extremely large areas and in some of the most remote, weakly administered and hostile territories on earth. The effort required for individual registration or detailed population surveys has far exceeded the skills and resources of either UNHCR or the host government.

As a refugee influx levels off and relief operations become more organized, the scope for accurate enumeration improves. This is particularly the case in emergencies where new arrivals move into established camps or settlements. Once people are concentrated in specific locations and programmes have been set up to provide them with food, water, shelter and medical services, it becomes easier to collect reasonably accurate demographic data.

In many parts of the world, however, refugees do not live in organized camps. Instead, they settle spontaneously, amongst local people with the same ethnic and linguistic background. In situations such as this, it is often difficult to prevent the local population from registering as refugees and to establish how many refugees are actually living in the area.

The difficulties do not end there. As a report by the US government's Bureau for Refugee Programmes states, "given the fluidity of most refugee situations, counting refugees is at best an approximate science". Refugees often come and go across international borders as well as within their countries of asylum, according to changing levels of assistance and security. They may move in and out of camps, or migrate between rural and urban areas. Some refugees register more than once in order to gain higher levels of assistance, and deliberately undermine subsequent efforts to undertake a more accurate census. Some family members remain in the country of asylum and continue to receive relief, while others return to their country of origin in order to tend the family farm or simply to assess the prospects for repatriation. It is very difficult for aid agencies and local authorities to keep track of such movements.

A refugee population, like any other, is a dynamic rather than a static entity. Refugees die, get married and give birth. Refugee families may split up, regroup or change their place of residence. However accurate they may have been at the time of their collection, statistical data about the size and composition of a refugee population can quickly become outdated. Updating this information is not a straightforward exercise either, particularly among refugees who record births, deaths, ages and family relationships in ways that do not correspond with standard Western practice.

Even in the industrialized countries, where individual screening procedures are the norm and where data collection presents fewer practical problems, refugee numbers are still fraught with inconsistencies and lack of precision.

Within Western Europe, for example, governments have been making a concerted effort to harmonize their asylum policies and procedures. For the time being, however, they continue to publish their refugee and asylum statistics at different times of the year, in different formats, and with varying degrees of detail. Accurate comparisons are therefore extremely difficult to make.

Much of the confusion surrounding refugee statistics undoubtedly stems from their sensitive and controversial nature. Refugees are in many ways a symbol of failure. No government likes to admit that its citizens have felt obliged to leave their own country. Similarly, returnees are a symbol of success. When people decide to go back to their homeland, the leaders of that country can legitimately claim that its citizens are expressing some kind of confidence in its government. Not surprisingly, therefore, the refugee and returnee figures issued by countries of asylum and countries of origin are rarely consistent.

Economic and political considerations also play a part in the statistical issue. It is no secret that the governments of some host countries have made inflated claims concerning the number of refugees or returnees living on their territory, in the hope that this will attract higher levels of international sympathy and material support.

On occasions, UNHCR has been obliged to compromise with such official claims, agreeing to a "planning figure" which is known to be higher than the actual number of people receiving assistance from the organization. In other situations, host governments have strenuously denied the arrival of refugees from a friendly neighbouring state, forcing UNHCR to engage in some tortuous verbal gymnastics. Mozambican refugees, for example, were referred to as "externally-displaced persons in a refugee-like situation," until the country of origin agreed to the use of more conventional terminology. And in Central America, the refugee figures used by host governments and UNHCR include substantial numbers of foreign nationals whose legal status is unclear.

Statistical creativity is not confined to the developing world. In many of the industrialized countries governments and politicians have a tendency to disseminate very selective information about refugee numbers. An administration which is seeking to justify the introduction of a more restrictive asylum policy, for example, may issue statistics which demonstrate a sharp increase in the number of people submitting requests for refugee status. But it may neglect to say what proportion of those asylum-seekers have actually been granted refugee status, and how many have moved on to other countries or returned to their homeland.

Governments and politicians are not the only people to act in this way. Pressure groups, voluntary organizations and journalists have all been known to publish refugee numbers which bear little resemblance to the probable reality – sometimes because they are unaware of the methodological problems associated with the available statistics, and sometimes because they are more concerned with policy positions than with statistical accuracy. In the 1980s, for example, it became commonplace for certain groups to claim that African or Asian asylum-seekers in Western Europe were much less likely to be recognized as refugees than claimants from the former Soviet bloc. Such assertions were not always founded on a demonstrably sound statistical basis.

While the barriers to the collection of accurate refugee statistics are formidable, they are not insurmountable. In many refugee situations, reasonably precise enumeration is possible. Given adequate resources, a degree of stability, efficient staff members and, most crucially, support from the host government authorities, it is generally feasible for UNHCR to obtain detailed information on the size, composition and characteristics of a refugee population. Recent shifts in the global balance of power and the increased authority of the United Nations have also enhanced UNHCR's ability to disseminate unbiased refugee and beneficiary statistics.

Serious statistical problems, however, will almost certainly continue to arise in large, complex and rapidly changing emergencies, particularly when relief supplies are scarce and when the presence of refugees is a matter of political controversy. A life and death struggle for food and influence is hardly ever compatible with accurate enumeration.

Annex I.1
Refugee Populations by Country or Territory of Asylum and by Origin: 1991 – 1992
1991 and 1992

Country or territory of asylum	Region, country or ethnic group of origin	Total 31 Dec. 1991		Total 31 Dec. 1992	
AFRICA					
Algeria		169,100		219,300	
	Malian/Niger		–		50,000
	Sahrawi		165,000		165,000
	Other		4,100		4,300
Angola		11,000		11,000	
	South African		300		200
	Zairian		10,800		10,800
Benin		500		300	
	Chadian		400		200
	Other		–		100
Botswana		900		500	
	South African		500		200
	Zimbabwean		100		–
	Other		300		300
Burkina Faso		300		5,700	
	Various		300		5,700
Burundi		270,100		271,700	
	Rwandese		243,900		245,600
	Ugandan		300		300
	Zairian		25,800		25,800
	Other		–		100
Cameroon		45,200		42,200	
	Chadian		44,800		41,700
	Other		400		500
Central African Rep.		12,200		19,000	
	Chadian		1,000		1,200
	Sudanese		11,100		17,700
	Other		100		100
Congo		3,400		9,500	
	Chadian		2,200		2,200
	Zairian		400		400
	Central African Rep.		300		300
	Other		400		6,600
Côte d'Ivoire		230,300		174,100	
	Liberian		229,900		173,700
	Other		400		400
Djibouti		96,100		28,000	
	Ethiopian		11,500		8,000
	Somali		84,600		20,000
Egypt		2,200		5,500	
	Ethiopian		600		400
	Somali		1,300		4,900
	Other		300		300
Ethiopia		527,000		431,800	
	Sudanese		15,000		25,600
	Somali		512,000		406,100
	Other		–		100
Gabon		200		300	
	Various		200		300
AFRICA (Cont.)					
Gambia		200		3,600	
	Liberian		200		300
	Senegalese		–		3,300
Ghana		8,100		12,100	
	Liberian		8,000		12,000
	Other		100		100
Guinea		548,000		478,500	
	Liberian		548,000		478,500
Guinea-Bissau		4,600		12,200	
	Senegalese		4,600		12,200
Kenya		120,200		401,900	
	Ethiopian		10,600		68,600
	Sudanese		–		21,800
	Somali		95,900		285,600
	Ugandan		9,800		3,300
	Other		3,900		22,600
Lesotho		200		100	
	South African		200		100
Liberia		–		100,000	
	Sierra Leonean		–		100,000
Malawi		981,800		1,058,500	
	Mozambican		981,800		1,058,500
Mali		13,100		13,100	
	Mauritanian		13,100		13,100
Mauritania		35,200		37,500	
	Various		35,200		37,500
Mozambique		400		300	
	South African		–		200
	Various		400		100
Morocco		300		300	
	Various		300		300
Namibia		100		200	
	Various		100		200
Niger		1,400		3,700	
	Chadian		1,400		3,400
	Other		–		300
Nigeria		3,600		4,800	
	Chadian		1,500		1,400
	Ghanaian		200		100
	Liberian		1,000		2,900
	Other		900		300
Rwanda		34,000		25,200	
	Burundi		34,000		25,200
Senegal		71,900		71,600	
	Guinea-Bissau		5,000		5,000
	Mauritanian		66,800		66,500
	Other		100		100

149

Country or territory of asylum	Region, country or ethnic group of origin	Total 31 Dec. 1991		Total 31 Dec. 1992	

AFRICA (Cont.)

Country or territory of asylum	Region, country or ethnic group of origin	Total 31 Dec. 1991		Total 31 Dec. 1992	
Sierra Leone		28,000		5,900	
	Various		28,000		5,900
Somalia		–		500	
	Ethiopian		–		500
Sudan		729,200		725,600	
	Chadian		20,700		16,000
	Ethiopian		700,000		703,500
	Ugandan		6,500		3,800
	Zairian		2,000		2,300
Swaziland		49,600		55,600	
	Mozambican		42,000		48,100
	South African		7,500		7,400
	Other		100		100
Togo		3,400		3,400	
	Ghanaian		3,200		3,200
	Liberian		100		100
	Other		100		100
Tunisia		100		100	
	Various		100		100
Uganda		162,500		196,300	
	Rwandese		84,000		85,800
	Sudanese		77,100		92,100
	Zairian		600		15,600
	Other		700		2,800
United Rep. of Tanzania		288,100		292,100	
	Burundi		148,700		149,500
	Mozambican		72,200		75,200
	Rwandese		50,000		50,000
	Zairian		16,000		16,000
	Other		1,300		1,500
Zaire		483,000		391,100	
	Angolan		278,600		198,000
	Burundi		41,200		9,500
	Rwandese		50,900		50,900
	Sudanese		90,800		109,400
	Ugandan		20,100		21,100
	Other		1,300		2,300
Zambia		140,700		142,100	
	Angolan		102,500		101,800
	Mozambican		23,500		26,300
	Namibian		100		–
	South African		1,800		600
	Other		12,700		13,400
Zimbabwe		197,600		137,200	
	Mozambican		197,100		136,600
	Other		500		600
Africa (other)		800		800	
	Various		800		800
AFRICA TOTAL		**5,274,600**		**5,393,200**	

ASIA

Country or territory of asylum	Region, country or ethnic group of origin	Total 31 Dec. 1991		Total 31 Dec. 1992	
Afghanistan		–		60,000	
	Tajik		–		60,000
Bangladesh		40,300		245,000	
	Myanmar & others		40,300		245,000
China		288,900		288,100	
	Vietnamese		284,500		285,500
	Lao		4,100		2,500
	Other		200		–
Hong Kong		60,000		45,300	
	Vietnamese [1]		60,000		45,300
India		210,600		258,400	
	Afghan		9,800		11,000
	Sri Lankan		200,000		113,400
	Chakma (Bangladeshi)		–		53,200
	Tibetan		N/A		80,000
	Other		800		800
Indonesia		18,700		15,600	
	Vietnamese [1]		17,000		15,000
	Other		1,700		600
Iran (Islamic Rep. of)		4,405,000		4,150,700	
	Afghan		3,186,600		2,900,700
	Iraqi		1,218,400		1,250,100
Iraq		88,000		95,000	
	Various		88,000		95,000
Japan		9,100		8,200	
	Indo-Chinese		9,100		8,200
Jordan		400		300	
	Various		400		300
Kuwait		125,000		124,900	
	Iraqi		20,000		19,900
	Bidoon		80,000		80,000
	Palestinian		25,000		25,000
Lebanon		5,200		6,000	
	Various		5,200		6,000
Macau		100		–	
	Vietnamese [1]		100		–
Malaysia		13,900		10,300	
	Vietnamese [1]		12,500		10,300
	Other		1,500		–
Nepal		9,600		75,500	
	Bhutanese		9,500		75,400
	Other		100		–
Pakistan		3,099,900		1,629,200	
	Afghan		3,098,000		1,627,000
	Iranian		500		300
	Other		1,400		1,900
Philippines		20,000		6,700	
	Vietnamese [1]		19,800		6,700
	Other		100		–

ASIA (Cont.)

Country or territory of asylum	Region, country or ethnic group of origin	Total 31 Dec. 1991		Total 31Dec. 1992	
Rep. of Korea		200		100	
	Vietnamese [1]		200		100
Saudi Arabia		33,100		28,700	
	Iraqi		32,900		27,700
	Various		200		1,000
Singapore		200		100	
	Various		200		100
Syrian Arab Rep.		4,200		5,700	
	Various		4,200		5,700
Tajikistan		–		3,000	
	Afghan		–		3,000
Thailand		88,200		63,600	
	Cambodian [2]		15,000		7,100
	Lao		57,300		40,900
	Vietnamese [1]		13,700		12,600
	Other		2,200		3,000
Turkey		29,400		28,500	
	Bosnia and Herzegovina		–		15,100
	Iranian		1,400		1,800
	Iraqi		28,000		11,400
	Other		–		200
Viet Nam		20,100		16,300	
	Cambodian		20,100		16,300
Yemen		30,000		59,700	
	Ethiopian		3,100		3,400
	Somali		26,700		56,200
	Other		100		100
Asia (other)		600		15,200	
	Somali		–		15,100
	Other		600		100
ASIA TOTAL		8,600,700		7,240,100	

EUROPE [3]

Country or territory of asylum	Region, country or ethnic group of origin	Total 31 Dec. 1991		Total 31Dec. 1992	
Albania		–		3,000	
	Various		–		3,000
Armenia		–		300,000	
	Azerbaijani		–		300,000
Austria [4]		18,700		60,900	
	Various		18,700		60,900
Azerbaijan		–		246,000	
	Armenian		–		195,000
	Other		–		51,000
Belgium		24,100		24,300	
	Various		24,100		24,300
Bosnia and Herzegovina [5]		–		810,000	
	Various		–		810,000
Bulgaria [6]		–		200	
	Various		–		200
Croatia [7]		–		648,000	
	Various		–		648,000
Czechoslovakia [8]		700		9,400	
	Various		700		9,400
Denmark		44,000		58,300	
	Various		44,000		58,300
Finland		7,700		12,000	
	Various		7,700		12,000
F. Y. R. of Macedonia [6]		–		32,000	
	Various		–		32,000
France		170,000		182,600	
	Various		170,000		182,600
Germany [9]		383,900		827,100	
	Various		383,900		827,100
Greece		9,000		8,500	
	Various		9,000		8,500
Hungary [10]		73,800		32,400	
	Various		73,800		32,400
Iceland		100		200	
	Various		100		200
Ireland		300		500	
	Various		300		500
Italy		12,200		12,400	
	Various		12,200		12,400
Luxembourg		700		2,200	
	Various		700		2,200
Netherlands		21,300		26,900	
	Various		21,300		26,900

Country or territory of asylum	Region, country or ethnic group of origin	Total 31 Dec. 1991		Total 31 Dec. 1992	

EUROPE (Cont.)

Country or territory of asylum	Region, country or ethnic group of origin	Total 31 Dec. 1991		Total 31 Dec. 1992	
Norway		29,100		35,700	
	Various		29,100		35,700
Poland		200		2,700	
	Various		200		2,700
Portugal		1,000		1,800	
	Various		1,000		1,800
Romania		700		500	
	Various		700		500
Russian Federation		–		17,100	
	Afghan		–		8,800
	Other		–		8,300
Slovenia [6]		–		47,000	
	Various		–		47,000
Spain		9,200		9,700	
	Various		9,200		9,700
Sweden		238,400		324,500	
	Various		238,400		324,500
Switzerland		27,600		26,700	
	Various		27,600		26,700
United Kingdom		100,000		100,000	
	Various		100,000		100,000
Yugoslavia, Fed. Rep. of [6]		500		516,500	
	Various		500		516,500
EUROPE TOTAL		1,173,200		4,379,100	

LATIN AMERICA

Country or territory of asylum	Region, country or ethnic group of origin	Total 31 Dec. 1991		Total 31 Dec. 1992	
Argentina		11,500		11,500	
	European		1,000		1,000
	Indo-Chinese		1,500		1,500
	Latin American		8,900		8,900
	Other		100		100
Bahamas		–		400	
	Haitian		–		400
Belize		19,400		20,400	
	Salvadorian		8,400		8,800
	Guatemalan		3,000		3,400
	Other		600		600
	Not identified [11]		7,400		7,400
Bolivia		300		500	
	Various		300		500
Brazil		5,400		5,400	
	European		2,000		2,000
	Latin American		2,500		2,500
	Other		900		900
Chile		100		100	
	Various		100		100
Colombia		500		500	
	Various		500		500
Costa Rica		117,500		114,400	
	Salvadorian		6,300		5,600
	Nicaraguan		28,100		27,800
	Latin American (other)		3,100		900
	Not identified [11]		80,000		80,000
Cuba		–		5,100	
	African		–		2,900
	Haitian		–		1,100
	Latin American (other)		–		1,100
Dominican Republic		1,600		500	
	Haitian		1,600		500
Ecuador		300		200	
	Various		300		200
El Salvador		20,100		19,900	
	Nicaraguan		400		200
	Other		19,700		19,700
French Guiana		5,900		1,700	
	Surinamese		5,900		1,700
Guatemala		223,200		222,900	
	Salvadorian		2,600		2,400
	Nicaraguan		2,400		2,300
	Other		100		100
	Not identified [11]		218,200		218,200
Honduras		102,000		100,100	
	Salvadorian		1,700		100
	Haitian		100		–
	Nicaraguan		100		–
	Not identified [11]		100,000		100,000

Country or territory of asylum	Region, country or ethnic group	Total 31 Dec. 1991		Total 31Dec. 1992	

LATIN AMERICA (Cont.)

Country or territory of asylum	Region, country or ethnic group	Total 31 Dec. 1991		Total 31Dec. 1992	
Mexico		354,500		361,000	
	Salvadorian		4,200		4,200
	Guatemalan		43,400		49,800
	Latin American (other)		1,100		1,100
	Not identified [11]		305,800		305,800
Nicaragua		14,900		14,500	
	Salvadorian		6,100		5,600
	Guatemalan		200		200
	Not identified [11]		8,600		8,600
Paraguay		100		–	
	Various		100		–
Panama		900		1,000	
	Salvadorian		400		400
	Nicaraguan		300		400
	Other		200		200
Peru		700		600	
	European		200		200
	Latin American		400		400
	Other		100		100
Suriname		–		100	
	Haitian		–		100
Uruguay		100		100	
	Various		100		100
Venezuela		1,700		2,000	
	Caribbean		1,600		1,900
	Other		100		100
Latin America (other)		2,600		2,600	
	Various		2,600		2,600
LATIN AMERICA TOTAL		883,300		885,500	

NORTH AMERICA

Country or territory of asylum	Region, country or ethnic group	Total 31 Dec. 1991		Total 31Dec. 1992	
Canada		538,100		568,200	
	Various		538,100		568,200
United States [12]		482,000		473,000	
	Various		482,000		473,000
NORTH AMERICA TOTAL		1,020,100		1,041,200	

OCEANIA

Country or territory of asylum	Region, country or ethnic group	Total 31 Dec. 1991		Total 31Dec. 1992	
Australia [12]		32,400		35,600	
	Various		32,400		35,600
New Zealand		16,800		17,300	
	Various		16,800		17,300
Papua New Guinea		6,100		6,700	
	Indonesian		6,100		6,700
OCEANIA TOTAL		55,300		59,600	
GRAND TOTAL		17,007,200		18,998,700	

Note: The figures are provided mostly by governments based on their own records and methods of estimation; in certain instances they include persons reported by governments as being in "refugee like" situations; these statistics do not cover Palestinian refugees who come under the mandate of the United Nations Relief and Works Agency for Palestinian Refugees in the Near East (UNRWA). The figures are rounded to the nearest hundred, a dash (–) indicates that the figure is less than 50 or that no figure is available.

1 Includes all Vietnamese asylum-seekers regardless of their refugee status.
2 Does not include some 370,000 Cambodians displaced on the Thai-Cambodian border of whom some 236,000 had been repatriated by 31 December 1992.
3 Refugee statistics provided by European governments do not normally indicate the specific scope or interpretation given to the term "refugee" in the respective country. A breakdown by type of refugee status is therefore not normally available.
4 1992 figure includes 42,100 from the former Yugoslavia.
5 Mainly internally displaced persons.
6 Majority from the republics of the former Yugoslavia.
7 Majority from the republics of the former Yugoslavia, of whom 245,000 internally displaced and approximately 87,000 in United Nations Protected Areas (UNPAs).
8 Of whom 8,500 from the former Yugoslavia. On 1 January 1993, Czechoslovakia separated into two states: the Czech Republic and Slovakia.
9 The figure of 827,100 at 31 December 1992 includes an estimated 640,000 *de facto* refugees, i.e. persons who either did not apply for asylum or whose application was rejected, but who were nevertheless not deported for political or humanitarian reasons. The figure does not include an estimated 577,600 asylum applicants whose claims are pending and who received government assistance.
10 The 1992 number includes 29,000 persons from the former Yugoslavia staying temporarily in Hungary, and Convention refugees.
11 Other Central Americans in refugee-like situations (government estimate)
12 Indicative figures.

Annex I.2

Top 50 Countries and Territories Ranked According to the Ratio of Refugee Population to Total Population

Annex I.2 provides a ranking of the countries and territories with the largest refugee populations relative to their total population.

Rank	Country or territory	Refugee population as at 31 Dec. 1992 (in thousands)	Total population estimate (in thousands)	Year of population estimate	Ratio refugee population/total population
1	Malawi	1,058	10,356	1992	1 : 9.8
2	Belize[1]	20	198	1992	9.9
3	Armenia	300	3,489	1992	11.6
4	Guinea	478	6,116	1992	12.8
5	Swaziland	56	792	1992	14.1
6	Iran (Islamic Rep. of)	4,151	61,565	1992	14.8
7	Croatia[2]	316	4,764	1991	15.1
8	Kuwait	125	1,970	1992	15.8
9	Djibouti	28	467	1992	16.7
10	Federal Rep. of Yugoslavia	516	10,630	1992	20.6
11	Burundi	272	5,823	1992	21.4
12	Sweden	324	8,652	1992	26.7
13	Liberia	100	2,751	1992	27.5
14	Costa Rica[1]	114	3,192	1992	28.0
15	Azerbaijan	246	7,283	1992	29.6
16	Sudan	726	26,656	1992	36.7
17	Slovenia	47	1,996	1992	42.5
18	Guatemala[1]	223	9,745	1992	43.7
19	Canada	568	27,367	1992	48.2
20	French Guiana	2	104	1992	52.0
21	Honduras[1]	100	5,462	1992	54.6
22	Mauritania	38	2,143	1992	56.4
23	Zambia	142	8,638	1992	60.8
24	Kenya	402	25,230	1992	62.8
25	FYR Macedonia	32	2,034	1991	63.6
26	Côte d'Ivoire	174	12,910	1992	74.2
27	Pakistan	1,629	124,773	1992	76.6
28	Zimbabwe	137	10,583	1992	77.2
29	Guinea Bissau	12	1,006	1992	83.8
30	Denmark	58	5,158	1992	88.9
31	Uganda	196	18,674	1992	95.3
32	United Rep. of Tanzania	292	27,829	1992	95.3
33	Germany	827	80,253	1992	97.0
34	Zaire	391	39,882	1992	102.0
35	Senegal	72	7,736	1992	107.4
36	Norway	36	4,288	1992	119.1
37	Algeria	219	26,346	1992	120.3
38	Ethiopia	432	52,981	1992	122.6
39	Austria	61	7,776	1992	127.5
40	Hong Kong[3]	45	5,800	1992	128.9
41	Central African Rep.	19	3,173	1992	167.0
42	Luxembourg	2	378	1992	189.0
43	Iraq	95	19,290	1992	203.1
44	New Zealand	17	3,455	1992	203.2
45	Yemen	60	12,535	1992	208.9
46	Gambia	4	908	1992	227.0
47	Congo	10	2,368	1992	236.8
48	Mexico[1]	361	88,153	1992	244.2
49	Switzerland	27	6,813	1992	252.3
50	El Salvador	20	5,396	1992	269.8

Note: This table does not include Bosnia and Herzegovina which had an estimated 810,000 internally displaced people on 31 December 1992.

Sources for total population estimates: *World Population Prospects: The 1992 Revision.* United Nations Population Division; *Population and Vital Statistics Report*, various issues. United Nations Statistical Division; *Monthly Bulletin of Statistics*, various issues. United Nations Statistical Division; *Statistics Bulletin No. 1934.* Belgrade: Federal Institute for Statistics, 1992.

1. Refugee population includes government estimate of Central Americans in refugee-like situations.
2. Refugee population does not include internally displaced Croatians or refugees in the UNPAs.
3. Refugee population includes all Vietnamese asylum-seekers regardless of their refugee status.

154

Annex I.3

Top 50 Countries Ranked According to the Ratio of Refugee Population to Gross National Product per Capita

Annex I.3 depicts the economic 'burden' of refugees. The chart compares a country's refugee population with its Gross National Product (GNP) per capita, a leading indicator of national economic development.

Rank	Country	Refugee population as at 31 Dec. 1992	GNP per capita ($)	Year of GNP estimate	Ratio refugee population/GNP per capita
1	Malawi	1,058,000	230	1991	4,600
2	Pakistan	1,629,000	400	1991	4,073
3	Ethiopia	432,000	120	1991	3,600
4	United Rep. of Tanzania	292,000	100	1991	2,920
5	Sudan	726,000	320	1985	2,269
6	Iran (Islamic Rep. of)	4,151,000	2,170	1991	1,913
7	Zaire	391,000	220	1990	1,777
8	Burundi	272,000	210	1991	1,295
9	Kenya	402,000	340	1991	1,182
10	Uganda	196,000	170	1991	1,153
11	Bangladesh	245,000	220	1991	1,114
12	Guinea	478,000	460	1991	1,039
13	India	258,000	330	1991	782
14	China	288,000	370	1991	778
15	Nepal	75,000	180	1991	417
16	Zambia	142,000	420	1990	338
17	Afghanistan	60,000	220	1988	273
18	Côte d'Ivoire	174,000	690	1991	252
19	Guatemala[1]	223,000	930	1991	240
20	Liberia	100,000	450	1987	222
21	Zimbabwe	137,000	650	1991	211
22	Honduras[1]	100,000	580	1991	172
23	Federal Rep. of Yugoslavia[2]	516,000	3,060	1990	169
24	Azerbaijan[3]	246,000	1,670	1991	147
25	Armenia[3]	300,000	2,150	1991	140
26	Mexico[1]	361,000	3,030	1991	119
27	Yemen	60,000	520	1991	115
28	Algeria	219,000	1,980	1991	111
29	Senegal	72,000	720	1991	100
30	Rwanda	25,000	270	1991	93
31	Mauritania	38,000	510	1991	75
32	Croatia[4]	316,000	4,399	1990	72
33	Viet Nam	16,000	230	1990	70
34	Guinea Bissau	12,000	180	1991	67
35	Costa Rica[1]	114,000	1,850	1991	62
36	Swaziland	56,000	1,050	1991	53
37	Djibouti	28,000	530	1978	53
38	Cameroon	42,000	850	1991	49
39	Central African Rep.	19,000	390	1991	49
40	Mali	13,000	280	1991	46
41	Thailand	64,000	1,570	1991	41
42	Germany[5]	827,000	23,650	1991	35
43	Nicaragua[1]	14,000	460	1991	30
44	Ghana	12,000	400	1991	30
45	Sierra Leone	6,000	210	1991	29
46	Canada	568,000	20,440	1991	28
47	Indonesia	16,000	610	1991	26
48	Iraq	95,000	4,110	1990	23
49	United States	473,000	22,240	1991	21
50	Burkina Faso	6,000	290	1991	21

Note: This table does not include Bosnia and Herzegovina which had an estimated 810,000 internally displaced people on 31 December 1992.

Sources for GNP per capita estimates: World Bank. *World Development Report 1993*.
Oxford University Press, 1993; World Bank. *World Tables 1992*. John Hopkins University
Press, 1992; Encyclopedia Britannica. *Britannica Book of the Year*, 1993.

1. Refugee population includes government estimate of Central Americans in refugee-like situations.

2. GNP estimate refers to Serbia and Montenegro only.

3. According to the World Bank, the GNP estimate should be regarded as very preliminary.

4. Refugee population does not include internally displaced Croatians or refugees in the UNPAs.

5. GNP estimate refers to the Federal Republic of Germany before unification.

Annex 1.4
Major Refugee Flows by Country or Territory of Asylum and by Origin: 1991–1992 [1]

Country or territory of asylum	Origin	Total 1991	Total 1992
AFRICA			
Djibouti		14,000	–
	Ethiopian	13,000	–
Ethiopia		–	18,000
	Sudanese	–	10,000
	Somali	–	8,000
Guinea		223,000	11,000
	Liberian	223,000	11,000
Kenya		106,000	120,000
	Ethiopian	6,000	
	Somali	96,000	93,000
	Sudanese	–	22,000
Liberia		–	110,000
	Sierra Leonean	–	110,000
Malawi		–	77,000
	Mozambican	–	77,000
Mauritania		–	20,000
	Various	–	20,000
Rwanda		11,000	–
	Burundi	11,000	–
Senegal		12,000	–
	Mauritanian	12,000	–
Sudan		51,000	–
	Ethiopian	51,000	–
Uganda		–	48,000
	Sudanese	–	14,000
	Zairian	–	30,000
Zaire		68,000	25,000
	Angolan	8,000	–
	Burundi	28,000	–
	Sudanese	21,000	19,000
	Ugandan	10,000	–
Zimbabwe		15,000	40,000
	Mozambican	15,000	40,000
ASIA AND OCEANIA			
Bangladesh		40,000	205,000
	Myanmar & others	40,000	205,000
ASIA AND OCEANIA (Cont.)			
Hong Kong		20,000	–
	Vietnamese	20,000	–
Iran (Islamic Rep. of)		1,410,000	–
	Iraqi	1,410,000	–
Nepal		19,000	59,000
	Bhutanese	19,000	56,000
Pakistan		21,000	60,000
	Afghan	21,000	60,000
Saudi Arabia		35,000	–
	Iraqi	35,000	–
Yemen Arab Republic		22,000	30,000
	Various	22,000	
	Somali	–	29,000
EUROPE [2]			
Armenia		–	300,000
	Azerbaijani	–	300,000
Azerbaijan		–	246,000
	Armenian	–	195,000
	Central Asian	–	51,000
Croatia		–	316,000
	Various	–	316,000
Federal Rep. of Yugoslavia [3]		–	516,000
	Various	–	516,000
Hungary		51,000	–
	Various	51,000	–
FYR Macedonia		–	32,000
	Various	–	32,000
Russian Fed.		–	17,000
	Afghan	–	9,000
	Iranian & Iraqi	–	6,000
Slovenia		–	47,000
	Various	–	47,000
Turkey		–	19,000
	Bosnian	–	15,000

1 Indicative figures
2 Excludes industralized countries listed in Annex 1.5
3 Figure includes 1991 and 1992

Annex I.5
Indicative Numbers of Asylum Applicants in 26 Industrialized Countries: 1983-1992 (in thousands)

Country of asylum application	1983	1984	1985	1986	1987	1988	1989	1990	1991	1992	Total
Germany	19.7	35.3	73.9	99.7	57.4	103.1	121.3	193.1	256.1	438.2	1397.7
United States[1]	26.1	24.3	16.6	18.9	26.1	60.7	101.7	73.6	56.3	104.0	508.3
France[2]	15.0	16.0	25.8	23.5	24.9	31.7	58.8	49.8	45.9	26.8	318.1
Sweden	3.0	12.0	14.5	14.6	18.1	19.6	30.4	29.4	27.4	83.2 *	252.0 *
Canada	5.0	7.1	8.4	23.0	26.0	40.0	21.8	36.6	30.6	37.7	236.0
Switzerland	7.9	7.5	9.7	8.6	10.9	16.8	24.4	35.9	41.7	18.2	181.3
Austria	5.9	7.2	6.7	8.7	11.4	15.8	21.9	22.8	27.3	16.3	143.9
United Kingdom[3]	4.3	3.9	5.5	4.8	5.2	5.3	15.6 *	25.3 *	44.8 *	24.5 *	139.0 *
Netherlands	2.0	2.6	5.7	5.9	13.5	7.5	13.9	21.2	21.6	17.5	111.2
Belgium	2.9	3.7	5.3	7.7	6.0	5.1	8.1	13.0	15.2	17.7	84.5
Italy	3.1	4.6	5.4	6.5	11.1	1.3	2.3	4.8	23.3	2.5	64.7
Denmark	0.8	4.3	8.7	9.3	2.8	4.7	4.6	5.3	4.6	13.9	58.9
Hungary	–	–	–	–	–	–	27.0	18.3	5.5	6.0	56.7
Spain	1.4	1.1	2.4	2.3	2.5	3.3	2.9	6.9	7.3	12.7	42.6
Norway	0.2	0.3	0.9	2.7	8.6	6.6	4.5	4.0	4.6	5.3	37.4
Greece	0.5	0.8	1.4	4.3	7.0	8.4	3.0	6.2	2.7	2.0	36.0
Yugoslavia[4]	1.9	2.8	2.0	2.8	3.1	4.3	7.1	2.5	1.6	4.1	28.2
Australia	–	–	–	–	–	–	0.5	3.6	16.0	4.1	24.2
Finland	..	..	..	..	0.1	0.1	0.2	2.8	2.2	3.7	8.9
Japan	0.8	0.6	0.5	0.4	0.2	0.3	0.8	0.2	0.4	0.1	4.3
Portugal	1.5	0.4	0.1	0.3	0.5	0.4	0.2	0.1	0.3	0.7	4.3
Poland	–	–	–	–	–	–	–	–	2.5	0.6	3.1
Czechoslovakia[5]	–	–	–	–	–	–	–	–	2.0	0.8 *	2.8 *
Luxembourg	..	..	..	..	..	..	..	..	..	2.0 *	2.0 *
Romania	–	–	–	–	–	–	–	..	0.5	0.8	1.3
Bulgaria	–	–	–	–	–	–	–	–	0.1	0.2	0.2
TOTAL	101.7	134.2	193.2	243.6	235.0	334.8	470.6 *	554.8 *	639.8 *	839.3 *	3747.1 *

Sources: Statistics from national governments provided to UNHCR and the Intergovernmental Consultations on Asylum, Refugee and Migration Policies in Europe, North America and Australia; United States Department of Justice, *1990 Statistical Yearbook of the Immigration and Naturalization Service*. Washington DC: 1991.

1 Data refer to the number of applications ("cases") filed with the Immigration and Naturalization Service (INS). Cases filed by apprehended aliens or those denied by the INS which were renewed with immigration judges are excluded. Data are reported by U.S. Fiscal Year (1 October to 30 September).
2 The 1992 figure includes refugees resettled under French resettlement quota, whereas previous years do not. Persons under the age of 16 are not included in the French data.
3 The number for 1992 refers to asylum applications ("cases") only.
4 The numbers refer to persons originating from outside the territory of former Yugoslavia. The number for 1992 refers to the Federal Republic of Yugoslavia (Serbia and Montenegro) only.
5 On 1 January 1993, Czechoslovakia separated into two states: the Czech Republic and Slovakia.

– Fewer than 50 applications   .. Not available   * Estimated figure

The numbers in Annex I.5 are indicative since countries of asylum record asylum applications in a variety of ways. First, while most data in the table refer to individuals applying for asylum, some countries report the number of asylum applications, or "cases". Second, limited numbers of resettled or "quota" refugees are included in some European countries' figures, but excluded by France (until 1992) and the United States. Third, it is not clear how many people from the former Yugoslavia, and other groups that have received temporary asylum, have been included in the asylum statistics as such people are often not required to submit a formal application. Increasingly, people originating from a country considered "safe", or who have travelled via a country which could have granted them asylum, are not allowed to submit an asylum claim. Such people are therefore likely to be excluded from the official asylum statistics.

Some general trends can be observed. In 1983-1992, Germany received most applications for asylum (1.4 million) followed by the United States (508,000), France (318,000), Sweden (252,000) and Canada (236,000). Germany has not only been the largest receiver of asylum applicants since 1984, but also increased its share. Thus, whereas during 1983-1992, some 37 per cent of all asylum-seekers in the 26 listed countries requested asylum in Germany, by 1992 Germany's share had increased to 52 per cent. Conversely, in France the number of asylum applicants dropped significantly following the reorganization of the French Office for the Protection of Refugees and Stateless Persons (OFPRA) in 1990, and the subsequent acceleration in the processing of asylum applications as well as the abolition of the right to work for asylum-seekers in October 1991. France's share of the total number of asylum applicants decreased from 12 per cent in 1989 to 3 per cent in 1992. During 1983-1992, Sweden received the third largest overall number of asylum-seekers in Europe. However, the numbers of asylum applicants fell sharply in 1990 and 1991, following the introduction of changes in the country's normal asylum procedure in December 1989, before rising substantially again in 1992.

Annex I.6
Leading Nationalities of Asylum Applicants in Ten European Countries (by year of asylum application): 1988-1992[1]

	1988 ('000)	1988 (%)		1989 ('000)	1989 (%)		1990 ('000)	1990 (%)
Poland	39.2	18	Turkey	57.5	19	Romania	60.4	15
Turkey	34.8	16	Poland	32.1	11	Turkey	47.0	12
Former Yugoslavia	24.0	11	Former Yugoslavia	26.0	9	Former Yugoslavia	33.0	8
Iran (Islamic Rep. of)	17.4	8	Sri Lanka	19.7	6	Lebanon	29.5	7
Sri Lanka	8.1	4	Lebanon	14.4	5	Sri Lanka	19.0	5
Romania	7.0	3	Romania	14.4	5	Iran (Islamic Rep. of)	17.6	4
Zaire	6.7	3	Iran (Islamic Rep. of)	14.3	5	Poland	13.3	3
Lebanon	6.6	3	Zaire	10.7	4	India	11.6	3
Chile	6.3	3	Somalia	8.6	3	Zaire	10.7	3
Hungary	5.9	3	Ghana	7.9	3	Somalia	10.1	3
Other	59.9	28	Other	97.9	32	Other	143.9	36
TOTAL	215.9	100	TOTAL	303.5	100	TOTAL	396.1	100

	1991 ('000)	1991 (%)		1992 ('000)	1992 (%)		Total ('000)	Total (%)
Former Yugoslavia	115.5	24	Former Yugoslavia	229.6	35	Former Yugoslavia	428.2	21
Romania	58.3	12	Romania	114.2	17	Romania	254.3	12
Turkey	44.7	9	Turkey	36.9	6	Turkey	221.1	11
Sri Lanka	23.5	5	Sri Lanka	19.0	3	Poland	96.2	5
Zaire	17.3	4	Zaire	17.4	3	Sri Lanka	89.3	4
Iran (Islamic Rep. of)	15.1	3	Somalia	14.0	2	Iran (Islamic Rep. of)	72.0	3
Pakistan	13.4	3	Viet Nam	13.6	2	Lebanon	65.3	3
Nigeria	12.5	3	Iraq	13.4	2	Zaire	62.8	3
India	11.7	2	Nigeria	12.1	2	Pakistan	44.7	2
Ghana	11.0	2	Ghana	10.5	2	India	43.8	2
Other	165.9	34	Other	180.8	27	Other	688.4	33
TOTAL	489.0	100	TOTAL	661.4	100	GRAND TOTAL	2065.9	100

1 This table is based on a list of the 22 most common nationalities of asylum applicants in Austria, Belgium, Denmark, France, Germany, Netherlands, Norway, Sweden, Switzerland and the United Kingdom. The category "Other" normally includes smaller national groups. However, in the case of some asylum countries, for example France, it may include larger groups which do not rank among the leading 22 nationalities of asylum applicants arriving in all ten of the listed asylum countries. Nigeria and Viet Nam were listed separately only as of 1990.

A number of observations can be made with regard to the origin of asylum applicants. Figures in Annexes I.6 and I.7 relate to asylum applications which may be founded or unfounded. They do not imply a presumption of refugee status. First, a small number of nationalities account for the majority of asylum applications: between 1988 and 1992, one-third of all asylum applications were submitted by only two nationalities (people from former Yugoslavia and Romania), while only four nationalities accounted for almost 50 per cent of all claims. Second, people tend to seek asylum in the region: most asylum applicants came from Europe and Western Asia. Third, the leading countries of origin of asylum applicants have been high on the list for a number of years: Turkey and the former Yugoslavia, for example, have been among the top three countries of origin every year since 1988. Likewise, Sri Lanka has consistently ranked fourth or fifth.

Annex I.6 reflects some of the important political changes that have taken place in the world. First, the break-up of former Yugoslavia, which began in 1991, has resulted in thousands of refugees fleeing to Western Europe. As citizens from former Yugoslavia are allowed to stay in several European countries on a group basis, the numbers in Annex I.6 may possibly be under-represented. On a more positive note, the end of the Cold War has led to Hungary and Poland disappearing from the list of leading countries of origin; and by 1992, two other "traditional" countries of origin during the 1980s, the Islamic Republic of Iran and Lebanon, had also dropped out of the "top-ten" list. On the other hand, the relaxation of exit restrictions in Romania has given rise to a major outflow: since 1990 the country has ranked either first or second in the list of leading countries of origin of asylum applicants in Europe.

Germany has been the biggest recipient of most major groups of asylum applicants during the period 1988-1992 in absolute terms (see Annex I.7). However, significant differences exist in the relative distribution of asylum applicants in Europe: whereas people from former Yugoslavia formed the single largest group of asylum applicants in Germany and the Nordic countries, Turks were the largest group in France (22 per cent of all applicants) and Switzerland (33 per cent); Romanians ranked second highest in Germany (17 per cent of all claimants) and highest in Austria (32 per cent). Annex I.7 also shows how in some countries of asylum the majority of claims are submitted by a very small number of nationalities, while other countries attract a more heterogeneous assortment of asylum applicants.

Leading Nationalities of Asylum Applicants in Ten European Countries (by country of asylum application): 1988-1992

Austria	'000	%	Belgium	'000	%	Denmark	'000	%
Romania	32.4	31	Zaire	8.1	14	Former Yugoslavia	9.9	30
Former Yugoslavia	15.7	15	Romania	7.9	13	Stateless	4.1	12
Turkey	9.3	9	Ghana	6.7	11	Iraq	3.3	10
Poland	8.9	9	Turkey	5.1	9	Iran (Islamic Rep. of)	2.7	8
Iran (Islamic Rep. of)	5.4	5	India	4.5	8	Somalia	2.0	6
Czechoslovakia[1]	5.2	5	Former Yugoslavia	4.4	8	Sri Lanka	1.8	5
Hungary	3.0	3	Pakistan	3.1	5	Poland	1.2	4
Iraq	2.3	2	Poland	2.1	4	Romania	1.0	3
Pakistan	2.1	2	Nigeria	1.8	3	Lebanon	1.0	3
Lebanon	2.0	2	Bangladesh	1.0	2	Afghanistan	0.3	1
Other	17.5	17	Other	14.1	24	Other	5.7	17
TOTAL	104.0	100	TOTAL	59.0	100	TOTAL	33.0	100

France	'000	%	Germany	'000	%	Netherlands	'000	%
Turkey	46.5	22	Former Yugoslavia	259.9	23	Somalia	10.4	13
Zaire	24.6	12	Romania	185.4	17	Sri Lanka	7.2	9
Sri Lanka	14.5	7	Turkey	109.2	10	Former Yugoslavia	6.7	8
Romania	9.3	4	Poland	71.9	6	Iran (Islamic Rep. of)	6.1*	7
Pakistan	7.1	3	Lebanon	37.2	3	Romania	5.4	7
Ghana	4.8	2	Iran (Islamic Rep. of)	33.4	3	Ethiopia	3.7	5
Angola	4.8	2	Viet Nam	29.8	3	Poland	3.4	4
India	4.5	2	Sri Lanka	26.4	2	Turkey	3.3	4
Former Yugoslavia	3.9	2	Afghanistan	26.1	2	Ghana	3.1	4
Poland	3.4	2	Nigeria	24.2	2	Lebanon	3.0	4
Other	89.6	42	Other	308.2	28	Other	29.4	36
TOTAL	212.9	100	TOTAL	1111.8	100	TOTAL	81.7	100

Norway	'000	%	Sweden	'000	%	Switzerland	'000	%
Former Yugoslavia	6.7	27	Former Yugoslavia	87.0	46	Turkey	32.5	24
Iran (Islamic Rep. of)	2.4	10	Iran (Islamic Rep. of)	15.9	8	Former Yugoslavia	28.3	21
Somalia	2.4	10	Iraq	10.4	5	Sri Lanka	21.3	16
Sri Lanka	2.1	8	Lebanon	7.9	4	Lebanon	10.3	8
Chile	2.0	8	Somalia	7.2	4	Romania	5.9	4
Ethiopia	1.1	5	Ethiopia	5.9	3	Pakistan	4.9	4
Lebanon	0.9	3	Romania	5.4	3	India	4.2	3
Poland	0.8	3	Turkey	3.9	2	Zaire	3.4	2
Turkey	0.7	3	Chile	3.7	2	Somalia	2.3	2
Iraq	0.6	2	Sri Lanka	3.3	2	Bangladesh	2.2	2
Other	5.1	21	Other	39.2	21	Other	21.6	16
TOTAL	24.8	100	TOTAL	189.8	100	TOTAL	136.8	100

United Kingdom	'000	%	Total	'000	%
Sri Lanka	11.7	10	Former Yugoslavia	428.2	21
Turkey	10.4	9	Romania	254.3	12
Zaire	10.0	9	Turkey	221.1	11
Somalia	8.5	8	Poland	96.2	5
Iraq	8.0	7	Sri Lanka	89.3	4
Angola	7.1	6	Iran (Islamic Rep. of)	72.0	3
Pakistan	6.9	6	Lebanon	65.3	3
India	5.9	5	Zaire	62.8	3
Former Yugoslavia	5.7	5	Pakistan	44.7	2
Ghana	5.2	5	India	43.8	2
Other	32.9	29	Other	688.4	33
TOTAL	112.1	100	GRAND TOTAL	2065.9	100

Note: This table is based on a list of the 22 most common nationalities of asylum applicants in the ten specified European countries. The category "Other" normally includes smaller national groups. However, in the case of some asylum countries, for example France, it may include larger groups which do not rank among the leading 22 nationalities of asylum applicants arriving in all ten of the listed asylum countries. Angola, Nigeria and Viet Nam were listed separately only as of 1990.

1 As of 1 January 1993, Czechoslovakia separated into two states: the Czech Republic and Slovakia.

Annex I.8
Indicative Numbers of Returnees During 1992

To	From	Total	
AFRICA			
Angola		96,000	
	Zaire		61,000
	Zambia		35,000
Burundi		40,000	
	Zaire		27,000
	United Rep. of Tanzania		8,000
	Rwanda		5,000
Chad		7,000	
	Sudan		6,000
	Cameroon		1,000
Eritrea		5,000	
	Sudan		5,000
Ethiopia		7,000	
	Kenya		4,000
	Djibouti		3,000
Liberia		7,000	
	Guinea		3,000
	Ghana		3,000
	Côte d'Ivoire		1,000
Mozambique [1]		178,000	
	Malawi		175,000
	Zimbabwe		3,000
Sierra Leone		21,000	
	Liberia		19,000
	Guinea		2,000
Somalia		200,000	
	Ethiopia		200,000
South Africa		5,000	
	United Rep. of Tanzania		2,000
	Zambia		1,000
	Zimbabwe		1,000
	Mozambique		1,000
Sudan		1,000	
	Central African Rep.		1,000
Uganda		4,000	
	Sudan		4,000
AFRICA TOTAL		571,000	
ASIA			
Afghanistan		1,518,000	
	Pakistan		1,268,000
	Iran (Islamic Rep. of)		250,000
Cambodia		237,000	
	Thailand		235,000
	Indonesia		1,000
	Viet Nam		1,000

To	From	Total	
ASIA (Cont.)			
Iran (Islamic Rep. of)		1,000	
	Iraq		1,000
Iraq		29,000	
	Turkey		17,000
	Iran (Islamic Rep. of)		11,000
	Saudi Arabia		1,000
Lao People's Democratic Rep.		5,000	
	Thailand		3,000
	China		2,000
Myanmar [2]		6,000	
	Bangladesh		6,000
Sri Lanka		29,000	
	India		29,000
Viet Nam		17,000	
	Hong Kong		12,000
	Thailand		3,000
	Indonesia		1,000
	Malaysia		1,000
ASIA TOTAL		1,842,000	
EUROPE			
Federal Rep. of Yugoslavia [3]		3,000	
	Hungary		3,000
EUROPE TOTAL		3,000	
LATIN AMERICA			
El Salvador		2,000	
	Honduras		2,000
Guatemala		2,000	
	Mexico		2,000
Haiti		4,000	
	Cuba		3,000
	Bahamas		1,000
Nicaragua		2,000	
	Costa Rica		2,000
Suriname		4,000	
	French Guiana		4,000
LATIN AMERICA TOTAL		14,000	
TOTAL		2,430,000	

Note: repatriations involving less than 500 persons have been excluded.

1 Updated estimate from government
2 1,000 of whom repatriated with UNHCR assistance
3 Full name: Federal Republic of Yugoslavia (Serbia and Montenegro)

Annex II

International Instruments and Their Significance

Annex II.1

The Statute of the Office of the United Nations High Commissioner for Refugees

Adopted by the United Nations General Assembly on 14 December 1950 as Annex to General Assembly resolution 428 (V).

Article 1

The United Nations High Commissioner for Refugees, acting under the authority of the General Assembly, shall assume the function of providing international protection, under the auspices of the United Nations, to refugees who fall within the scope of the present Statute and of seeking permanent solutions for the problem of refugees by assisting Governments and, subject to the approval of the Governments concerned, private organizations to facilitate the voluntary repatriation of such refugees, or their assimilation within new national communities.

Article 2

The work of the High Commissioner shall be of an entirely non-political character; it shall be humanitarian and social and shall relate, as a rule, to groups and categories of refugees....

Annex II.2

The 1951 Convention and 1967 Protocol relating to the Status of Refugees

The Convention was adopted by the United Nations Conference on the Status of Refugees and Stateless Persons at Geneva from 2-25 July 1951 and entered into force on 22 April 1954. The Protocol relating to the Status of Refugees was adopted by the UN General Assembly on 16 December 1966 and came into force on 4 October 1967.

The Convention and the Protocol are the main international instruments that regulate the conduct of States in matters relating to the treatment of refugees. While the Convention does not create a right of asylum, it is important for the legal protection of refugees and the definition of their status. It attempts to establish an international code of rights for refugees on a general basis. It embodies principles that promote and safeguard their rights in the fields of employment, education, residence, freedom of movement, access to courts, naturalization and above all the security against return to a country where they may risk persecution.

The importance of the 1967 Protocol lies in the fact that it extends the scope of the 1951 Convention by removing the dateline of 1 January 1951 contained in the definition of the term refugee in Article 1 A(2), thus making the Convention applicable to people who become refugees after that date. The 1967 Protocol also provides that the Protocol be applied by States Parties without any geographic limitation. However if States have opted, when acceding to the 1951 Convention, to limit its application to events occurring in Europe [Article 1B(1)(a)], that limitation also applies to the 1967 Protocol.

Article 1 – Definition of the term "Refugee"

A(2) [Any person who]... owing to well-founded fear of being persecuted for reasons of race, religion, nationality, membership of particular social group or political opinion, is outside the country of his nationality and is unable to or, owing to such fear, is unwilling to avail himself of the protection of that country; or who, not having a nationality and being outside the country of his former habitual residence..., is unable or, owing to such fear, is unwilling to return to it. (as amended by Article 1(2) of the 1967 Protocol)

Article 33 – Prohibition of expulsion or return ("refoulement")

(1) No Contracting State shall expel or return ("refouler") a refugee in any manner whatsoever to the frontiers of territories where his life or freedom would be threatened on account of his race, religion, nationality, membership of a particular social group or political opinion.

Annex II.3

Universal Declaration of Human Rights

Adopted and proclaimed by United Nations General Assembly resolution 217 A (III) of 10 December 1948.

Article 9

No one shall be subjected to arbitrary arrest, detention or exile.

Article 13

(1) Everyone has the right to freedom of movement and residence within the borders of each state.

(2) Everyone has the right to leave any country, including his own, and to return to his country.

Article 14

(1) Everyone has the right to seek and enjoy in other countries asylum from persecution.

Article 15

(1) Everyone has the right to a nationality.

(2) No one shall be arbitrarily deprived of his nationality nor denied the right to change his nationality.

Annex II.4
International Covenants on Human Rights

The Covenant on Economic, Social and Cultural Rights and the Covenant on Civil and Political Rights were adopted by the UN General Assembly and opened for signature in December 1966. Both Covenants entered into force in early 1976.

The United Nations has set international human rights standards in some 70 covenants, conventions and treaties. The two International Covenants (on Economic, Social and Cultural Rights and on Civil and Political Rights) are among the UN treaties that impose legally binding obligations on states parties concerning the rights of people under their jurisdiction.

International Covenant on Civil and Political Rights

Article 2

(1) Each State Party to the present Covenant undertakes to respect and to ensure to all individuals within its territory and subject to its jurisdiction the rights recognized in the present Covenant, without distinction of any kind, such as race, colour, sex, language, religion, political or other opinion, national or social origin, property, birth or other status.

Article 12

(1) Everyone lawfully within the territory of a State shall, within that territory, have the right to liberty of movement and freedom to choose his residence.

(2) Everyone shall be free to leave any country, including his own.

(3) The above-mentioned rights shall not be subject to any restrictions except those which are provided by law, are necessary to protect national security, public order *(ordre public)* public health or morals or the rights and freedoms of others, and are consistent with the other rights recognized in the present Covenant.

(4) No one shall be arbitrarily deprived of the right to enter his own country.

Article 13

An alien lawfully in the territory of a State Party to the present Covenant may be expelled therefrom only in pursuance of a decision reached in accordance with law and shall, except where compelling reasons of national security otherwise require, be allowed to submit the reasons against his expulsion and to have his case reviewed by, and be represented for the purpose before, the competent authority or a person or persons especially designated by the competent authority.

Annex II.5
Convention Against Torture and Other Cruel, Inhuman or Degrading Treatment or Punishment

Approved by consensus by the UN General Assembly on 10 December 1984 as Annex to GA resolution 39/46.

The Convention extends the principle of *non-refoulement* and non-extradition to any State.

Article 3

(1) No State Party shall expel, return ("*refouler*") or extradite a person to another State where there are substantial grounds for believing that he would be in danger of being subjected to torture. For the purpose of determining whether there are such grounds, the competent authorities shall take into account all relevant considerations including, where applicable, the existence in the State concerned of a consistent pattern of gross, flagrant or mass violations of human rights.

Annex II.6
African Charter on Human and Peoples' Rights

Adopted by the 18th Assembly of the Heads of State and Government of the Organization of African Unity (OAU) on 27 June 1981 at Nairobi.

Article 12

(3) Every individual shall have the right, when persecuted, to seek and obtain asylum in other countries in accordance with the law of those countries and international conventions.

Annex II.7
Organization of African Unity (OAU) Convention Governing the Specific Aspects of Refugee Problems in Africa

Adopted by the Assembly of Heads of State and Government at its 6th Ordinary Session, Addis Ababa, 10 September 1969.

The OAU Convention adopts a broader definition of the term "refugee" than the internationally accepted definition found in the 1951 Convention and the 1967 Protocol relating to the Status of Refugees. It does not include any temporal or geographical limitations, nor any reference to earlier categories of refugees. The OAU Convention also regulates the question of asylum. In addition, it unambiguously stipulates that repatriation must be a voluntary act.

Article I – Definition of the term "Refugee"
1. [Definition as in Article 1 A (2) of the 1951 Convention]
2. The term "refugee" shall also apply to every person who, owing to external aggression, occupation, foreign domination or events seriously disturbing public order in either part or the whole of his country of origin or nationality, is compelled to leave his place of habitual residence in order to seek refuge in another place outside his country of origin or nationality.

Article II – Asylum
1. Member States of the OAU shall use their best endeavours consistent with their respective legislations to receive refugees and to secure the settlement of those refugees who, for well-founded reasons, are unable or unwilling to return to their country of origin or nationality.
3. No person shall be subjected by a Member State to measures such as rejection at the frontier, return or expulsion, which would compel him to return to or remain in a territory where his life, physical integrity or liberty would be threatened for the reasons set out in Article I, paragraphs 1 and 2.

Article V – Voluntary Repatriation
1. The essentially voluntary character of repatriation shall be respected in all cases and no refugee shall be repatriated against his will.

Article VIII – Co-operation with the Office of the United Nations High Commissioner for Refugees
1. Member States shall co-operate with the Office of the United Nations High Commissioner for Refugees.

Annex II.8
American Convention on Human Rights "Pact of San José, Costa Rica"

Signed on 22 November 1969 at the Inter-American Specialized Conference on Human Rights, held at San José, Costa Rica.

Article 22
(2) Every person has the right to leave any country freely, including his own.
(5) No one can be expelled from the territory of the state of which he is a national or be deprived of the right to enter it.
(7) Every person has the right to seek and be granted asylum in a foreign territory, in accordance with the legislation of the state and international conventions, in the event he is being pursued for political offenses or related common crimes.
(8) In no case may an alien be deported or returned to a country, regardless of whether or not it is his country of origin, if in that country his right to life or personal freedom is in danger of being violated because of his race, nationality, religion, social status or political opinion.

Annex II.9
Cartagena Declaration on Refugees

Adopted at the Colloquium, entitled "Coloquio Sobre la Protección Internacional de los Refugiados en América Central, México y Panamá: Problemas Jurídicos y Humanitarios" held from 19 – 22 November 1984 Cartagena, Colombia.

In 1984, experts and representatives from ten governments met at a Colloquium in Cartagena, Colombia, to search for solutions to the acute refugee problems in the region. The Colloquium subsequently adopted the Cartagena Declaration on Refugees.

The Declaration seeks, inter alia, *to promote the adoption of national laws and regulations that facilitate the application of the 1951 Convention and the 1967 Protocol relating to the Status of Refugees. It emphasizes that repatriation of refugees must be voluntary, and embodies principles for their protection, assistance and reintegration.*

Like the OAU Convention (see 7 above), the Cartagena Declaration broadens the definition of the term "refugee" found in the 1951 Convention. Although a non-binding instrument, the Declaration has been accepted and is being applied by the Latin American States to the degree that it has entered the domain of international law.

Conclusion 3

To reiterate that, in view of the experience gained from the massive flows of refugees in the Central American area, it is necessary to consider enlarging the concept of a refugee, bearing in mind, as far as appropriate and in the light of the situation prevailing in the region, the precedent of the OAU Convention (article 1, paragraph 2) and the doctrine employed in the reports of the Inter-American Commission on Human Rights. Hence the definition or concept of a refugee to be recommended for use in the region is one which, in addition to containing the elements of the 1951 Convention and the 1967 Protocol, includes among refugees persons who have fled their country because their lives, safety or freedom have been threatened by generalized violence, foreign aggression, internal conflicts, massive violation of human rights or other circumstances which have seriously disturbed public order.

Annex II.10
Convention Determining the State Responsible for examining Applications for Asylum lodged in one of the Member States of the European Communities

Signed by the Member States of the European Communities at Dublin on 15 June 1990.

The treaty, known as the Dublin Convention, was signed as one of the collective measures taken by Member States towards the realization of a single market and the elimination of controls at internal Community borders.

In its preamble, the signatories to the Dublin Convention express their determination to guarantee adequate protection to refugees in keeping with their common humanitarian tradition. The Dublin Convention also contains an expression of the signatories' awareness of the need to take measures to avoid leaving applicants for asylum in doubt for too long as regards the likely outcome of their applications. The signatories also state their concern to provide all applicants for asylum with a guarantee that their applications will be examined by one of the Member States and to ensure that applicants for asylum are not referred successively from one Member State to another.

In accordance with these objectives, the Dublin Convention sets rules for determining the State responsible for examining applications for asylum. The Dublin Convention also elaborates the circumstances and the conditions which govern the transfer or re-admission of applicants between Member States. It provides, moreover, for the mutual exchange between Member States of general information and of information on individual cases. A number of safeguards are included concerning the protection of personal data.

In Article 2 of the Dublin Convention, Member States of the European Communities reaffirm their obligations under the 1951 Convention and 1967 Protocol relating to the Status of Refugees, with no geographic restriction of the scope of these instruments, and restate their commitment to co-operate with the United Nations High Commissioner for Refugees in applying them.

List of 120 States party to the 1951 Convention and/or the 1967 Protocol Relating to the Status of Refugees

113 States are Party both to the 1951 Convention and the 1967 Protocol

Albania	Czech Republic	Jamaica	Rwanda
Algeria	Denmark[2]	Japan	Sao Tome and Principe
Angola	Djibouti	Kenya	Senegal
Argentina	Dominican Republic	Korea, Republic of	Seychelles
Australia[1]	Ecuador	Lesotho	Sierra Leone
Austria	Egypt	Liberia	Slovak Republic
Azerbaijan	El Salvador	Liechtenstein	Slovenia
Belgium	Equatorial Guinea	Luxembourg	Somalia
Belize	Ethiopia	Malawi	Spain
Benin	Fiji	Mali	Sudan
Bolivia	Finland	Malta *	Suriname
Botswana	France[3]	Mauritania	Sweden
Brazil	Gabon	Morocco	Switzerland
Bulgaria	Gambia	Mozambique	Togo
Burkina Faso	Germany	Netherlands[4]	Tunisia
Burundi	Ghana	New Zealand	Turkey *
Cambodia	Greece	Nicaragua	Tuvalu
Cameroon	Guatemala	Niger	Uganda
Canada	Guinea	Nigeria	United Kingdom[5]
Central African Republic	Guinea-Bissau	Norway	United Republic of Tanzania
Chad	Haiti	Panama	Uruguay
Chile	Holy See	Papua New Guinea	Yemen
China	Honduras	Paraguay	Yugoslavia
Colombia	Hungary *	Peru	Zaire
Congo	Iceland	Philippines	Zambia
Costa Rica	Iran, Islamic Republic of	Poland	Zimbabwe
Côte d'Ivoire	Ireland	Portugal	
Croatia	Israel	Romania	
Cyprus	Italy	Russian Federation	

3 States are Party only to the 1951 Convention

Madagascar *
Monaco *
Samoa

4 States are Party only to the 1967 Protocol

Cape Verde
Swaziland
United States of America
Venezuela

---

* These States have made a declaration in accordance with Article 1 (B) (1) of the 1951 Convention to the effect that the words "events occurring before 1 January 1951" in Article 1, Section A, should be understood to mean "events occurring in Europe before 1 January 1951". All other States Parties apply the Convention without geographical limitation. Malta and Turkey have expressly maintained their declarations of geographical limitation with regard to the 1951 Convention upon acceding to the 1967 Protocol.

1 Australia extended application of the Convention to Norfolk Island.
2 Denmark declared that the Convention was also applicable to Greenland.
3 France declared that the Convention applied to all territories for whose international relations France was responsible.
4 The Netherlands extended application of the Protocol to Aruba.
5 The United Kingdom extended application of the Convention to the following territories for the conduct of whose international relations the Government of the United Kingdom is responsible: Channel Islands, Falkland Islands (Malvinas), Isle of Man, St. Helena. The United Kingdom declared that its accession to the Protocol did not apply to Jersey, but extended its application to Montserrat.

This list does not include any states who may have become State Parties to the 1951 Convention and/or the 1967 Protocol after 1 June 1993.

The Work of UNHCR

Annex III

Establishment of UNHCR

The Office of the United Nations High Commissioner for Refugees (UNHCR) was set up by the UN General Assembly. Since 1 January 1951, UNHCR has been responsible for protecting refugees and promoting lasting solutions to their problems.

Although the organization was initially established as a temporary one – its lifespan was originally to be three years – it soon became clear that refugee issues would require continued attention. The Assembly has consequently renewed UNHCR's mandate for successive five-year periods. The most recent extension prolongs UNHCR's existence from 1 January 1994 to 31 December 1998.

The High Commissioner

The High Commissioner for Refugees is elected by the UN General Assembly on the nomination of the Secretary-General. There have been eight High Commissioners since UNHCR was established in 1951 (see Box III.1). The current incumbent, Mrs Sadako Ogata of Japan, took up office on 1 January 1991. The High Commissioner acts under the authority of the General Assembly. She also reports to UNHCR's Executive Committee, a body composed at present of 46 governments which oversees UNHCR's assistance budgets and advises on refugee protection (see Box III.2).

UNHCR's mandate

UNHCR's founding statute[33] makes it clear that the organization's work is humanitarian and entirely non-political. It entrusts UNHCR with two main and closely related functions – to protect refugees and to promote durable solutions to their problems.

According to its Statute, UNHCR is competent to assist: *Any person who, "owing to well-ounded fear of being persecuted for reasons of race, religion, nationality, or political opinion, is outside the country of his nationality and is unable or, owing to such fear or for reasons*

169

High Commissioners

Eight High Commissioners have served since UNHCR was established in 1951. They are:

Mr Gerrit J. van Heuven Goedhart (Netherlands)
December 1950 – July 1956

Mr Auguste R. Lindt
(Switzerland)
December 1956 – December 1960

Mr Felix Schnyder
(Switzerland)
December 1960 – December 1965

Sadruddin Aga Khan
(Iran)
December 1965 – December 1977

Mr Poul Hartling
(Denmark)
January 1978 – December 1985

Mr Jean-Pierre Hocké
(Switzerland)
January 1986 – November 1989

Mr Thorvald Stoltenberg
(Norway)
January 1990 – November 1990

Mrs Sadako Ogata
(Japan)
January 1991 – present

other than personal convenience, is unwilling to avail himself of the protection of that country; or who, not having a nationality and being outside the country of his former habitual residence, is unable or, owing to such fear or for reasons other than personal convenience, is unwilling to return to it."

While this definition still forms the core of UNHCR's mandate, additional criteria have been progressively introduced to accommodate the evolving nature of refugee flows in recent decades. In typical situations today, UNHCR provides protection and assistance to groups of refugees fleeing combinations of persecution, conflict and widespread violations of human rights. In such circumstances, UNHCR usually bases its intervention on a general assessment of conditions in the refugee-producing country rather than on an examination of each person's individual claim to asylum.

Initially, UNHCR's mandate was limited to people outside their country of origin. Over time, however, as part of its duty to ensure that voluntary repatriation schemes are sustainable,[34] it has become involved in assisting and protecting returnees in their home countries. In recent years, moreover, the General Assembly and the Secretary-General have increasingly frequently called on UNHCR to protect or assist particular groups of internally displaced people who have not crossed an international border but are in a refugee-like situation inside their country of origin. In November 1991, for example, the Secretary-General asked UNHCR to assume the role of lead UN agency for humanitarian

Composition of UNHCR's Executive Committee

UNHCR's Executive Committee is made up of governments which have a particular interest in refugee matters. Many are either important asylum countries or major donors to UNHCR programmes. Following the election of Ethiopia and Hungary in 1992, the Executive Committee is composed of the following 46 member states:

Algeria, Argentina, Australia, Austria, Belgium, Brazil, Canada, China, Colombia, Denmark, Ethiopia, Finland, France, Germany, Greece, Holy See, Hungary, the Islamic Republic of Iran, Israel, Italy, Japan, Lebanon, Lesotho, Madagascar, Morocco, Namibia, Netherlands, Nicaragua, Nigeria, Norway, Pakistan, Philippines, Somalia, Sudan, Sweden, Switzerland, Thailand, Tunisia, Turkey, Uganda, United Kingdom, United Republic of Tanzania, United States of America, Venezuela, Yugoslavia and Zaire.

In 1993, Spain made a formal application to become the 47th member of the Committee.

assistance to victims of the conflict in former Yugoslavia. By July 1993, it was continuing to provide massive humanitarian relief to roughly 2.3 million internally displaced people and war victims in Bosnia and Herzegovina. .

Additional functions of UNHCR

At first, material aspects of refugee relief were seen to be the responsibility of the government which had granted asylum. However, as many of the world's more recent major refugee flows have occurred in less developed countries, UNHCR has acquired the additional role of co-ordinating material assistance for refugees, returnees and, in specific instances, displaced people. Although not mentioned in the organization's Statute, this has become one of its principal functions alongside protection and the promotion of solutions.

As of June 1993, UNHCR employed 3,703 staff members to carry out its functions. Of these, 810 were stationed at its Geneva headquarters and 2,893 deployed in some 177 field offices in 106 countries. The map of UNHCR's presence throughout the world changes rapidly as new refugee situations emerge or possibilities for solutions are consolidated.

Refugee protection

The protection of refugees remains UNHCR's *raison d'être*. Protection lies at the heart of the organization's efforts to find lasting solutions to the plight of refugees and provides the context in which it carries out its relief activities.

In performing its protection function, UNHCR tries to ensure that refugees are granted asylum and a legal status which takes account of their particular situation and needs. Crucial to this legal status is the widely accepted principle of *non-refoulement*, which prohibits the expulsion or forcible return of refugees to a country where they may have reason to fear persecution or other threats to their lives, liberty or security.

In order to promote and safeguard the rights of refugees UNHCR tries particularly:

• To encourage governments to subscribe to international and regional conventions and arrangements concerning refugees, returnees and displaced people, and to ensure that the standards they set out are effectively put into practice.

• To promote the granting of asylum to refugees i.e. to ensure that they are admitted to safety and protected against forcible return to a country where they have reason to fear persecution or other serious harm.

• To ensure that applications for asylum are examined fairly and that asylum-seekers are protected, while their requests are being examined, against forcible return to a country where their freedom or lives would be endangered.

• To ensure that refugees are treated in accordance with recognized international standards and receive an appropriate legal status, including, wherever possible, the same economic and social rights as nationals of the country in which they have been given asylum.

• To help refugees to cease being refugees either through voluntary repatriation to their countries of origin, or, if this is not feasible, through the eventual acquisition of the nationality of their country of residence.

• To help reintegrate refugees returning to their home country in close consultation with the government concerned and to monitor amnesties, guarantees or assurances on the basis of which they have returned home.

• To promote the physical security of refugees, asylum-seekers and returnees, particularly their safety from military attacks and other acts of violence.

• To promote the reunification of refugee families.

Recent trends

Refugee numbers have been increasing dramatically. By early 1993, the world's refugee population had grown to 18.2 million. Millions more people had been uprooted within their own countries. Whilst maintaining its non-political stance, UNHCR has reacted by trying to address the refugee problem in its totality – from exodus to return and reintegration, through a strategy which particularly emphasizes emergency preparedness and response, the pursuit of solutions, and the development of preventive activities.

Responding to emergencies

When large-scale refugee influxes occur, it is vital to be able to respond rapidly despite difficult conditions. Since the start of the 1990s, UNHCR has mounted emergency operations in an accelerating series of crises. These have included the flight of 1.8 million Iraqi Kurds to the Islamic Republic of Iran and the border between Turkey and Iraq; the war that has produced some 3.6 million refugees, displaced people and victims of conflict in the former Yugoslavia; the arrival of about 420,000 refugees in Kenya; an exodus of around 260,000 refugees from Myanmar into Bangladesh and an influx of over 85,000 asylum-seekers from Bhutan into Nepal. In addition, crises in the Transcaucasus and Central Asia led the organization to dispatch Emergency Response Teams to Armenia, Azerbaijan and Tajikistan in early December 1992, making these countries, with their 1.5 million displaced

people and refugees, a new focus of UNHCR concern and activity. In early 1993, UNHCR began to deal with a new exodus of some 280,000 refugees from Togo into Benin and Ghana.

A $25 million emergency fund allows UNHCR to provide a rapid response to new refugee situations. If this initial assistance proves insufficient to meet the full range of needs arising from a large-scale movement of refugees, special appeals are launched to raise funds from the international community.

The enormous challenges posed by the refugee emergency in the Persian Gulf in the spring of 1991 revealed weaknesses in UNHCR's emergency response capacity, prompting the High Commissioner to take a number of corrective measures. A structure of emergency response teams was introduced and arrangements made to pre-position and stockpile relief supplies to be drawn on in emergencies. To provide yet further flexibility, standby arrangements were made with the Danish and Norwegian Refugee Councils and the United Nations Volunteers (UNV) for the quick deployment of staff to emergency operations in any part of the world. As a result, UNHCR has been able to respond with increasing speed to subsequent crises.

Promoting solutions

In seeking durable solutions to refugees' problems, UNHCR attempts to help those who wish to go home to do so, and tries to assist them to reintegrate into their home communities. Where this is not feasible, it works to help them integrate in countries of asylum or, failing that, to resettle them in other countries.

(a) Voluntary repatriation

Voluntary repatriation has long been regarded as the preferred solution to refugee problems. In 1992, UNHCR helped some 2.4 million refugees to return home voluntarily. Return movements have continued in 1993. UNHCR's approach to voluntary repatriation depends on a number of factors, most importantly conditions in the country of origin. Unless it is convinced that refugees can return in reasonable safety, the organization does not actively promote return. It may, however, facilitate existing spontaneous movements – as, for example, through the travel and in-kind grants it has provided to 1.7 million people who have gone back to Afghanistan from Pakistan and the Islamic Republic of Iran since April 1992. In some cases, where conditions in the country of origin permit, it may actively promote and organize the return movement – as was the case with the 41,000 refugees airlifted home to Namibia in 1989 or the 365,000 Cambodian refugees who went home from Thailand in 1992 and early 1993. In other instances, it promotes repatriation and provides assistance to returnees, but only organizes transport for people unable to make their own arrangements. Such has been the approach to the repatriation of some 1.3 million Mozambican refugees that got under way in mid-1993, presaging a resolution of the largest single refugee problem on the African continent.

Where voluntary repatriation is organized or facilitated by UNHCR, the Office attempts, wherever possible, to ensure that a legal framework is set up to protect the returnees' rights and interests. Steps taken include negotiating amnesties and guarantees of non-recrimination against returnees. Wherever possible, these form the substance of written repatriation agreements. Frequently, tripartite agreements are drawn up between the country of origin, the country of asylum and UNHCR, specifying the conditions of return and setting out safeguards for returnees.

Nevertheless, optimism about voluntary repatriation has been tempered by the fact that many refugees return to situations of devastation and uncertainty – or even outright insecurity. Until recently, it was assumed that reintegration would occur spontaneously or that governments, assisted by development agencies, would address the needs of returnees and their communities via national development programmes. These assumptions have largely proved ill-founded, and it is now clear that relief assistance and longer-term development programmes are separated by a wide gap, which threatens the successful reintegration of returnees and the viability of their communities.

UNHCR is therefore adopting new approaches. In south-eastern Ethiopia, where the situation is one of general deprivation, it has ceased to distinguish between refugees, returnees and affected local people. In a co-operative effort with other UN and non-governmental agencies, the organization has moved beyond its traditional mandate in an effort to meet the needs of the entire community, stabilize the population and pre-empt renewed displacement. In other repatriation operations, from Central America to Cambodia and Somalia, UNHCR has increasingly opted for "quick impact projects" – often in collaboration with UNDP – to help returnees and their communities regain self-sufficiency.

(b) Local settlement

In cases where voluntary repatriation is unlikely to take place in the foreseeable future, the best solution is often to settle refugees within the host country. This can only be done, however, with the agreement of the government of the asylum country concerned and, as refugee numbers have escalated, local settlement opportunities have tended to become increasingly restricted.

In industrialized countries, government welfare systems and NGOs provide the bulk of the resources necessary to integrate refugees. Elsewhere, UNHCR furnishes varying degrees of support for local settlement projects in both rural and urban settings. Traditionally, local integration projects in rural areas have taken the form of settlements such as those supported by UNHCR in Ethiopia, Mexico, the People's Republic of China, Uganda, Zaire and Zambia. In urban or semi-urban areas, assistance is given to individual refugees to help them integrate. When possible, UNHCR provides education, vocational training and counselling to help refugees gain access to employment and the means to become independent (see Box III.4).

(c) Third country resettlement

For refugees who can neither return to their country of origin nor safely remain in their country of refuge, the only solution is to resettle in a third country. A number of countries offer

Refugee Education

UNHCR supports four kinds of education programmes for refugees: primary, secondary, tertiary and non-formal. These programmes are managed by either the governments of asylum countries or by NGOs, both of which often provide part of the financial support required. Unfortunately, however, only a minority of the world's refugee children go to school. Education programmes are often the first victims of any cuts in assistance budgets, with higher priority being given to food, shelter and medical care. Sadly, if exile and suffering often deprive young refugees of their childhood, lack of educational opportunities can also rob them of their future.

Wherever possible, refugee children receive a basic primary education. In 1992, UNHCR supported 86 primary school projects around the world. These covered an estimated 36 per cent of primary-school-age refugee children. Some 60 per cent of those enrolled in schools were boys and 40 per cent girls. Approximately 70 per cent of those in school were in the first two grades of the primary cycle which varies in length, but which usually consists of six grades.

Assistance at secondary and tertiary levels takes the form of scholarships and is linked to UNHCR's search for durable solutions. Only about 10 per cent of the refugees eligible for secondary and tertiary education were assisted. 79 per cent of those enrolled in secondary schools were boys and 21 per cent girls, while at tertiary level, 85 per cent were men and only 15 per cent were women.

Non-formal programmes aim to help refugees acquire skills useful in the context of repatriation, local settlement or resettlement in third countries. They usually include a variety of vocational and technical courses, adult literacy and foreign language training.

asylum to refugees only on a temporary basis, on condition that they are subsequently resettled. Even in countries that do not impose this condition, local economic, political or security factors may sometimes make it necessary to move the refugee elsewhere. The decision to resettle a refugee is normally taken only in the absence of other options and when there is no alternative way to guarantee the legal or physical security of the person concerned.

In 1991 and 1992, UNHCR sought resettlement opportunities for about 75,600 and 42,300 people respectively – much less than half a per cent of the total world refugee population. But resettlement countries could not accommodate even this tiny proportion: there was a shortfall of 55 per cent in 1991 and of 20 per cent in 1992 (see Figure III.A).

In 1989, following the introduction of the Comprehensive Plan of Action, blanket resettlement for Indo-Chinese refugees ceased, and the major focus of resettlement activity shifted to the Middle East. In 1992, UNHCR sought to resettle some 30,000 Iraqis from Saudi Arabia after efforts to explore possibilities for voluntary repatriation had failed. Between April 1992 and June 1993, approximately 10,880 Iraqis had been accepted for resettlement, several thousand of them in the Islamic Republic of Iran.

Another major challenge arose in 1992 concerning the resettlement of inmates from places of detention in Bosnia and Herzegovina. An emergency operation started on 1 October 1992 to transfer detainees to a UNHCR centre at Karlovac in Croatia. By early July 1993, 22 countries had offered temporary protection or resettlement to the ex-detainees and their families and over 11,000 people had left for third countries.

Fig. III.A
Shortfall of Resettlement Places in 1990, 1991 and 1992

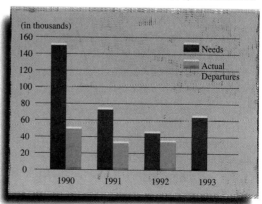

Resettlement efforts in Africa in 1992 continued to focus on countries of the Horn. With civil strife and ethnic warfare widespread, resettlement for especially vulnerable refugees in Africa – including women-at-risk, victims of torture and disabled refugees – remains a serious concern for UNHCR. Although governments responded generously to the resettlement needs of African refugees in 1992, UNHCR had to make a special appeal in August for resettlement places, particularly for Somali war victims. Just over 6,000 African refugees were resettled during the year, but at the end of the year a further 6,000 were still awaiting placement.

The overall numbers of refugees being resettled under UNHCR auspices has declined since 1989. Nevertheless, resettlement remains an important solution for refugees of many nationalities who cannot be guaranteed protection in the country or territory to which they have fled, as well as for vulnerable groups with special needs.

Prevention in countries of origin

In the 1990s, UNHCR has begun to undertake preventive initiatives in countries which currently produce refugees or which may do so in the future. A wide range of preventive activities are carried out both before and during refugee crises. In the latter case, they frequently take place in the broader context of the United Nations' peace-keeping or peace-making efforts.

Preventive action being developed by UNHCR includes initiatives to forestall and manage possible refugee flows through institution-building and training in countries likely to produce refugees and in those which may need to offer asylum. This has been a growing focus of UNHCR activity in Eastern Europe and the countries of the former Soviet Union. In situations where economically motivated migrants may seek to take advantage of refugee channels, mass information programmes – such as those run by UNHCR in Viet Nam and Albania – have been launched to provide a clearer understanding of refugee status. Such programmes aim to discourage people who may seek to use asylum channels for economic reasons, while keeping them open for those who flee persecution.

Where refugee crises have already erupted, UNHCR has become more directly involved with internally displaced people, and even – as in Bosnia and Herzegovina and Somalia – with other local people. Although UNHCR's general mandate does not extend to the internally displaced, it has increasingly undertaken humanitarian action on their behalf, with a view not only to providing relief but also to averting further internal displacement and the need to seek refuge abroad.

The massive humanitarian assistance operation run by UNHCR in Bosnia and Herzegovina falls into this category. Almost 600 UNHCR staff in the former Yugoslavia have helped not only to distribute relief to displaced and besieged populations, but also to meet their protection needs. In Somalia, UNHCR has channelled assistance across the border from Kenya in an effort to stabilize population movements and eventually create conditions conducive to the return of refugees. UNHCR's Open Relief Centres in Sri Lanka have become havens of safety, accepted and respected by both warring parties.

In responding to refugee crises, UNHCR attempts, wherever possible, to link prevention of further displacement to the promotion of solutions. In Tajikistan, for example, it has been actively participating in integrated UN efforts to restore peace by providing relief to the internally displaced and helping people return to their places of origin. In this way it hopes to prevent the escalation of displacement problems whilst providing solutions for the 60,000 Tajik refugees who fled to Afghanistan, as well as for the much larger numbers who have left their homes but stayed in Tajikistan.

Providing material assistance

Most of the world's 18.2 million refugees have found asylum in the least developed countries or in states which cannot be expected to shoulder the refugee presence unassisted. In such cases, UNHCR – in consultation with the government of the asylum country concerned – provides material assistance including food, shelter, medical aid and, in many situations, education and other social services.

The rapid growth in refugee numbers around the world has led to a many fold increase in UNHCR's assistance budgets in recent years. By 1992, the organization's total annual budget had risen to $1,093,058,700 (see Figure III.B).

In 1991 and 1992, UNHCR's largest assistance programmes were as follow s (Fig. III.C):

Fig III.C
UNHCR Ten Largest Programmes in 1991 and 1992
(in thousands of US dollars)

Country or territory	Level of assistance	Situation
1991		
Ethiopia	86,706.9	Assistance to Somali and Sudanese refugee, and Ethiopian returnees
Western Asia	84,558.9	Emergency assistance in the Persian Gulf
Iraq	74,918.0	Emergency assistance in the Persian Gulf
Iran (Islamic Rep.of)	59,455.0	Assistance to Afghan and Iraqi refugees
Malawi	49,915.2	Assistance to Mozambican refugees
Pakistan	45,475.1	Assistance to Afghan refugees
Sudan	42,995.8	Assistance to Ethiopian and Chadian refugees
Thailand	34,155.1	Assistance to Indo-Chinese refugees
Hong Kong	24,206.0	Assistance to Vietnamese refugees
Guinea	15,763.1	Assistance to Liberian refugees
1992		
Former Yugoslavia	296,518.6	Assistance to displaced people
Kenya	65,370.4	Assistance to Somali refugees
Pakistan	60,092.6	Assistance to Afghan refugees
Ethiopia	48,292.5	Assistance to Somali and Sudanese refugee, and Ethiopian returnees
Cambodia	37,273.5	Assistance to returnees
Malawi	27,924.1	Assistance to Mozambican refugees
Thailand	26,762.7	Assistance to Indo-Chinese refugees
Hong Kong	24,540.8	Assistance to Vietnamese refugee
Iraq	22,733.1	Emergency assistance in the Persian Gulf
Iran (Islamic Rep.of)	21,911.5	Assistance to Afghan and Iraqi refugees

Fig III.B
UNHCR Budget by Region for 1991 and 1992
– all sources of funds (in thousands of US dollars)

Region	1991	1992
Africa	303,338.9	298,169.9
Asia	425,310.0	327,463.9
Europe	26,845.0	327,998.3
Latin America	43,744.6	46,983.5
North America	2,711.4	2,823.7
Oceania	2,624.8	1,078.1
Headquarters/Global projects	78,363.4	88,541.3
TOTAL	882,938.1	1,093,058.7

Funding UNHCR programmes

With the exception of a very limited subsidy from the UN Regular Budget (which is used exclusively for administrative costs), UNHCR's assistance programmes are funded by voluntary contributions from governments, intergovernmental and non-governmental organizations, and individuals (see Figures III.D and III.E).

These so-called "voluntary funds" finance all UNHCR assistance programmes worldwide. UNHCR's annual voluntary funds expenditure has risen rapidly over the last 25 years (see Figure III.F) reaching $1,071,884,345 in 1992.

Building partnerships

From the outset, UNHCR's work was intended to be undertaken jointly with other members of the international community. As its activities have increased and diversified, UNHCR's relations with other organs and agencies of the UN system, with intergovernmental organizations and NGOs, and even with the armed forces, have become increasingly important.

UNHCR draws on the expertise of other UN organizations in matters such as food production (FAO), health measures (WHO), education (UNESCO), child welfare (UNICEF) and vocational training (ILO). The World Food Programme (WFP) plays an important part in supplying food until refugees arc able to grow their own crops or become self-sufficient through other activities. In Central America, Cambodia and elsewhere, UNHCR and UNDP are co-operating increasingly closely as returnees frequently need development

176

Fig. III.D
**Top 22 Contributors to UNHCR
in Absolute Terms in 1992**

Governments and the European Community	Contributions ($US millions)
1 United States of America	240.69
2 European Community	228.87
3 Japan	119.62
4 Sweden	91.75
5 Germany	85.00
6 United Kingdom	67.59
7 Norway	50.38
8 Netherlands	44.65
9 Canada	41.72
10 Denmark	39.39
11 France	35.19
12 Finland	30.14
13 Switzerland	24.34
14 Italy	21.99
15 Australia	8.42
16 Belgium	6.05
17 Spain	3.77
18 Oman	3.20
19 Austria	2.34
20 Morocco	1.98
21 Luxembourg	1.25
22 Ireland	1.02

(Contributions as recorded up to 23 June 1993)

Fig. III.E
**Top 22 Contributors to UNHCR
Per Capita in 1992**

Governments and the European Community	Population[1] (millions)	Contributions[2] ($US millions)	Per Capita ($US)
1 Norway	4.3	50.38	11.72
2 Sweden	8.6	91.75	10.67
3 Denmark	5.2	39.39	7.57
4 Finland	5.0	30.14	6.03
5 Switzerland	6.8	24.34	3.58
6 Luxembourg	0.4	1.25	3.13
7 Netherlands	15.1	44.65	2.96
8 Liechtenstein	0.03	0.067	2.23
9 Oman	1.6	3.20	2.00
10 Canada	27.0	41.72	1.55
11 United Kingdom	57.7	67.59	1.17
12 Germany	80.4	85.00	1.06
13 Japan	123.9	119.62	0.97
14 United States of America	252.7	240.69	0.95
15 European Community	345.5	228.87	0.66
16 France	57.0	35.19	0.62
17 Belgium	9.8	6.05	0.62
18 Australia	17.3	8.42	0.49
19 Italy	57.1	21.99	0.39
20 Iceland	0.3	0.094	0.31
21 Austria	7.8	2.34	0.30
22 Ireland	3.5	1.02	0.29

1 Based on latest official estimates of 1991 population figures in United Nations Statistical Division, *Monthly Bulletin of Statistics*, Vol. XLVII No. 4, April 1993
2 As recorded up to 26 June 1993

Fig. III.F
UNHCR Expenditure: 1967 – 1992 (in US dollars)

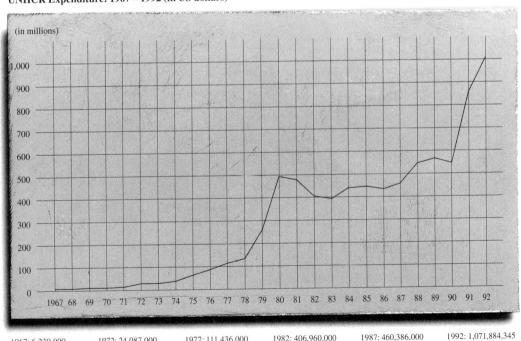

1967: 6,230,000	1972: 24,087,000	1977: 111,436,000	1982: 406,960,000	1987: 460,386,000	1992: 1,071,884,345
1968: 7,041,000	1973: 24,456,000	1978: 134,681,000	1983: 397,663,200	1988: 545,497,400	
1969: 8,651,000	1974: 34,826,000	1979: 269,995,000	1984: 444,200,300	1989: 570,328,400	
1970: 8,308,000	1975: 69,006,000	1980: 496,956,000	1985: 457,849,000	1990: 544,009,200	
1971: 9,427,000	1976: 90,862,000	1981: 474,256,500	1986: 440,725,000	1991: 862,547,700	

assistance in order to reintegrate effectively into their home communities. In a number of situations where refugees have not been able to return home, the World Bank, the International Fund for Agricultural Development (IFAD) and UNHCR have joined forces to plan, finance and implement projects which aim to pro-mote self-reliance. These include agricultural activities and schemes to create employment opportunities for refugees in their country of asylum.

More than ever before, success in redressing and preventing refugee problems depends on the effective co-ordination of all concerned actors: governmental, intergovernmental and non-governmental. This has sometimes been achieved by designating a lead agency responsible for the co-ordination of a particular operation, notably at the field level. In early 1992, to further enhance emergency response, the United Nations created the Department of Humanitarian Affairs (DHA) with a mandate to co-ordinate UN response in complex humanitarian emergencies.

Over the decades, the most sustained and devoted service to the cause of refugees has been provided by NGOs. NGOs not only provide substantial aid from their own resources but also frequently act as UNHCR's operational partners in carrying out specific projects (see Figure III.G). They are also important partners in advocating for the refugee cause.

Fig. III.G
Non-Governmental Organizations
UNHCR's Operational Partners in 1992 by Region of Implementation

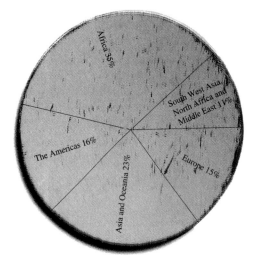

Africa: 125 NGOs
The Americas: 54 NGOs
Asia and Oceania: 76 NGOs

Europe: 52 NGOs
South West Asia, North Africa and
the Middle East: 38 NGOs

Annex IV

Chronologies

IV.1 Significant Events In Cambodia:
July 1988 - July 1993

IV.2 Significant Events in Somalia:
January 1991 - July 1993

IV.3 Significant Events in the Former
Yugoslavia: June 1991 – July 1993

Significant Events In Cambodia:
July 1988 - July 1993

1988

July 26-28	The four Cambodian political parties hold their first meeting (JIM 1) at Bogor, Indonesia.

1989

Feb. 6-21	A second meeting (JIM 2) in Jakarta focuses on national reconciliation.
July	UN Secretary-General designates UNHCR lead agency for repatriation of Cambodian refugees and displaced persons within the framework of a comprehensive peace settlement.

1990

Feb. 3	Prince Norodom Sihanouk issues a declaration reinstating the name of "Cambodia".
Feb. 21	Prince Sihanouk and Prime Minister Hun Sen issue a joint communiqué calling for a supreme national body to represent Cambodia's sovereignty and unity. They also request UN participation in the transition period following cessation of hostilities.
Feb. 26-28	Informal consultations towards a political settlement are held in Jakarta (JIM 3).
Aug. 28	A framework document is accepted by the Cambodian parties as the basis for settling the Cambodia conflict. The document is unanimously endorsed by Security Council resolution 668 on 20 September and General Assembly resolution 45/3 on 15 October, 1990.
Sept. 9-10	At a meeting in Jakarta, the Supreme National Council of Cambodia (SNC) is set up.

1991

July 16-17	A meeting in Beijing elects Prince Norodom Sihanouk as the President of the SNC.
Sept. 27	Following meetings held in Paris (21-23 December 1990), Pattaya, Thailand (24-26 June and 26-29 August 1991), Jakarta (4-6 June 1991) and New York (19 September 1991), agreement is reached on a comprehensive political settlement to the Cambodian conflict. The agreement establishes the United Nations Transitional Authority in Cambodia (UNTAC).
Oct. 23	Signing of the Paris Peace Accords.

1992

Jan. 24	First SNC meeting on voluntary repatriation.
Mar. 27	A contingent of 850 UNTAC infantrymen arrives in Battambang to provide protection for the first convoy of returnees.
Mar. 30	First repatriation convoy crosses the border from Thailand en route to Battambang Province. It transports 527 returnees from six camps.
Apr. 2	In a meeting between UNHCR and State of Cambodia (SOC) officials, agreement is reached on the repatriation of Cambodians from countries other than Thailand.
Apr. 24	A first group of Cambodians return by air from Indonesia.
Apr. 27	Official opening of Phnom Penh reception centre.
Apr. 30	First train convoy, the "Sisophon Express", arrives in Phnom Penh with 612 returnees aboard. The train is scheduled to travel from Sisophon to Phnom Penh every four days until the end of the operation.
May 6	Opening of Siem Reap Reception Centre.
May 9	UNTAC announces the launching of phase 2 of the UNTAC peace plan (cantonment and demobilization), scheduled for 13 June 1992.
May 21	Opening of Pursat Reception Centre.
May 23	Opening of Tuol Makak Reception Centre in Battambang Province.
May 30	Party of Democratic Kampuchea (PDK – "Khmer Rouge") prevents the Secretary-General's Special Representative, Mr Y. Akashi from entering Pailin, the PDK stronghold.
June 1	In Thailand, 2,000 refugees seize the staging area in Site 2, demanding increased repatriation allowances.
June 12	Security Council appeals to all four Cambodian parties to abide by the Paris Peace Accords.
June 13	Cantonment begins with the arrival at 32 of the 82 sites by roughly 5,000 soldiers from three of the four Cambodian factions. The PDK refuses to demobilize.
June 21-22	Ministerial Conference on the Rehabilitation and Reconstruction of Cambodia takes place in Tokyo with the government of Japan and UNDP as co-hosts. Two declarations on Rehabilitation, Reconstruction and the Cambodia Peace Process are adopted. Total contributions of $880 million are announced.
June 22	SNC meeting is held to break the deadlock with the PDK on the implementation of the Paris Peace Accords. Khieu Samphan, PDK leader, requests additional time to respond.

June 27	Conciliatory PDK note welcomes "international consensus" that emerged at Tokyo.
July 1	De-mining of route 69 from Sisophon to Thmar Pouk is completed. The road opens up access between zones controlled by opposing factions.
July 2	PDK demands the abolition of the SOC Government. Prime Minister Hun Sen rejects the PDK demand on 6 July.
July 22	Indonesian battalion takes on provision of security to reception centres and repatriation convoys.
July 14	PDK proposes gradual disarming of its entire army in stages over a period of four weeks, coinciding with the resignation of SOC ministers. At the same time, they launch a major attack on two villages near Phum Khulen.
July 18	Government cantonment site at Kulen (northern Preah Vihear) is subjected to sustained bombardment, allegedly by the PDK, despite the presence of UNTAC military advisers.
Aug. 5	SNC adopts Electoral Law.
Sept. 5	First return takes place to north-east Cambodia.
Sept. 12	UNTAC issues Electoral Regulations relating to the right of political parties to open offices throughout Cambodia.
Sept. 15	First return takes place to areas under the control of the Front national pour un Cambodge indépendant, neutre, pacifique et coopératif (FUNCINPEC). A total of 1,000 families return to this area over the next months.
Sept. 22	SNC accedes to the 1951 Convention and 1967 Protocol relating to the status of refugees.
Oct. 2	The first two camps in Thailand are closed – Sok Sann (KPNLF) and Site K (PDK).
Oct. 19	Official closure of O'Trao, the third Thai border camp.
Oct. 30	UNTAC Electoral Component begins to register returnees for elections.
Nov. 16	First convoy of Cambodian returnees from Viet Nam, (101 persons) arrives in Phnom Penh. A total of 850 Cambodian refugees in Viet Nam had requested to return to Cambodia.
Dec. 14	Official closure of the FUNICPEC administered Site B camp in Thailand.
Dec. 21	A decision is taken to extend voter registration until 31 January 1993.

1993

Jan. 7	UNTAC directive 93/1 establishes procedures for the prosecution of those responsible for human rights violations.
Jan. 14	First group of 256 people returns to Yeah Ath settlement site, under PDK control but to which UNHCR, NGOs and UNTAC have free access.
Jan. 22	Official closure of Site 8, the largest PDK-administered camp in Thailand.
Jan. 29	Pre-registration of voters is completed in the Thai border camps.
Feb. 5	Completion of voter registration. Total number of registered voters reached 4.7 million .
Feb. 15	The 300,000th returnee crosses the border from Thailand.

Mar. 3	Official closing of Khao-I-Dang camp near the Thai border.
Mar. 24	The last "Sisophon Express" travels to Phnom Penh with some 1,050 returnees on board. Since its launch on 30 April 1992, it had transported 95,000 returnees.
Apr. 7	Start of election campaign.
Apr. 8	A Japanese volunteer working as a district electoral supervisor is killed.
Apr. 30	Voluntary repatriation from Site 2 comes to an end, leaving 573 persons refusing to return to Cambodia. UNHCR is denied further access to the camp and the Thai government decides to consider those remaining as illegal immigrants.
May 3	PDK soldiers launch full-scale attack on the town of Siem Reap, hitting the airport and parts of the city.
May 4	An UNTAC convoy is attacked. One Japanese Civil Policeman is killed, and three more wounded, along with five Dutch soldiers.
May 7	The Thai government deports the remaining 573 residents from Site 2 to Cambodia.
May 19	Closure of electoral campaign.
May 23	Start of UNTAC-supervised Cambodian elections.
May 26	Over four million Cambodians cast their vote (85 per cent) without any major incidents. The voting is declared free and fair.
June 15	Election results are announced by UNTAC. The new Constituent Assembly comprises 58 seats for FUNICIPEC, 51 seats for the Cambodia People's Party (CPP), 10 seats for the Buddhist Liberal Democratic Party (BLDP) and 1 seat for the Movement de Libération National du Kampuchea (MOLINAKA).
July 1	A new interim government is formed under the presidency of Prince Norodom Sihanouk.

Significant Events in Somalia: January 1991-July 1993

1991

Jan. 1	President Siad Barre is ousted amidst widespread violence. International personnel of the UN and diplomatic missions are evacuated.
Jan.	Somali National Movement forces gain control of north-west Somalia, setting the scene for the subsequent independence bid by "Somaliland".
Feb. 4	UNHCR staff member Ahmed Liban Ainanshe is killed by bandits while on duty in Mogadishu.
Mar. 6	A joint UN mission returns to Mogadishu to re-establish presence. The UN and other relief organizations begin to return to north-west Somalia.
Apr. 10	The UN re-evacuates all staff from Somalia after several senior officials are attacked by gunmen in Mogadishu and two policemen escorting them are assassinated.
May	Fighting breaks out between the two rival groups of the Hawiye clan under the respective leaderships of warlord General Mohamed Farah Aideed and the self-proclaimed interim President Mohamed Ali Mahdi.

May 18	North-west Somalia proclaims unilateral independence.	Apr. 24	Security Council resolution 751 establishes a United Nations Operation in Somalia (UNOSOM). It requests the Secretary-General to deploy 50 military observers and foresees the establishment of a security force to be deployed as soon as possible.
June 26	UN needs assessment mission composed of 23 officials from different agencies visits Mogadishu 26 June – 4 July 1991.		
July 2	UNHCR staff member Abdillahi Sheikh Omar is killed by bandits while on duty in Mogadishu.	June	Eleven Somali organizations and factions from Somalia participate in an All Party Meeting on Somalia in Ethiopia. They sign the Bahir Dar Declaration and Agreement to lay the groundwork for a lasting political solution in Somalia. Sporadic fighting continues.
July 10	A second inter-agency mission of specialists travels to other areas of Somalia from 10 to 17 July 1991.		
July	UNHCR and CARE International undertake a fact-finding mission to north-west Somalia to prepare a Comprehensive Plan of Operations in anticipation of the return of Somali refugees from Ethiopia.	July	Advance party of UNOSOM arrives in Mogadishu in early July.
July 19	UN launches joint Appeal for Somalia, seeking $64 million in aid as part of the Special Emergency Programme for the Horn of Africa (SEPHA).	Aug. 28	Following a report by the Secretary-General on serious security problems hindering the delivery of relief, Security Council resolution 775 increases the strength of UNOSOM in order to protect humanitarian assistance.
Sept.	UNHCR re-establishes an international presence in Hargeisa in north-west Somalia but the security situation deteriorates. UN agencies and NGOs become targets of attacks.	Sept. 10	Under-Secretary-General for Humanitarian Affairs, Jan Eliasson, leads high level inter-agency mission to Somalia which decides establishment of 100-day Action Plan for Accelerated Humanitarian Assistance.
Dec.	In preparation for the possible return of Somali refugees from eastern Ethiopia to north-west Somalia, UNHCR intensifies de-mining operations, with particular focus on major access routes and areas of return.	Sept 14	First group of UNOSOM security personnel arrives in Mogadishu. The situation continues to deteriorate with several thousands reported to have died of starvation.
1992		Sept.	UNHCR launches a cross-border assistance programme from Kenya in an effort to stabilize famine-related population movements in southern Somalia.
Jan.	Inter-clan fighting intensifies in southern Somalia. Increasing numbers of Somalis flee into Kenya and Ethiopia or into the interior of Somalia. Those arriving in neighbouring countries are frequently in very poor physical condition.	Nov. 24	As situation deteriorates, Secretary-General reports to Security Council on the failure of the various factions to co-operate with UNOSOM; the extortion, blackmail and robbery to which the international relief effort is subjected; and the repeated attacks on UN personnel and equipment.
Jan. 5	Dr Marta Pumpalova of UNICEF is killed by unidentified gunmen in Bossasso, a port town in north-east Somalia.		
Jan. 23	Security Council resolution 733 urges all parties to the conflict to cease hostilities and imposes a general and complete arms embargo on Somalia.	Nov. 26	US government informs the UN that it is ready to provide troops to protect humanitarian relief in Somalia.
Feb.	Armed elements belonging to different factions continue to fight for territory. Reports of starvation and looting of emergency aid start to hit the world news. Relief workers are constantly threatened. In north-west Somalia, the unstable security and political situation make it virtually impossible for the UN and other relief agencies to implement planned activities. UNHCR is compelled to evacuate international staff from Hargeisa to Djibouti.	Dec. 3	Acting under Chapter VII of the Charter, the Security Council unanimously adopts resolution 794 authorizing "use of all necessary means" to establish a secure environment for humanitarian relief operations in Somalia, on the grounds that the "magnitude of the human tragedy caused by the conflict in Somalia" constitutes a threat to international peace and security.
Mar. 3	A UN-brokered cease-fire is signed.	Dec. 4	President Bush makes available up to 28,000 US troops to participate in Operation Restore Hope.
Mar. 17	Security Council resolution 746 is adopted in support of the Secretary-General's decision to despatch a team to prepare a plan for a cease-fire monitoring mechanism and for the urgent and unimpeded delivery of humanitarian relief.	Dec. 8	The first US marines land in Somalia as part of the Unified Task Force (UNITAF) established under Security Council resolution 794. They meet with no resistance.
Mar. 24	UN staff member Abdi Maalim Garad is killed.	Dec. 26	The leaders of Somalia's two principal armed factions, Mohamed Farah Aideed and Mohamed Ali Mahdi, agree to a cease-fire and to the elimination of the so-called green line that divided Mogadishu into two warring camps.
Apr. 8-9	Regional heads of government meet in Addis Ababa to attend a Summit on Humanitarian Issues in the Horn of Africa and sign a Framework of Cooperation and Action Programme to address the region's problems.		
		Dec. 31	President Bush visits US troops in Mogadishu and inspects a number of relief programmes.

1993

Jan.	Security improves with the arrival of the US troops and coalition forces. Food is reported to be reaching the needy in the interior. Isolated incidents of coalition forces engaging Somali gunmen are reported.
Jan. 2	UNICEF staff member, Sean Devereux is killed by a gunman in Kismayo.
Jan. 4	The Informal Preparatory Meeting on National Reconciliation in Somalia opens in Addis Ababa. Attended by representatives of 14 Somali factions, it establishes an Ad Hoc Committee to resolve the question of criteria for participation in the planned National Reconciliation Conference.
Jan. 24	In north-west Somalia, a Peace and Reconciliation Conference called by clan elders begins to discuss the future government structure of "Somaliland".
Mar. 11	The third Co-ordination Meeting on Humanitarian Assistance for Somalia opens in Addis Ababa. UN requests $166.5 million to fund 1993 operations.
Mar. 15	The Conference on National Reconciliation in Somalia opens in Addis Ababa. The peace talks agree on a multi-party political structure to run Somalia during an interim period leading to national elections. The parties also commit themselves to disarmament within a 90-day period.
May 5	The Peace and Reconciliation Conference in North-west Somalia is successfully concluded with the election of Mr Mohamed Ibrahim Egal as President of Somaliland and Mr Abdirahman Aw Ali as Vice-President.
June 5	Twelve cabinet ministers and seven vice-ministers of Somaliland are sworn in at the presidential building in Hargeisa.
June 5	Premeditated armed attacks launched by forces led by Mohamed Farah Aideed result in the death of 24 Pakistani troops serving with UNOSOM in Mogadishu.
June 6	Security Council resolution 837 is passed unanimously to express the world's outrage at the Mogadishu killings.
June 11	UNOSOM begins decisive action to restore security in Mogadishu in pursuance of Security Council Resolution 837. The Security Council also authorizes the investigation of the attacks of 5 June and the arrest and detention of those responsible.
June 12	Four journalists on assignment in Mogadishu are attacked and killed by Somali mobs. UN Secretary-General says the UN will do everything in its power to bring those responsible to justice.

Significant Events in the Former Yugoslavia: June 1991 – July 1993

1991

June 25	Croatia and Slovenia proclaim independence. Fighting breaks out.
Sept. 7	EC establishes the Peace Conference on Yugoslavia chaired by Lord Carrington.
Sept. 25	UN Security Council resolution 713 imposes an arms embargo on Yugoslavia.
Oct. 8	UN Secretary-General appoints Cyrus Vance as his Personal Envoy.
Oct. 25	UN Secretary-General asks UNHCR to assist displaced persons in Yugoslavia.
Nov. 8	EC suspends Hague Peace Conference and agrees a package of sanctions against Yugoslavia.
Nov. 23	Meeting at the request of Cyrus Vance in Geneva., the Serbian and Croatian presidents agree a cease-fire and the establishment of a UN peace-keeping operation. The cease-fire breaks down almost immediately.
Nov. 26	UNHCR begins to aid people displaced by the war in Croatia.
Nov. 27	Security Council Resolution 721 paves the way for deployment of peace-keeping forces.
	Representatives of Yugoslav republics meet in Geneva under ICRC auspices to discuss adherence to Geneva Conventions.
Dec. 17	First UNHCR relief shipments reach Belgrade and Zagreb.
Dec. 23	Germany recognizes Croatia and Slovenia.

1992

Jan. 2	Cyrus Vance negotiates Sarajevo Accord, the first lasting cease-fire in the war in Croatia.
Jan. 7	Five EC monitors are killed when their helicopter is shot down by an aircraft north of Zagreb.
Jan. 14	An initial group of 51 UN Military Liaison Officers (MLOs) arrive to assess conditions for deployment of a UN peace-keeping force.
Jan. 15	EC recognizes Croatia and Slovenia.
Feb. 7	Security Council resolution 740 requests the Secretary-General to expedite preparations for a UN peace-keeping operation.
Feb. 13	UN Secretary-General announces that he will recommend to the Security Council the deployment of a UN peace-keeping force in three proposed UN protected areas (UNPAs) to be established in Croatia.
Feb. 21	Security Council resolution 743 establishes a UN Protection Force (UNPROFOR).
Feb. 29	More than 99 per cent of those voting in a referendum in Bosnia and Herzegovina cast ballots in favour of independence. Bosnian Serbs boycott the vote.
Mar. 3	Bosnia and Herzegovina proclaims independence. Fighting intensifies and reports of ethnic cleansing begin.
Mar. 27	The UN High Commissioner for Refugees, Sadako Ogata, appeals to all parties to refrain from actions that cause new displacement of civilians.

Apr. 6	EC recognizes Bosnia and Herzegovina as independent. Fighting in eastern Bosnia intensifies.
Apr. 7	US recognizes independence of Slovenia, Croatia and Bosnia and Herzegovina.
	Security Council resolution 749 authorizes deployment of UNPROFOR.
Apr. 11	The three Bosnian parties to the conflict, meeting under UNHCR auspices, agree to facilitate the work of humanitarian organizations aiding the displaced. UNHCR begins distributing food aid to displaced people from the war in Bosnia and Herzegovina.
Apr. 12	A cease-fire is signed under the auspices of the EC but fighting continues in many regions. ·
Apr. 27	Yugoslavia's Serbian-led parliament proclaims the Federal Republic of Yugoslavia (Serbia and Montenegro).
May 15	Security Council resolution 752 demands an end to the fighting in Bosnia and Herzegovina and to "ethnic cleansing".
May 16	UNHCR temporarily evacuates staff from Sarajevo as the capital becomes engulfed in the conflict.
May 18	An ICRC delegate is killed in a mortar attack on a convoy entering Sarajevo.
May 22	General Assembly admits Bosnia and Herzegovina, Croatia and Slovenia as members of the UN.
May 24	UNHCR temporarily suspends operations in Bosnia after 11 trucks are hijacked.
May 27	ICRC announces temporary withdrawal from Bosnia and Herzegovina.
May 30	Security Council resolution 757 imposes mandatory sanctions against Yugoslavia (Serbia and Montenegro) in the form of restrictions on commercial activities, petroleum imports and freezing of assets abroad, and demands that all parties immediately allow unimpeded delivery of humanitarian supplies to Sarajevo and other parts of Bosnia and Herzegovina.
June 16	UNHCR resumes operations with land deliveries in Bosnia to Sarajevo, Mostar and Banja Luka.
June 28	President Mitterand of France visits Sarajevo.
June 29	Security Council resolution 761 authorizes reinforcement of UNPROFOR to ensure the security and functioning of Sarajevo airport and the delivery of humanitarian assistance.
June 30	Security Council resolution 762 urges the Croatian government to cease military activities in or adjacent to UNPAs.
July 3	UNHCR airlift of humanitarian assistance to Sarajevo begins.
July 7	G7 leaders threaten use of force to ensure that relief reaches Sarajevo.
July 9	Bosnian President Izetbegovic reports 60,000 Bosnians killed by Serb forces and 1.4 million displaced.
July 17	A cease-fire is signed within the framework of the EC Conference on Yugoslavia but is not implemented.
July 24	Security Council suggests broadening and intensifying the EC Conference on Yugoslavia.
July 29	UN High Commissioner for Refugees convenes a ministerial-level International Meeting in Geneva. More than two million people are said to have been displaced. A comprehensive humanitarian strategy is adopted centred on access to safety and assistance for survival.
Aug. 4	Security Council expresses deep concern at abuse of civilians in camps, prisons and detention centres, particularly in Bosnia and Herzegovina, and calls for unimpeded access for ICRC and other international organizations.
Aug. 7	Security Council resolution 769 condemns abuses against civilian population, particularly on ethnic grounds.
Aug. 10	European Commission President Jacques Delors criticizes the EC for inaction in Yugoslavia and calls for realistic military intervention.
Aug. 13	Security Council resolutions 770 and 771 foreshadow the use of force as last resort to ensure relief aid for Bosnia and compliance with its call for a halt to "ethnic cleansing".
	Following reports of atrocious living conditions in detention camps, the international community denounces crimes against humanity at an extraordinary session of the UN Human Rights Commission, which appoints Tadeusz Mazowiecki to investigate human rights violations.
Aug. 26	UN Secretary-General and UK Prime Minister, John Major, as President of the EC Council of Ministers, co-chair International Conference on the former Yugoslavia in London. A framework for an overall political settlement is established and a Steering Committee set up. Lord Carrington steps down as EC mediator and is replaced by Lord Owen
Sept. 3	Shooting down of Italian relief plane and death of four crew members leads to month-long suspension of Sarajevo airlift.
	The Steering Committee of the International Conference on the former Yugoslavia opens in Geneva under the co-chairmanship of Cyrus Vance (UN) and Lord Owen (EC).
Sept. 10	UN Secretary-General requests Security Council to enlarge UNPROFOR's mandate to include the protection of humanitarian assistance provided by UNHCR and others.
Sept. 14	Security Council decides to send 5,000 additional troops to Bosnia and Herzegovina.
Sept. 19	Security Council Resolution 777 recommends that the Federal Republic of Yugoslavia (Serbia and Montenegro) shall not participate in the work of the UN General Assembly.
Sept. 29	UN High Commissioner for Refugees predicts that 400,000 could die during the winter without emergency aid and a resumption of the airlift.
Oct. 3	Resumption of Sarajevo airlift.
Oct. 5	Cyrus Vance criticizes the slow deployment of UN forces to protect relief convoys. UNHCR estimates the number of refugees, internally displaced and victims of conflict to number three million.
Oct. 6	Security Council resolution 780 calls for the establishment of an impartial Commission of Experts to examine grave breaches of the Geneva Conventions and other violations of humanitarian law in former Yugoslavia.

Oct. 9	Security Council resolution 781 imposes a ban on military flights over Bosnia and Herzegovina.
Nov. 4	Croatia turns back hundreds of Bosnian Muslim refugees, saying it can absorb no more.
Nov. 16	Security Council resolution 787 asks the Secretary-General, in consultation with UNHCR, to study the establishment of safe areas for affected populations.
Nov. 29	A UNHCR convoy reaches the Muslim town of Srebrenica, cut off since April by Serbian forces.
Dec. 11	Security Council resolution 795 authorizes the deployment of UNPROFOR in the former Yugoslav Republic of Macedonia to avoid the spread of the conflict.
Dec. 19	Following reports of widespread atrocities against women in Bosnia and Herzegovina, an EC delegation visits the region to investigate allegations of mass rape.
Dec. 20	President Milosevic of Serbia defeats Milan Panic in the presidential election.

1993

Jan. 11	Peace talks resume in Geneva in the framework of the International Conference on former Yugoslavia and a comprehensive peace plan is put forward by the co-chairmen.
Feb. 2	A local interpreter is killed in an attack on a UNHCR relief convoy.
Feb. 9	Peace talks resume at UN Headquarters in New York.
Feb. 17	UNHCR temporarily suspends many of its operations in Bosnia and Herzegovina in face of widespread blockages of humanitarian assistance.
Feb. 22	Security Council resolution 808 establishes an international war crimes tribunal to prosecute persons responsible for humanitarian law violations in former Yugoslavia.
Feb. 23	President Clinton and the UN SecretaryGeneral agree on a plan to parachute relief supplies to eastern Bosnia as a temporary effort to supplement land convoys. The air drop operation is under UNHCR co-ordination.
Mar. 17	France joins the US in the airdrop operation. Germany follows on 28 March.
Mar. 25	Peace talks continue in New York where some progress is reported. Bosnian Muslim president and Bosnian Croat leader sign a revised map dividing the republic into 10 semi-autonomous provinces known as the Vance-Owen Plan.
	UN High Commissioner for Refugees convenes a meeting in the framework of the Humanitarian Issues Working Group of the International Conference on former Yugoslavia to seek support for the UN's revised appeal for funds. The cumulative budget requirement amounts to US$1,335,329,097.
Mar. 30	Security Council resolution 815 renews for three months the presence of its 22,000 peace-keeping force in former Yugoslavia.
Mar. 31	Security Council resolution 816 reinforces the no-fly zone over Bosnia by authorizing the use of all

	necessary measures to ensure compliance with the ban on flights.
Apr. 1	It is announced that Cyrus Vance plans to relinquish his responsibilities as UN negotiator. He is replaced by the Norwegian Foreign Minister and former UN High Commissioner for Refugees, Thorvald Stoltenberg.
Apr. 7	Following a compromise between Greece and the former Yugoslav Republic of Macedonia, the Security Council recommends that the latter be admitted to the UN under the temporary name of Former Yugoslav Republic of Macedonia.
Apr. 16	Security Council resolution 819 declares Srebrenica a safe area.
Apr. 17	Security Council adopts resolution 820 which proclaims a strict enforcement of sanctions against Serbia and Montenegro to come into effect on 26 April if a peace plan is not signed.
Apr. 28	Security Council resolution 821 recommends to the General Assembly that the Federal Republic of Yugoslavia be excluded from participating in the work of the UN Economic and Social Council.
May 6	Security Council resolution 824 declares Sarajevo, Tuzla, Zepa, Gorazde, Bihac and Srebrenica safe areas.
May 15	In a two day referendum, the Bosnian Serbs overwhelmingly reject the Vance-Owen plan.
May 25	Pursuant to resolution 808, UN Security Council resolution 827 adopts the statute of the international war crimes tribunal.
June 1	A UNHCR convoy is hit by shells killing two Danish drivers and a local interpreter. Three days earlier, three Italian volunteers were shot dead .
June 2	A Belgian journalist is killed by a sniper. His death adds to over 30 journalists and 50 UNPROFOR personnel killed in the conflict.
June 4	Security Council resolution 836 authorizes UNPROFOR to deter attacks against the safe areas and, acting in self defence, to use force.
June 16	In a summit held in Geneva between the presidents of Bosnia, Serbia and Croatia, the Serbs and Croats propose another peace plan: a three-part division of Bosnia and Herzegovina along ethnic lines.
June 18	The UN High Commissioner for Refugees states that "The intensification of the war, the absence of decisive political breakthrough, the restrictions on asylum and the virtual depletion of resources for the humanitarian efforts constitute an explosive mixture which may cause a massive humanitarian disaster with even greater consequences for Europe."
June 30	Security Council resolution 847 extends UNPROFOR's mandate for an interim period of three months.

184

Bibliography

The range of scholarly literature on refugees is vast. This bibliography is not intended to be exhaustive. Rather than attempt to cover all aspects of refugee protection and assistance, it focuses on policy and legal issues, particularly as they relate to asylum. While the emphasis is on recent developments, a number of works are cited for historical background.

Adelman, H. "Humanitarian intervention: The case of the Kurds." *International Journal of Refugee Law* 4.1 (Jan. 1992): 4-38.

Adelman, H., ed. *Refugee Policy: Canada and the United States.* Toronto: York Lanes Press, 1991.

Aguilar Zinser, A. *CIREFCA: The promises and reality of the International Conference on Central American Refugees.* Washington DC: Center for Immigration Policy and Refugee Assistance, Georgetown University, 1991.

Amnesty International. *Europe: Harmonization of asylum policy: Accelerated procedures for "manifestly unfounded" asylum claims and the "safe country" concept.* Brussels: Amnesty International, Nov. 1992.

Amnesty International. *Europe: Human rights and the need for a fair asylum policy.* London: Amnesty International, Nov. 1991.

Appleyard, R. and C. Stahl, eds. *International Migration Today.* Paris; Nedlands (Australia): UNESCO, University of Western Australia, Centre for Migration and Development Studies, 1988.

Appleyard, R. *International Migration: Challenge for the nineties.* Geneva: International Organization for Migration, 1991.

Arboleda, E. "Refugee definition in Africa and Latin America: The lessons of pragmatism." *International Journal of Refugee Law* 3.2 (Apr. 1991): 185-207.

Argent, T. *Croatia's Crucible: Providing Asylum for Refugees from Bosnia and Hercegovina.* Washington DC: US Committee for Refugees, Oct. 1992.

Bettati, M., and B. Kouchner, eds. *Le devoir d'ingérence: Peut-on les laisser mourir?* Paris: Editions Denoël, 1987.

Beyer, G.A. "Human rights monitoring and the failure of early warning: A practitioner's view." *International Journal of Refugee Law* 2.1 (1990): 56-82.

Blaschke, J. and A. Germershausen, eds. *Sozialwissenschatliche Studien über das Weltflüchtlingsproblem.* Berlin: Edition Parabolis, 1992.

Boutros-Ghali, B. *An agenda for peace: Preventive diplomacy, peacemaking and peace-keeping.* Report of the Secretary-General pursuant to the statement adopted by the Summit Meeting of the Security Council on 31 Jan. 1992. New York: United Nations, June 1992.

Bramwell, A.C., ed. *Refugees in the age of total war.* London: Unwin Hyman, 1988.

Brown, M., ed. *Ethnic conflict and International Security.* Princeton (US): Princeton University Press, 1993.

Bulcha, M. *Flight and integration: Causes of mass exodus from Ethiopia and problems of integration in the Sudan.* Uppsala (Sweden): Scandinavian Institute of African Studies, 1988.

Chipman, J. "Managing the Politics of Parochialism." *Survival* 35.1 (Spring 1993).

Cohen, R. *Human rights and humanitarian emergencies: new roles for UN human rights bodies.* Washington DC: Refugee Policy Group, Sept. 1992.

Coles, G.J.L. *The Question of a general approach to the problem of refugees from situations of armed conflict and serious internal disturbance.* Collection of Publications 9. San Remo (Italy): International Institute of Humanitarian Law, 1989.

Coles, G.J.L., P. Nobel, I. Khokhlov and J.C. Hathaway. "Human Rights and Refugee Law." *Bulletin of Human Rights* 1: 63-123. Geneva: United Nations, Centre for Human Rights.

Corten, O. and P. Klein. *Droit d'ingérence ou obligation de réaction?: Les possibilités d'action visant à assurer le respect des droits de la personne face au principe de non-intervention.* Collection de Droit International 26. Bruxelles: Bruylant, Editions de l'Université de Bruxelles, 1992.

Cuny, F.C., B.N. Stein, and P. Reed, eds. *Repatriation during conflict in Africa and Asia.* Dallas: Center for the Study of Societies in Crisis, 1992.

de Jong, D. and A. Voets, eds. *Refugees in the World: The European Community's Response.* Utrecht: Netherlands Institute of Human Rights, 1990.

Delissen, A.J.M. and G.J. Tanja, eds. *Humanitarian Law of Armed Conflict: Challenges Ahead.* Dordrecht (Netherlands): Martinus Nijhoff, 1991.

Deng, F. "Comprehensive Study on the Human Rights Issues Related to Internally Displaced Persons." Geneva: United Nations, 1993.

Dmitrichev, T.F. "Conceptual approaches to early warning - mechanisms and methods: A view from the United Nations." *International Journal of Refugee Law* 3.2 (Apr. 1991): 264-271.

Feller, E. "Carrier sanctions and international law." *International Journal of Refugee Law* 1.1 (Jan. 1989): 48-66.

Forbes Martin, S. *Refugee Women.* London; Atlantic Highlands (US): Zed Books, 1991.

Frelick, B. *Yugoslavia Torn Asumder: Lessons for protecting refugees from civil war.* Washington DC: US Committee for Refugees, February 1992.

Gallagher, D. and S. Forbes Martin. *The Many Faces of the Somali Crisis: Humanitarian Issues in Somalia, Kenya and Ethiopia.* Washington DC: Refugee Policy Group, 1993.

Garbarino, J., K. Kostelny and N. Dubrow. *No place to be a child: Growing up in a war zone.* Lexington (US); Toronto: Lexington Books, 1991.

Goodwin-Gill, G.S. "The Language of Protection. " *The International Journal of Refugee Law* 1.1 (Jan. 1989).

Goodwin-Gill, G.S. *The Refugee in International Law.* Oxford: Clarendon Press, 1983.

Goodwin-Gill, G.S., ed. "The 1951 Convention Relating to the Status of Refugees: Principles, Problems and Potential." Special issue of *The International Journal of Refugee Law.* 3.3 (July 1991).

Goodwin-Gill, G.S., ed. *International human rights law: The new decade: Refugees - Facing crisis in the 1990s.* Oxford: Oxford University Press, 1990.

Gordenker, L. and T.G. Weiss, eds. *Soldiers, peacekeepers and disasters.* Basingstoke (UK); London: Macmillan, International Peace Academy, 1991.

Gordenker, L. *Refugees in international politics.* Beckenham (UK); Sydney: Croom Helm, 1987.

Gros Espiell, H., S. Picado and L. Valladares Lanza. "Principles and criteria for the protection of and assistance to Central American refugees, returnees and displaced persons in Central America." *International Journal of Refugee Law* 2.1 (Jan. 1990): 83-117.

Hamilton, K., ed. *The Security Dimensions of International Migration in Europe.* Washington DC: Center for Strategic and International Studies, 1993.

Harrell-Bond, B.E. *Imposing Aid: Emergency Assistance to Refugees.* Oxford: Oxford University Press, 1986.

Hathaway, J.C. *The Law of Refugee Status.* Toronto: Butterworths, 1991.

Helton, A.C. "The Comprehensive Plan of Action for Indo-Chinese refugees: An experiment in refugee protection and control." *New York Law School Journal of Human Rights* 8.1 (1990): 111-148.

Holborn, L.W. *Refugees, A Problem of our Time: the Work of the United Nations High Commissioner for Refugees, 1951-1972.* 2 vols. Metuchen (US): Scarecrow, 1975.

Holborn, L.W. *The International Refugee Organization: A specialized agency of the United Nations, its history and work, 1946-1952.* London; New York; Toronto: Oxford University Press, Geoffrey Cumberlege, 1956.

Independent Commission on International Humanitarian Issues. *Refugees: The dynamics of displacement.* London; Atlantic Highlands (US): Zed Books, 1986.

Independent Commission on International Humanitarian Issues. *Winning the human race?* The report of the Independent Commission on International Humanitarian Issues. London; Atlantic Highlands (US): Zed Books, 1988.

Johnsson, A.B. "The International protection of women refugees: A summary of principal problems and issues." *International Journal of Refugee Law* 1.2 (Apr. 1989): 221-232.

Joly, D. and R. Poulton. *Refugees: Asylum in Europe?.* London: Minority Rights Group, 1992.

Keen, D. *Refugees - Rationing the Right to Life: The Crisis in Emergency Relief.* London: Zed Books, 1992.

Khokhlov, I. "The rights of refugees under international law." *Bulletin of Human Rights* 91.1 (1992): 85-97.

Kjaerum, M., ed. *The Effects of Carrier Sanctions on the Asylum System.* Copenhagen: Danish Refugee Council, Danish Center of Human Rights, October 1991.

Knowles, M. *Afghanistan: Trends and prospects for refugee repatriation.* Washington DC: Refugee Policy Group, 1992.

Koehn, P. *Refugees from Revolution: U.S. Policy and Third World Migration.* Boulder (US): Westview Press, 1991.

Kouchner, B. *Le malheur des autres.* Paris: Odile Jacob, 1991.

Larkin, M.A., F.C. Cuny and B.N. Stein, eds. *Repatriation under conflict in Central America.* Washington DC: Georgetown University, Center for Immigration Policy and Refugee Assistance, 1991.

Lassailly-Jacob, V., and M. Zmolek, eds. "Environmental refugees." Special issue of *Refuge* 12.1. North York (Canada): York University, Centre for Refugee Studies, June 1992.

Lawyers Committee for Human Rights. *Temporary protected status in the United States: An assessment of a new humanitarian remedy.* New York: Sept. 1992.

Lawyers Committee for Human Rights. *The human rights of refugees and displaced persons: Protections afforded refugees, asylum seekers and displaced persons under international human rights, humanitarian and refugee law.* New York: 1991.

Lawyers Committee for Human Rights. *The implementation of the Refugee Act of 1980: A decade of experience.* New York: Mar. 1990.

Lawyers Committee for Human Rights. *The UNHCR at 40: Refugee protection at the crossroads.* New York: 1991.

Loescher, G. and J. Scanlon. *Calculated Kindness: Refugees and America's Half-Open Door. 1945 to Present.* New York; London: Free Press, Collier-Macmillan, 1986.

Loescher, G. *Beyond Charity: International Cooperation and the Global Refugee Problem.* New York; Oxford: Oxford University Press, 1993.

Loescher, G. *Refugee movements and international security.* Adelphi Paper 268. London; Riverside (US): International Institute for Strategic Studies, 1992.

Loescher, G., ed. *Refugees and the Asylum Dilemma in the West.* University Park, Pennsylvania: Pennsylvania State Press, 1992.

Marrus, M. *The Unwanted: European Refugees in the Twentieth Century.* New York: Oxford University Press, 1985.

Mayotte, J. *Disposable People: The Plight of Refugees.* New York: Orbis Books, 1992.

Minear, L., T.G. Weiss and K.M. Campbell. *Humanitarianism and war: Learning the lessons from recent armed conflicts.* Providence (US): Brown University, Thomas J. Watson Jr. Institute for International Studies, 1991.

Muntarbhorn, V. *The Status of Refugees in Asia.* London: Clarendon, 1992.

Newland, K. "Ethnic Conflict and Refugees." *Survival* 35.1 (Spring 1993).

Noiriel, G. *La tyrannie du national: Le droit d'asile en Europe (1793-1993).* Paris: Calmann-Lévy, 1991.

Ramcharan, B.G. *The International Law and Practice of Early-Warning and Preventive Diplomacy: The emerging global watch.* Dordrecht (Netherlands); Boston; London: Martinus Nijhoff, 1991.

Ressler, E.M., N. Boothby and D.J. Steinbock. *Unaccompanied Children: Care and Protection in Wars, Natural Disasters, and Refugee Movements.* New York; Oxford: Oxford University Press, 1988.

Rupesinghe, K. and M. Kuroda, eds. *Early Warning and Conflict Resolution.* New York; Basingstoke (UK): St. Martin Press, MacMillan, 1992.

Rystad, G., ed. *The Uprooted: Forced Migration as an International Problem in the Post-War Era.* Lund (Sweden): Lund University Press, 1990.

Salomon, K. *Refugees in the cold war: Toward a new international refugee regime in the early postwar era.* Lund (Sweden); Bromley (UK): Lund University Press, Chartwell-Bratt , 1991

Sandoz, Y., M. Torrelli and D. Plattner. "Humanitarian assistance." *International Review of the Red Cross* 288 (1992).

Stavehagen, R. *The Ethnic Question: Conflict, Development and Human Rights.* Tokyo: United Nations University Press, 1990.

Suhrke, A and A. Zolberg. "Beyond the refugee crisis: Disengagement and durable solutions for the developing world." *Migration: A European Journal of International Migration and Ethnic Relations* 5: 69-119. Berlin: Edition Parabolis, 1989.

Takkenberg, A. and C.C. Tahbaz, eds. *The collected Travaux préparatoires of the 1951 Geneva Convention relating to the Status of Refugees.* Amsterdam: Dutch Refugee Council, 1990.

Thornberry, P. *Minorities and Human Rights Law.* London: Minority Rights Group, 1991.

United Nations High Commissioner for Refugees. *Collection of International Instruments Concerning Refugees.* Geneva: UNHCR, 1979.

United Nations, Centre for Human Rights, ed. *A Compilation of International Instruments.* New York: United Nations, 1988.

United States Department of State, Bureau for Refugee Programs. *World Refugee Report 1991.* A report submitted to the Congress as part of the consultations on FY 1992 admissions to the United States. Washington DC: Department of State Publications, 1991.

United States Department of State, Bureau for Refugee Programs. *World Refugee Report 1992.* A report submitted to the Congress as part of the consultations on FY 1993 admissions to the United States. Washington DC: Department of State Publications, 1992.

US Committee for Refugees. *World Refugee Survey 1992.* Washington DC: US Committee for Refugees, 1992.

US Committee for Refugees. *World Refugee Survey 1993.* Washington DC: US Committee for Refugees, 1993.

Vichniac, I. *Croix Rouge: Les Stratèges de la bonne conscience.* Paris: Alain Moreau, 1988.

Walker, J. "International Mediation of Ethnic Conflict." *Survival* 35.1 (Spring 1993).

Weiss, T. E. and L. Minear, eds. *Humanitarianism Across Borders.* Boulder (US): Lynne Rienner, 1993.

Yundt, K.W. "The Organization of American States and legal protection to political refugees in Central America." *International Migration Review* 23.2 (1989): 281-218.

Zarjevski, Y. *A Future Preserved: International Assistance to Refugees.* Oxford; New York: Pergamon, 1988.

Zolberg, A.R., A. Suhrke and S. Aguayo. *Escape from Violence: Conflict and the refugee crisis in the developing world.* New York; Oxford: Oxford University Press, 1989.

Zucker, N. and N. Zucker. *The Guarded Gate: The Reality of American Refugee Policy.* San Diego (US): Harcourt Brace Jovanovich, 1987.

The following are a few of the leading journals covering refugee issues:

International Journal of Refugee Law. Published quarterly by Oxford University Press.

International Migration Review. Published quarterly by the Centre for Migration Studies.

International Migration. Published quarterly by IOM.

Journal of Refugee Studies. Published quarterly by Oxford University Press.

Refugee Abstracts. Published quarterly by UNHCR.

Refugees. Published three times a year by UNHCR.

World Refugee Survey. Published annually by the US Committee for Refugees.

Endnotes

1   Unless otherwise indicated, all figures in the text are based on UNHCR statistics.

2   Francis Deng, *Protecting the Internally Displaced: A Challenge for the United Nations*. Report by the Special Representative of the Secretary-General on Internally Displaced Persons to the UN Commission on Human Rights, 1993.

3   The World Bank, *The World Development Report 1991*. New York: Oxford University Press, 1991.

4   Rodolfo Stavehagen, *The Ethnic Question: Conflict, Development, and Human Rights*. Tokyo: United Nations University Press, 1990.

5   See Reginald Appleyard, "International Migration: Challenge for the nineties." Geneva: International Organization for Migration, 1991.

6   Walter Kalin, *Das Prinzip des Non-refoulement*. Frankfurt: Peter Lang, 1982. Cited in W. Gunther Plaut, *Refugee Determination in Canada*. Ottawa: 1985.

7   James B. Pritchard, ed., *Ancient Near Eastern Texts relating to the Old Testament*. Princeton (US): Princeton University Press, 1969.

8   Astri Suhrke, "Safeguarding the Right to Asylum." Unpublished paper prepared for the Expert Group Meeting on Population Distribution and Migration (Santa Cruz, Bolivia: 18-22 January 1993), preparatory to the International Conference on Population and Development, 1994, organized by the Population Division of the Department of Economic and Social Development, United Nations Secretariat, in collaboration with the UN Population Fund.

9   Intergovernmental Consultations on Asylum and Refugee Policies in Europe, North America and Australia, "Towards international recognition of the need for consistent removal policies with respect to rejected asylum-seekers." Unpublished working paper. Geneva: 1992.

10 Antonio Cruz, *Carrier Sanctions in Five Community States: Incompatibilities Between International Civil Aviation and Human Rights Obligations*. Church Committee for Migrants in Europe, 1991.

11 The rate was slightly higher for Europe as a whole. In 1991, some 283,000 requests for Convention refugee status were adjudicated in the EC countries, the Nordic countries, Austria and Switzerland. Some 33,000 people (12 per cent) were granted Convention status while an additional 40,000 were allowed to stay on humanitarian grounds.

12 Intergovernmental Consultations on Asylum and Refugee Policies in Europe, North America and Australia, "Towards international recognition of the need for consistent removal policies with respect to rejected asylum-seekers." Unpublished working paper. Geneva: 1992.

13 Cecilia Hall, "Language Barrier Hits Refugees' Health Care." London: *The Independent*, 25 November 1992.

14 Henry Kamm, "Refugees Are Big Business on Moscow-Nordic Route." *International Herald Tribune*, 16 February 1993.

15 "Cinq refugiés tamouls retrouvés morts au sud de Vienne." Paris: *Libération*, 18 January 1993.

16 The Dublin Convention spells out the obligations of signatory states to share data on trends in asylum applications, country-of-origin assessments, legal issues and individual cases. The Schengen Supplementary Agreement foresees the creation of an information system containing computerized data on individual asylum applicants, although some states are insisting that measures to protect the privacy of individuals must be added before the agreement is put into force. The Organization for Economic Co-operation and Development includes a demographic monitoring unit, SOPEMI, which tracks migration flows. The Maastricht Summit, of December 1991, endorsed a clearing house for information on asylum, including laws

and statistics, which will be implemented by the General Secretariat of the Council of Ministers of the European Community in Brussels. In February 1993, European governments agreed to set up a Migration Information Unit to collect and disseminate information on migration trends in Central and Eastern Europe and the newly independent states of the former Soviet Union. The Economic Commission for Europe and the Council of Europe are also engaged in similar data-collection exercises.

17 The first systematic codification of human rights, based on the Universal Declaration of Human Rights of 1948, is contained in the International Covenant on Economic, Social and Cultural Rights of 1966 and the International Covenant on Civil and Political rights of the same year (see Annex II.4).

18 The First Geneva Convention for the Amelioration of the Condition of the Wounded in Armies in the Field.

19 Boutros Boutros-Ghali, *An Agenda for Peace: Preventive diplomacy, peacemaking and peacekeeping*. Report of the Secretary-General pursuant to the statement adopted by the summit meeting of the Security Council on 31 January 1992. New York: United Nations, June 1992.

20 Report of the Secretary-General on the Work of the Organization. New York: United Nations, 1991.

21 Report of the Secretary-General on the Work of the Organization. New York: United Nations, 1992.

22 See John Mackinlay, "Military Force in the Service of Humane Values," in Thomas E. Weiss and Larry Minear (eds.). *Humanitarianism Across Borders*. Boulder (US): Lynne Rienner, 1993.

23 "Famine-Affected, Refugee and Displaced Populations: Recommendations for Public Health Issues." *Morbidity and Mortality*

Weekly Report 41.RR-13, 24 July 1992. US Dept. of Health and Human Resources, Public Health Service.

24 See UNHCR, *Guidelines on the Protection of Refugee Women*. Geneva: UNHCR, July 1991.

25 See Hiram A. Ruiz, *El Retorno: Guatemalans' Risky Repatriation Begins*. Washington DC: US Committee for Refugees, February 1993.

26 Council of Europe, *Report on population movements between the republics of the former USSR*. January 1993.

27 Immigration and Refugee Board Documentation Centre, Ottawa, Canada, "USSR Country Profile." October 1991.

28 The Russian Federation acceded to the 1951 Convention and the 1967 Protocol on 2 February 1993 and, on 19 February 1993, promulgated a Law on Refugees and Displaced Persons. Azerbaijan acceded to both the 1951 Convention and the 1967 Protocol on 12 February 1993.

29 Helsinki Watch, *Yugoslavia: Human rights abuses in Kosovo 1990-1992*. New York: Helsinki Watch, October 1992.

30 *The Human Development Report 1992*. New York: United Nations Development Programme, 1992.

31 See Francis Deng, *Protecting the Internally Displaced: A Challenge for the United Nations*. Report by the Special Representative of the Secretary-General on Internally Displaced Persons to the UN Commission on Human Rights, 1993.

32 Court Robinson, *Sri Lanka: Island of Refugees*. US Committee for Refugees: Washington, 1991.

33 General Assembly resolution 428(V) of 14 December 1950.

34 Notably in accordance with General Assembly resolution 40/118 of 13 December 1985.

Abbreviations

CIREFCA
International Conference on Central American Refugees

CIS
Commonwealth of Independent States

DHA
Department of Humanitarian Affairs

EC
European Communities

ECLAC
Economic Commission for Latin America and the Caribbean

ECOSOC
Economic and Social Council

ECOWAS
Economic Community of West African States

FAO
Food and Agriculture Organization of the United Nations

IBRD
International Bank for Reconstruction and Development (World Bank)

ICAO
International Civil Aviation Organization

ICRC
International Committee of the Red Cross

ILO
International Labour Organisation

IMF
International Monetary Fund

IOM
International Organization for Migration

JIU
Joint Inspection Unit

NGO
Non-governmental organization

OAS
Organization of American States

OAU
Organization of African Unity

ODP
Orderly Departure Programme

OECD
Organization for Economic Co-operation and Development

ORC
Open Relief Centre

QUIP
Quick Impact Project

UNCHS
United Nations Centre for Human Settlements

UNDP
United Nations Development Programme

UNDRO
Office of the United Nations Disaster Relief Co-ordinator

UNESCO
United Nations Educational, Scientific and Cultural Organization

UNHCR
Office of the United Nations High Commissioner for Refugees

UNICEF
United Nations Children's Fund

UNIDO
United Nations Industrial Development Organization

UNIFIL
United Nations Interim Force in Lebanon

UNOCHA
United Nations Office for the Co-ordination of Humanitarian Assistance Relating to Afghanistan

UNOSAL
United Nations Observer Mission in El Salvador

UNOSOM
United Nations Operation in Somalia

UNPROFOR
United Nations Protection Force

UNTAC
United Nations Transitional Authority in Cambodia

UNRWA
United Nations Relief and Works Agency for Palestine Refugees in the Near East

UNV
United Nations Volunteers

WFP
World Food Programme

WHO
World Health Organization

FOR THE BEST IN PAPERBACKS, LOOK FOR THE

In every corner of the world, on every subject under the sun, Penguin represents quality and variety—the very best in publishing today.

For complete information about books available from Penguin—including Pelicans, Puffins, Peregrines, and Penguin Classics—and how to order them, write to us at the appropriate address below. Please note that for copyright reasons the selection of books varies from country to country.

In the United Kingdom: For a complete list of books available from Penguin in the U.K., please write to *Dept E.P., Penguin Books Ltd, Harmondsworth, Middlesex, UB7 0DA*.

In the United States: For a complete list of books available from Penguin in the U.S., please write to *Consumer Sales, Penguin USA, P.O. Box 999— Dept. 17109, Bergenfield, New Jersey 07621-0120*. VISA and MasterCard holders call 1-800-253-6476 to order all Penguin titles.

In Canada: For a complete list of books available from Penguin in Canada, please write to *Penguin Books Canada Ltd, 10 Alcorn Avenue, Suite 300, Toronto, Ontario, Canada M4V 3B2*.

In Australia: For a complete list of books available from Penguin in Australia, please write to the *Marketing Department, Penguin Books Ltd, P.O. Box 257, Ringwood, Victoria 3134*.

In New Zealand: For a complete list of books available from Penguin in New Zealand, please write to the *Marketing Department, Penguin Books (NZ) Ltd, Private Bag, Takapuna, Auckland 9*.

In India: For a complete list of books available from Penguin, please write to *Penguin Overseas Ltd, 706 Eros Apartments, 56 Nehru Place, New Delhi, 110019*.

In Holland: For a complete list of books available from Penguin in Holland, please write to *Penguin Books Nederland B.V., Postbus 195, NL-1380AD Weesp, Netherlands*.

In Germany: For a complete list of books available from Penguin, please write to *Penguin Books Ltd, Friedrichstrasse 10-12, D-6000 Frankfurt Main 1, Federal Republic of Germany*.

In Spain: For a complete list of books available from Penguin in Spain, please write to *Longman, Penguin España, Calle San Nicolas 15, E-28013 Madrid, Spain*.

In Japan: For a complete list of books available from Penguin in Japan, please write to *Longman Penguin Japan Co Ltd, Yamaguchi Building, 2-12-9 Kanda Jimbocho, Chiyoda-Ku, Tokyo 101, Japan*.